Effective Economic Education

Effective Economic Education
in the Schools

William B. Walstad and John C. Soper, Editors

Reference & Resource Series

Published by
The Joint Council on Economic Education
and The National Education Association

nea PROFESSIONAL LIBRARY
National Education Association
Washington, D.C.

Printing History
First Printing: February 1991

Library of Congress Cataloging-in-Publication Data

Effective economic education in the schools / William B. Walstad and
John C. Soper, editors.
    p.   cm. — (Reference & resource series)
    Includes bibliographical references and index.
    ISBN 0–8106–1840–0
    1. Economics—Study and teaching (Secondary)—United States.
    2. Economics—Study and teaching (Elementary)—United States.
    I. Walstad, William B.   II. Soper, John Charles.   III. Series:
Reference and resource series.
    HB74.8.E34   1990
    330'.071'073—dc20   90–35474
                                                               CIP

CONTENTS

FOREWORD I

This book tells an optimistic and courageous story about curriculum reform undertaken by unique partnerships among professional economists and educators, volunteers from business and labor, and both the private and public sectors. It is not another plea to reform the way we do undergraduate education in the United States, nor is it an expose' of who is to blame for apparent inadequacies within our national schooling enterprise. It is a story about success.

The story of curriculum change in economic education is a courageous story because the fight to overcome a lack of economic understanding has been joined by dedicated professionals who believe that they, by using modest resources appropriately targeted, can make a positive difference in the capacity of young people to cope with their economic worlds. It is also an optimistic story in that during the 25-year history of the Developmental Economic Education Program (DEEP) the place of economics in school curricula has greatly expanded. DEEP has meant that where teachers have taught economics well, students have learned. DEEP has provided the requisite instructional tools, teacher education, and curriculum services to cause significant positive change in what schools teach to students about economics.

Readers will find that when using DEEP processes, the Joint Council on Economic Education and its network of state affiliated councils and university-based service centers team productively with dedicated local school professionals to provide young people with high-quality economic instruction in classrooms. Teaching economic understanding to young people is a noble goal because understanding history, understanding our government, and understanding many other forces in our great democracy that come into play in our lives are based on understanding economics.

I commend these efforts and urge readers to become active participants in the movement to provide future generations of Americans with high-quality economic instruction in our schools.

Terrel H. Bell
Salt Lake City, Utah

FOREWORD II

This volume explores the history, the successes, and the challenges of what has become a model of business and education partnerships. The Developmental Economic Education Program (DEEP) demonstrates what is possible in elementary and secondary schools when efforts are made to improve curriculum by involving teachers, administrators, universities, and business in a curriculum change partnership. DEEP is a process that brings high-quality teaching and materials into the classroom and attempts to make that process a permanent one.

The history and expansion of the DEEP program as outlined in this volume are impressive. No other single curriculum change process has expanded to school systems covering 40 percent of the nation's student population. No other curriculum change process has sustained success for such a long period of time. Chapters summarizing research and focusing on specific case studies show that DEEP works.

The challenges for DEEP are to further expand and improve the quality of the developmental process. Delivering effective and permanent curriculum change to large urban areas is an immense task. To continue that expansion and to improve the quality of the process will require not only enhanced efforts on the part of education and business to change the curriculum, but also increased resources from education and business in order to be successful.

Empirical evidence provided by nationwide studies demonstrates that we have not achieved the goal of universal economic literacy. However, those same studies show that when economics is infused throughout the kindergarten through twelfth grade curriculum, when students take a separate high school economics course, and when teachers have sufficient background in economic education, students will understand how our economic system works. These are the essential components of the Developmental Economic Education Program.

Educators should look to this model process as a guide for future changes in economic education and in all parts of the curriculum. Business and foundations should use this model process as an ideal way to work together to improve overall education.

To business leaders interested in participating in educational reform, I commend this volume for its wealth of ideas and as a plan for future educational involvement.

Edgar S. Woolard, Jr.
E. I. duPont de Nemours and Company
Wilmington, Delaware

ACKNOWLEDGMENTS

This book owes its publication to many people and organizations. We must first recognize Michael MacDowell who gave strong support to the creation of the volume and offered many constructive ideas for its contents when he served as president of the Joint Council of Economic Education. We are also appreciative of the advice we received from the Joint Council's DEEP office, under the direction of S. Stowell Symmes, and from representatives of the National Association of Economic Educators who served on the Joint Council's DEEP Planning Committee during the creation phase of the project.

Further development of the volume was significantly enhanced by the opportunity for chapter authors to present papers at a national conference, held in Cleveland, Ohio. The conference was hosted by the Federal Reserve Bank of Cleveland and supported by a grant from the Ameritech Foundation to the Joint Council and its affiliated state councils on economic education in Illinois, Indiana, Michigan, Ohio, and Wisconsin. In addition, the National Federation of Independent Business Foundation, Price Waterhouse, and the Cleveland Center for Economic Education provided generous conference support.

We are also indebted to the following professional economic educators who provided thorough review and discussion of the papers presented at the Cleveland conference: Cheryl Allen (Wichita State University), Jeffrey Blais (Rhode Island College), Jean Caldwell (Central State University), David A. Dieterle (Northern Illinois University), Vera Freeman (University of Missouri–Kansas City), Jerry D. Johnson (University of Wisconsin, Eau Claire), Abbejean Kehler (The Ohio State University), Calvin A. Kent (Baylor University), Peter R. Moore (Rhode Island College), Frank J. Navratil (John Carroll University), Robert Ristau (Eastern Michigan University), Francis W. Rushing (Georgia State University), Phillip Saunders (Indiana University–Bloomington), Robert J. Strom (Federal Reserve Bank of Kansas City), and George M. Vredeveld (University of Cincinnati).

In completing editing and publication tasks, we had much help from Stephen Buckles and Joan Sullivan Baranski at the Joint Council on Economic Education and from Gordon Felton at the National Education Association. Both the University of Nebraska–Lincoln and John Carroll University also supported our work on this project. Sharon Nemeth at the National Center for Research in Economic Education at the University of Nebraska–Lincoln provided great assistance with typing manuscripts, with preparing the microcomputer disks, and with proofreading.

We especially appreciate having had the generous financial and emotional support for this publishing project provided by the Ameritech Foundation. Without commitments from foundation President John Koten and Director Mike Kuhlin, copublication and wide distribution of this book by the Joint Council and the NEA would not have been possible.

Finally, we gratefully thank all the chapter authors, whose names are listed in the table of contents, for their hard work and invaluable contributions to this volume.

William B. Walstad
John C. Soper

1. EFFECTIVE ECONOMIC EDUCATION: AN INTRODUCTION

by William B. Walstad and John C. Soper

The Developmental Economic Education Program (DEEP) was launched in 1964 by the Joint Council on Economic Education as an experimental program in three school districts. By 1989 there were 1,836 school districts enrolled in DEEP, covering some 39 percent of the precollege student population. The 1985–89 period was one of especially impressive growth for DEEP, with 1,176 districts added to the rolls and with DEEP coverage rising from 22 percent to 39 percent of the precollege student population. The DEEP experience, however, is much more than a simple count of enrolled school districts. As the chapters in this volume illustrate, DEEP is a tested model of curriculum change and teacher education that has shaped economic education in the nation's schools over the past 25 years.

DEEP basically embodies three principles intended to achieve *effective* economic education in the schools. First, DEEP requires a commitment on the part of a school district to provide economics instruction from the elementary through the secondary grades. The district commitment is voluntary, but enrolling in DEEP means that administrators, teachers, and parents in a community recognize the need for students to receive a nonpartisan education in economics. Second, DEEP is a cooperative and flexible model of curriculum change. It involves a partnership among college and university economic educators and school personnel working on needs identified in the school district, such as the revision of the curriculum, and on the dissemination or development of new instructional materials. Third, and most critical to the success of DEEP, is teacher education in economics. Economics is a challenging subject, and it must be taught well for students to improve their understanding. That means that teachers must have a mastery of basic economic concepts and know how to teach the subject to students. DEEP improves the economic education of teachers through in-service courses or workshops, which are often sponsored cooperatively by school districts, college and university centers for economic education, and state councils on economic education.

11

This current look at the DEEP experience is divided into five major parts. Part I consists of four chapters that give a rationale for economic education and explain in more detail the features of the DEEP model. Part II focuses on research and evaluation that have been conducted over the 25-year history of DEEP and on related studies of economic understanding among students in secondary and elementary grades. The next two parts offer case studies of how DEEP works. Part III looks at DEEP operations and issues in four diverse states. Part IV shows how the DEEP process works in six different school districts. In Part V the focus shifts from the present to the future; these chapters discuss the future of DEEP in the context of educational reform, requirements for new curriculum materials, needs of school districts, and leadership from the Joint Council.

RATIONALE

Stephen Buckles, Joint Council president, opens the volume by defining economic education as the process of teaching students the "method" of applying basic economic concepts to analyze personal and social economic issues. He then turns to the question of the justification for teaching economics in the school curriculum. From Buckles's perspective, economic education deserves a place in the school curriculum because the economic method gives students training in critical thinking. The opportunity for students to practice careful, logical thinking when analyzing economic issues represents a significant contribution that economic education makes to the major goals of elementary and secondary education.

Economics instruction also gives students insights into how to function better in various economic roles as consumers, workers, or citizens, and it develops the economic literacy needed to understand the complex interrelationships in our economic world. A key component of economic literacy is the mastery of basic concepts. Thus, a major section of the chapter is devoted to outlining 22 basic concepts to be taught to students by the time they graduate from high school and to discussing how the concepts can be used in a five-step method for solving economic problems. Economic education is not a collection of facts, statistics, or opinions about economic events, nor is it a course in check writing or comparison shopping; it is primarily a decision-making method that we teach to students.

With this background on what economic education is and what it is not, Buckles suggests some guidelines that teachers and administrators should follow in adopting classroom programs and selecting classroom materials in economics. The guidelines come in the form of ten important questions to be answered about economic education programs or materials. Positive responses to these questions indicate that the publications and programs are likely to be suitable for use with students; negative answers are grounds for rejection of the materials and programs.

In Chapter 3, Steven Miller offers us an expanded discussion of the case for economic education. Miller, like Buckles, defines economics and economic education as a method or process of decision making, of making reasoned judgments about economic issues. In his explanation, he offers an eight-step model of economic decision making and then describes how this model can be applied to the energy problems facing the United States in the 1970s. Miller believes that if this economic decision-making process is taught well in schools, it should promote more responsible and effective citizenship, which is a major goal of social studies education. He argues persuasively that economic education is "indispensable" to citizenship education and therefore should be considered "basic" to social studies education in the schools. The final section of the chapter describes the problem with "infusing" economics in the school curriculum, a problem also discussed in several later chapters.

Chapter 4 is the first of many chapters that focus specifically on DEEP. Stowell Symmes, executive director for DEEP at the Joint Council, describes the main features and tenets of the DEEP model of curriculum change in the chapter. DEEP is basically a process-oriented model that stresses interaction as college and university economists and educators work with teachers and administrators to improve the K–12 curriculum in economics. This work often involves the revision of curriculum guidelines to include more economics, the in-service education of teachers in economics and in how to teach the subject, and the development of instructional materials in economics for various grade levels. Flexibility is a major strength of the DEEP process model and probably explains why it has survived over the past 25 years, in contrast to the product-oriented models of curriculum change so prevalent in other social studies subjects during the 1960s and early 1970s.

After discussing DEEP in the context of curriculum theory and history, Symmes turns his attention to the historical record for DEEP since it was initiated on an experimental basis in 1964. He first explains how the DEEP process reflects acceptance of the goals of economic education and how school districts have made a commitment over time to deliver economic education through DEEP. The chapter next describes the qualitative improvement in curriculum materials available to DEEP schools and highlights some of the research findings on DEEP that will be reported in greater detail in Chapter 6. The chapter concludes with nine recommendations for actions to fulfill the promise of DEEP.

Teacher education is a key component of DEEP. Henry Hermanowicz discusses teacher education in depth in Chapter 5. The chapter begins with a background review of proposals for educational reform of the nation's schools that started with the publication of *A Nation at Risk*. In light of these reforms, the Joint Council decided to establish the Committee on Teacher Education, which Hermanowicz chaired, that would develop a general policy statement on the preparation in economics necessary for prospective elementary and secondary teachers enrolled in institutions of higher education. The chapter gives a complete listing of the major recommendations for teacher education made by the distinguished committee of economists, educators, and business leaders. Hermanowicz concludes by offering convincing arguments that the recommendations, if they are enacted, would meet a critical national need for more teachers who have the knowledge and skill to teach economics to students.

RESEARCH STUDIES

Research on DEEP and precollege economic education is reviewed in the four chapters of Part II. Chapter 6, by Michael Watts, is a comprehensive essay on DEEP history and research. Watts classifies DEEP in three phases:

1. 1964–67: experimental development

2. 1968–83: cooperating school enrollment

3. 1984–90: expansion and enhancement

For each phase, he reviews the major qualitative and quantitative findings from evaluation reports and research articles and offers interpretive comments. Watts finds that the research and evaluation results for DEEP are mixed, in large part because the program is voluntary and because researchers find it difficult to control for other factors, such as teacher training or district commitment to the program, without overstating or understating DEEP effects. The chapter ends with a look to the future based on Watts's assessment of the lessons from the past 25 years of DEEP history and of the major barriers to DEEP in the schools. Some of the points Watts makes are also discussed in Chapter 21 by Francis Rushing.

In Chapter 7 we expand the review of precollege research in economic education beyond the study of DEEP to examine the level of economic understanding among senior high school students. One major reason that economic education programs such as DEEP are important, if not essential for the basic education of students, is that most students nearing graduation from high school show a low level of economic literacy. To document this assertion, we report extensive data from our work to revise and norm the *Test of Economic Literacy* with a national sample of eleventh and twelfth grade students. On this test, students with a separate course in economics could correctly answer only about half the questions and showed the weakest understanding of macroeconomic and international economic subjects, the subjects most often covered on a daily basis by the news media. We believe that these and other deficiencies in economic understanding can be corrected if teachers, curriculum developers, school administrators, and economic educators work together through DEEP to improve the condition of economic education in senior high schools.

The assessment of student knowledge of economics is also our focus in Chapter 8, but in this chapter we report test results for junior high and elementary school students. The economic knowledge of eighth and ninth graders was measured with the new *Test of Economic Knowledge*, while the economic understanding of fifth and sixth graders was assessed with the recently revised *Basic Economics Test*. Both measures were normed with samples of thousands of students from schools across the nation. The results show that junior high and intermediate elementary students can and do learn a significant amount of economics when they are given instruction in the subject. If economics is taught at all these levels, it is usually "infused" into the social studies curriculum instead of being taught in a separate economics course. No doubt some of the low level of student performance is explained by the use of the infusion approach to economics, which is a more difficult way for students to

15

make significant gains in economic understanding.

The research section concludes with a chapter by Mark Schug on the development of economic thinking in students and its implications for classroom instruction. The research findings in this chapter are based on the use of qualitative research techniques, such as personal interviews and observations with small samples of students, in contrast to the quantitative approach taken in Chapters 7 and 8, which based results on the analysis of test data from large samples of students. In this chapter Schug reviews about 25 developmental studies, some cross-cultural, that illustrate how students' thinking about such notions as ownership, profit, and price follows a developmental pattern. Schug cites examples of classroom programs and materials that are effective with young children and offers suggestions about how to use the qualitative research on the psychological development of students to improve economic instruction.

DEEP IN THE STATES

Part III consists of four chapters dealing with how DEEP works in different kinds of statewide programs. In the first of these chapters, "DEEP Across the State," Bonnie Meszaros and James O'Neill discuss the DEEP model as it has been implemented successfully in the state of Delaware. Beginning in 1971 the Delaware Center for Economic Education gradually built a statewide economic education program for the schools. The authors discuss in detail seven principles that guided the program:

1. involving committed professional educators
2. taking one step at a time, rather than trying to "do it all at once"
3. stressing quality rather than quantity, initially emphasizing the economics training of teachers
4. offering schools a wide variety of options
5. organizing teaching resources and objectives together in a logical sequence
6. building a solid support base within the school districts
7. defining the goals of DEEP

The success of the Delaware program can be assessed, in part, by noting that thus far 7 of Delaware's 17 public school districts have won

16

Exemplary School Awards from the Joint Council, more awards than any other state has received.

Chapter 11, "DEEP and Core Competencies in Economics for Missouri School Districts" by Karen Hallows and Warren Solomon, reviews the experience of one state with a mandated competency-testing program for students. The test, the Missouri Mastery Achievement Test (MMAT), is a criterion-referenced instrument used at grades 3, 6, 8, and 10. The authors conclude that such a testing program, when developed with input from teachers and administrators, can raise the priority of economics teaching in the schools. One indirect effect of the test was that teachers requested additional workshops on economics teaching and more materials to help them accomplish the task of preparing students. Teachers also increased their reliance on the Missouri Council on Economic Education and its network of centers for economic education. As the test is administered at multiple grade levels, it should encourage administrators and teachers to integrate economics throughout the curriculum, rather than leaving it to a senior high capstone course. The testing program, however, is not without problems, and preliminary research indicates that the impact of DEEP on student MMAT performance is relatively weak.

There are now 28 states with some form of mandate for economic instruction. Of these, 15 require a separate course in economics for high school graduation. In Chapter 12, Sanford Gordon and Kenneth Wade discuss this critical issue of state mandates and explain what happens to DEEP when the state mandates economics in the curriculum. Gordon and Wade first offer reasons for and against state mandates in light of the changes in the Joint Council's position on this issue. They next describe the political process of securing state funding to implement the mandate in New York. They also explain the effects of the New York mandate on the DEEP process of revising the curriculum, conducting in-service education, and building partnerships among educational organizations. The final sections of the chapter briefly describe the experiences of Florida and California with state mandates in economics.

In the final chapter of Part III, Michael MacDowell and Peter Harrington provide some observations on the past and future prospects for the funding of DEEP. They speak with authority as MacDowell was recently president of the Joint Council and Harrington is the executive director of the Indiana Council on Economic Education, one of the Joint Council's stronger statewide affiliates. Both have extensive experience

17

with fund raising for the recent rapid expansion of DEEP over the 1984–89 period. Their insights in this chapter include a set of suggested guidelines for state and local fund-raising efforts for DEEP and a checklist of hints to assist DEEP fund raisers in the expansion of unrestricted giving. They conclude with a brief discussion of their views on the potential for public sector funding of economic education and DEEP. They see less potential for successful funding of DEEP at the national and state levels and argue that local funding sources will be the most to likely provide the expansion funds for DEEP.

DEEP IN SCHOOL DISTRICTS

Part IV offers five different models of how DEEP has worked in individual school districts. These are real-world implementations of DEEP which discuss some of the problems encountered in the attempt to install economics as a viable part of the regular curriculum in urban, suburban, and rural school settings. Particular emphasis is placed on the urban district, with three separate chapters on different kinds of urban school environments.

In Chapter 14, Judith Brenneke reviews the DEEP experiences in two inner-city districts (Cleveland and East Cleveland, Ohio), both of which have large minority populations. In both subcases, DEEP implementation was hampered by problems in the form of teacher and student mobility, low performance expectations, and administrative roadblocks. Significant resources were devoted to DEEP in both districts, but the outcomes have been less than fully satisfying. Nevertheless, these experiences provide rich background for the problems of dealing with the increasing at-risk school population and the school environment in inner cities.

Continuing with DEEP in the urban school setting, in Chapter 15 Howard Yeargan relates the experience of the Southwest Texas State University (SWTSU) Center for Economic Education with DEEP schools in the San Antonio metropolitan area. A potential "problem" for economic education in this area is the large Hispanic population, which constitutes more than 50 percent of the area population. Yeargan describes the process of gradual growth of DEEP affiliation in five area school districts between 1982 and 1989. Each of the five DEEP districts is different in size and structure, and the SWTSU Center had to proceed carefully in enlisting teacher and administrator support for DEEP. The author provides anecdotal evidence of the effectiveness of DEEP in the

San Antonio area. He points out that DEEP implementation has been tentative, primarily because of the perceived limitation of the SWTSU Center in delivering programs and services to the schools. Yeargan concludes that the largely Hispanic population is *not* a significant factor in the DEEP expansion effort: Hispanics appear to be no different from their Anglo counterparts in their attitudes toward economic education, although language difficulties may affect DEEP results.

With Chapter 16, James Dick completes the urban case studies of DEEP by describing the experience of the University of Nebraska–Omaha (UNO) Center for Economic Education and the Omaha Public Schools. The Omaha school system was one of the original DEEP systems from the mid-1960s and now has an enrollment of more than 41,000 students, about one-third of whom are members of minorities. Dick describes the district's renewal of its DEEP commitment during the 1980s, which culminated in 1988 with the district's selection by the Joint Council as an exemplary DEEP system. Factors contributing to DEEP success were the administrative support from the social studies supervisor and district superintendent and the involvement of key teachers. DEEP also worked in the Omaha system because of personnel support and financial incentives from the UNO Center and from the Nebraska Council on Economic Education. Dick concludes with recommendations for providing additional teacher training, forming closer ties between UNO Center personnel and Omaha curriculum supervisors, assessing students with national tests, and expanding the use of new curriculum materials.

In Chapter 17, Don Leet and Peter Mehas explore the planning, implementation, and evaluation of DEEP in a large suburban district in central California. In a real sense, the Clovis DEEP experience is an idyllic one. The school system grew from 14,000 students when DEEP began to more than 20,000 students today. The district has no obvious problems of low-income families or racial/ethnic imbalance. At the time DEEP was started, the district was also led by "a very talented superintendent." In addition, the CEO of a local business initiated the push for more and better economic education in the district and agreed to provide financial support for DEEP for three years.

In the planning stage for DEEP, a survey of the current curriculum was made to determine where economics was, or was not, taught. Then an objective test was developed and administered to evaluate student economic understanding at the ninth and twelfth grade levels. Based on

19

the analysis of strengths and weaknesses of student performance on the test, recommendations were submitted to the school board (and accepted). The implementation phase included in-service training for key teachers, curriculum writing by these key teachers, pilot testing of the curriculum units, and districtwide in-service training. After a three-year implementation, the DEEP steering committee recommended minimal competency testing of students at grades 3, 6, 8, and 11. During the maintenance phase of DEEP, the Clovis system built a $10,000 line item into the budget for DEEP so that the program will be sustained into the future.

The authors conclude with a set of recommendations for schools contemplating DEEP. They suggest that whenever possible there needs to be both private sector funding for DEEP and district funding for DEEP in a separate budget. It is also necessary to monitor student achievement in the program. The infusion model should be used to integrate economics throughout the curriculum, and teacher training should combine content in economics with teaching methods. The key ingredients in a successful DEEP are partnership, human capital, and evaluation.

In Chapter 18, the final case study in this volume, Lucien Ellington and Willie Mae Beattie describe DEEP in the Marion County (Tennessee) schools, which have an enrollment of about 5,000 students. DEEP was initiated in this rural district in 1984 by the University of Tennessee–Chattanooga (UTC) Center for Economic Education, primarily because key teachers had been involved in UTC Center programs. A proposal was developed by the district and funded for $10,000 by the UTC Center for training teachers, purchasing curriculum materials, and providing on-site UTC Center consulting support. In subsequent years the UTC Center provided $3,000 DEEP grants annually, and in return the district agreed to evaluate DEEP and to provide release time for teachers. After the first year a retired economics teacher was hired as a part-time consultant to maintain district support of DEEP. DEEP has gradually expanded to additional schools in the district (so that seven out of ten are now involved in DEEP). Evaluation results generally show students in DEEP schools score 20–30 percent higher on various economics tests, compared to students in non-DEEP schools in Marion County.

FUTURE DIRECTIONS

In Part V—"What's Next?"—four chapters examine different aspects of the future of DEEP. In Chapter 19, Marilyn Kourilsky and Lory Quaranta focus on four major imperatives arising from the educational reform movement growing out of *A Nation at Risk* and on the potential contributions of economic education to the advancement of educational reform. Kourilsky and Quaranta think that the Joint Council's approach excels in promoting collegialism and that it provides a role model for other subject disciplines. They also argue that economic educators could do a better job of enhancing professionalism in teaching, and they offer suggestions for changes. As for research-based practice in the classroom, the authors believe that the economic education movement could go much farther in applying current educational and psychological research about developmental levels and age appropriateness in the teaching and learning of economic concepts and that economic educators should role-model this repertoire for teachers in workshops and courses. The promotion of the fourth imperative, educational equity, can be accomplished by setting uniformly high learning expectations for *all* students, by devoting special attention to at-risk students, and by teaching from a multicultural perspective. The chapter contains much to recommend it because of its thought-provoking ideas and its many suggestions for improving economic education.

In Chapter 20, June Gilliard makes explicit a number of past assumptions underlying the Joint Council's programs and materials. She next discusses how changing conditions in the schools and in the school-age population may influence education and curriculum development in the next decade. Educational reform is one major variable that may influence educational outcomes by the year 2000, but this factor is unpredictable at this time. A more certain variable is the changing demographic nature of the school-age population. At the end of the 1980s, some 30 percent of school-age children were members of minority racial or ethnic groups; by 2001 it is estimated that 48 percent will be in these categories. The implications of this demographic shift have yet to be confronted by the educational system in the United States, and, as Gilliard notes, the demographic changes will most certainly affect the assumptions curriculum and materials developers must make in economic education.

In "The Next Stage of the DEEP Process," Francis Rushing looks at the DEEP model from a 25-year perspective and contrasts DEEP with other social studies and science education programs. Based on Marker's research into "new social studies" innovations, Rushing identifies major reasons why curriculum innovations are unlikely to last. Rushing's recommendations from these observations are that economic educators ought to

1. validate through testing what learning the materials can really deliver and not oversell them,

2. make certain that inside advocates are in place for the proposed curriculum innovation, and

3. be sure that teachers are trained in the effective use of programs or materials and that teacher modification of intended uses is carefully monitored to avoid errors.

Rushing thinks, based on his review of problems with the science education curriculum in the 1960s and 1970s, that a consistent and coherent economics curriculum for all students is a crucial element in the survival of economic education in the schools.

Rushing also reviews the five case studies contained in Part IV and concludes that they provide evidence of the diversity among school systems in the United States and of the many possible approaches toward the establishment of DEEP. He states that DEEP receives high marks as a model for curriculum change because of its needed structure and its flexibility of implementation. As to the need for major initiatives to change DEEP for the 1990s, Rushing argues that a *national* "Case for Economic Education" has not been made to establish economics as part of the educational imperative. He believes that the Joint Council needs to take a leadership position in selling the nation on the need for economic education and urges an expansion of research into DEEP and its connections to best-practice teacher training, scope and sequence preparation, pedagogical methods, and materials evaluation. The chapter concludes with many insightful recommendations for how to improve the focus of DEEP.

As editors of this volume, we reserved the last word for Stephen Buckles, Joint Council president. In Chapter 22 he shares his "Visions for the Future." Buckles believes that the Joint Council and its network not only must continue to emphasize growth in the number of DEEP systems, but also, more importantly, must increase efforts to improve the quality of new and existing DEEP systems. To achieve the overall goals of both quantity and quality, Buckles, like Rushing, believes that the Joint Council must increase national awareness of the need for economic education and the need for economics in the school. Improvements are also necessary in the set of teaching and curriculum materials in the field and in the delivery capability of the national network of state councils and centers. With some 40 percent of the nation's precollege students now enrolled in DEEP schools, Buckles projects an annual growth rate of at least 2 percent for the next five years. This growth, however, will require significant new resources at the council and center levels because marginal costs will increase as the Joint Council network tries to reach more of the nation's schools.

CONCLUSION

The DEEP experience with economic education is a rich and varied one, as the following chapters will reveal. The DEEP model of curriculum change has been successfully used to strengthen the economics curriculum in school districts, and many teachers have a better understanding of economics and how to teach it because of the DEEP stimulus. What DEEP represents, therefore, is effective economic education in the schools. The value of the DEEP process should not be underestimated in the decades ahead. Economics should not be excluded from the school curriculum or be given inadequate study when the subject is included in the classroom. An understanding of economics is vital for students facing the many challenges of our complex world. DEEP contributes to better education by preparing students for their economic future.

2. GUIDELINES FOR ECONOMIC CONTENT IN SCHOOL PROGRAMS

by Stephen Buckles

Teachers and administrators are confronted with countless options in terms of programs and materials to use in efforts to increase economic understanding. Yet time in the curriculum is limited. This chapter offers guidance that is intended to assist teachers and administrators in making the time devoted to economic education the most effective it can be. To achieve this end, the chapter discusses why sound economic education is important, what economic content should be included in economic education programs, and what guidelines teachers and administrators should use in making decisions about which materials and programs to include in the school curriculum.

WHAT IS ECONOMIC EDUCATION?

Public understanding of what economics is ranges from a vague "having something to do with money" to a *Webster's* (9th Collegiate Edition, 1985) definition of "a social science concerned chiefly with description and analysis of the production, distribution, and consumption of goods and services" (p. 395) to the somewhat serious "economics is what economists do." The best description, however, is offered by John Maynard Keynes (1930): "The theory of economics does not furnish a body of settled conclusions immediately applicable to policy. It is a method rather than a doctrine, an apparatus of the mind, a technique of thinking, which helps its possessor to draw correct conclusions" (p. 6).

Our teaching of economics can be most effective if we focus on the ideas that economics is a "method," an "apparatus," and a "technique." The best activities, readings, audiovisual materials, and presentations by outside experts are designed to go beyond the memorization of definitions and concepts or the presentation of value judgments. An understanding of basic concepts is necessary, and there is a role for value judgments. But just as economics as a discipline exists because of the necessity for making choices, the true goal of economic education should be to teach students how to make choices and decisions. If the goal of economic education is to enable students to use economic concepts in a reasoned manner to analyze personal and societal economic issues, then the "method" of economics is where we should concentrate.

Many materials and programs state that they include economics in the context of history and social studies. Some do so effectively, but others simply describe issues without using the power of economics to understand the issues and to instill the methods of analysis. For example, students often study the adventures of the explorers and the opening of the New World in the fifteenth and sixteenth centuries. There may be no discussion of the concepts of cost, investment, and profits that applied to those events and that are still relevant today. The full role of tariffs as a government revenue source and their effects on production in the eighteenth and nineteenth centuries are often ignored. The development of central banking is studied as a change in an institution without comparing the events to banking today. The Industrial Revolution and its effects on productivity can lead to an understanding of many of today's problems, but many materials miss that opportunity. These textbooks and supplementary materials discuss economic events, but they do not use the opportunities to teach economic understanding.

At the most fundamental and perhaps most important level, the economic way of thinking is best exemplified by this adage: "There is no such thing as a free lunch." An economically literate person, in making personal and family decisions and in forming opinions on issues and problems facing society, recognizes that there are benefits and costs to every choice. The economic method is first to recognize those benefits and costs and then to make choices that will make the individual or society as well off as possible.

It is very easy to favor rent controls on apartments in order to hold rents at a "fair" level, to vote for increased agricultural price supports to provide farmers with higher incomes, and to support limits on how high car insurance rates can go. These decisions become more difficult when one recognizes that there are costs to each. That recognition is necessary if we are to make rational decisions.

WHY TEACH ECONOMICS?

The most important justification for economic education is that it is training in logical, careful thinking. To the extent that it can enhance our students' abilities to analyze situations and problems in a rational manner, it contributes to the major goals of elementary and secondary education. And because economic understanding can be used to solve personal and societal problems, it becomes exciting for teachers to teach and for students to learn.

There are also other reasons for teaching economics. Many have made arguments that an understanding of economics allows individuals to function better as consumers, producers, workers, and citizens. Others argue that without knowledge of economics, students cannot fully understand history or the social studies. As Boulding (1969) states in the first issue of the *Journal of Economic Education*:

> An accurate and workable image of the social system in general, and the economic system in particular is . . . increasingly essential to human survival. If the prevailing images of the social system are unrealistic and inaccurate, decisions which are based on them are likely to lead to disaster. . . . Economic education, therefore, along with education in other aspects of the social system may well be one of the most important keys for man's survival. . . . In a complex world, unfortunately, ignorance is not likely to be bliss, and a society in which important decisions are based on fantasy and folk tales may well be doomed to extinction. (pp. 10–11)

Economic literacy is also required for finding answers to the multitude of questions that face the public. As Stigler (1983) notes: "Yet this last point—that the public does concern itself most frequently with economic questions—is a true and persuasive reason for its possessing economic literacy. . . . The public has chosen to speak and vote on economic problems so the only question is how intelligently it speaks and votes" (p. 64).

Teaching economics also provides a fuller understanding of institutions and historical events. Students find economic events interesting and of daily concern. If economic analysis is included in social studies, history, and other courses, those courses can be enriched, and the significance of the topics studied can be completely revealed and used to achieve better understanding of the economic questions facing today's world.

There is no doubt that adding economics to a curriculum has costs, but much work has been done by economic educators to minimize these costs. On the plus side, as stated by Keynes, Boulding, and Stigler, there are significant benefits from economic education. These benefits to students are likely to outweigh the curricular costs.

WHAT CONCEPTS SHOULD BE COVERED?

A Framework for Teaching the Basic Concepts (Saunders et al., 1984) is the best starting point for anyone interested in obtaining an overview of the relevant concepts necessary to build economic understanding. The *Framework* is part of the Joint Council on Economic Education's *Master Curriculum Guide* series and was written by a group of distinguished economists and educators. The *Framework* offers a detailed description of the basic concepts in economics, describes the necessary understandings of the structure of the economy, and outlines the effective decision-making process.

A second essential component for developing an understanding of what should be included in an economic curriculum is also a part of the *Master Curriculum Guide* series. *Economics: What and When* (Gilliard et al., 1988) takes the concepts from the *Framework* and places them into a recommended scope and sequence. The basic concepts are divided into six broad categories: fundamental economic concepts, microeconomic concepts, macroeconomic concepts, international economic concepts, measurement concepts and methods, and broad social goals. The concepts within each category are listed in Table 2.1.

The fundamental economic concepts are necessary for understanding the rationale for why all economic systems exist. They are also crucial in understanding whether such a system is directed by markets, by government decisions, or by a mixture of both market and government decision making.

The microeconomic concepts are essential for understanding our own economic system. These concepts explore how the questions of what we produce, how we produce, and for whom we produce are answered by markets. The successes and failures of markets are analyzed, and the proper role for government in regulating and changing markets is explored.

The macroeconomic concepts look at the economy as a whole. Measurement of our economic well-being and what influences our well-being, along with the causes of inflation and unemployment, are included. The use of government policy to change overall economic conditions is an important part of these concepts.

The international economic concepts explore why countries trade and how that trade takes place. The determination of exchange rates and the balance of trade are included. In most surveys of what teachers do and what materials include, these latter two areas, macroeconomic and

27

international economic concepts, do not receive the emphasis that they need. This may be due to the lack of teacher education in these areas.

The measurement concepts and methods category includes mathematical concepts that can be used to explain economic performance and events. Many of these concepts are often included in mathematics courses. Applications within economics permit these concepts to be reinforced and their usefulness in real problem solving to be emphasized.

The broad social goals group of concepts is a listing of national goals for any system. The important understandings to be developed are that there are often trade-offs among these goals and that different individuals and economic systems place varying degrees of importance on each goal. Understanding the goals, the trade-offs, and how value judgments influence the choice of policies and types of systems is really the capstone to adequate economic understanding.

TABLE 2.1
A Framework of Concepts

Fundamental Economic Concepts
    Scarcity
    Opportunity Cost and Trade-Offs
    Productivity
    Economic Systems
    Economic Institutions and Incentives
    Exchange, Money, and Interdependence

Microeconomic Concepts
    Markets and Prices
    Supply and Demand
    Competition and Market Structure
    Income Distribution
    Market Failures
    The Role of Government

Macroeconomic Concepts
    Gross National Product
    Aggregate Supply
    Aggregate Demand
    Unemployment
    Inflation and Deflation
    Monetary Policy
    Fiscal Policy

International Economic Concepts
    Absolute and Comparative Advantage and Barriers to Trade
    Exchange Rates and the Balance of Payments
    International Aspects of Growth and Stability

Measurement Concepts and Methods
  Tables
  Charts and Graphs
  Ratios and Percentages
  Percentage Changes
  Index Numbers
  Real vs. Nominal Values
  Averages and Distributions Around the Average

Broad Social Goals
  Economic Freedom
  Economic Efficiency
  Economic Equity
  Economic Security
  Full Employment
  Price Stability
  Economic Growth

Source: Saunders et al. (1984, p. 11, Exhibit 3).

AN EXAMPLE

These six categories do fit into a whole. Economic literacy is really a story that a high school graduate ought to be able to tell. An economically literate student understands the economic problem, how we approach that problem through our economic system, and how that system results in teaching or not teaching our social goals.

As an example of the economic story, I will use one economic concept to describe why we specialize, why markets and money exist, and why government has an economic role to play in our economy. Economics exists as a discipline because every society faces the basic economic problem of scarcity. Our wants for goods, services, and time are greater than the resources we have. Because of this condition, we cannot satisfy all of our wants at once; we must choose which wants to satisfy, and in so doing, we must give up others. Economics enables us to examine how we, as individuals, organizations, and a society, make these choices. And, more important, the discipline assists us in determining whether we are as well off as we can possibly be, given our resources. This question means asking ourselves whether we are using our resources in such a manner that we cannot be made any better off by an alternative allocation of resources. Economists call this condition *economic efficiency.*

As economic systems have evolved, the path has been from a system where each family unit produces all it needs to a system where each

29

worker specializes in particular production activities. The advantage of specialization has been that overall production can be increased, and, thus, more of our wants can be satisfied. That is, we can be more economically efficient. The disadvantage of specialization is that economic agents must then trade what they produce for things they want more. Thus, markets are created. Primitive economies engage in barter. However, money makes the trading of goods and services easier. Less time and effort are devoted to trading and more to production if money is used. Again, we can be more economically efficient.

Markets themselves can lead to an efficient allocation of resources. If our wants change so that we want and are willing to pay for more travel and fewer hot tubs, competitive markets will respond with increased profits in the travel industry and lower profits in the hot tub industry. That is, the market responds to better satisfy our wants and thus is more economically efficient.

But even very competitive markets will not always be efficient. That leads to an economic role for government. Government may need to ensure that markets remain competitive through antitrust laws. Other forms of government regulation may be appropriate when consumers do not have the abilities to fully determine the nature or quality of products.

Some goods and services are characterized by benefits received by persons other than the producers and the consumers. Competitive markets will not by themselves produce enough of these goods for economic efficiency. In some cases—national defense, for example— private markets would produce very little, if any. A private market production of national defense would fail because consumers would realize that if some others buy defense, they will also be protected without buying defense. Thus, most of us would probably be unwilling to voluntarily pay for defense. Private businesses, unable to sell defense, would not produce defense. In these instances, government either produces the goods and services or subsidizes their production.

The production of other goods and services creates costs that are borne by persons other than the producers and the consumers. Economic efficiency calls for a reduction in the output of these goods. The most obvious example of this situation is an instance where significant pollution is caused.

Markets do not appear to be totally stable when left alone. Business cycles occur in market economies, causing periods of high unemployment, or high inflation, or both. High unemployment and high inflation are not economically efficient because we could be better off if unemployment and inflation were lower. A legitimate, although controversial, role for government is to attempt to reduce instability. The principal areas of controversy are how much stability should be the goal of policy and how we should go about ensuring stability.

Economic efficiency is one of a set of societal goals relevant to economic decision making. If that goal is pursued, other goals may not be fully satisfied. For example, an efficient market may result in an income distribution that some would see as inequitable. That is, a portion of the goal of equity is given up for efficiency. Markets allocate incomes based on the supply and demand for different types of labor. This means that some individuals will earn high incomes and others will earn relatively low incomes. Some individuals, depending on their value judgments, will argue that it is unfair or inequitable. The underlying theme of the economic way of thinking is that when we make a choice, we give up something else. The comparison of the benefits of what we choose with the costs (what we give up) leads to rational decision making. If that theme can be made part of our students' working tool kits, then we will have accomplished perhaps the most important goal of economic education.

A common activity in many economic education materials and a useful test to see if students are really mastering economic concepts and their use is a problem-solving approach that is derived from the scientific method. This five-step approach emphasizes a logical analysis that is applicable in many disciplines. The procedure asks students to

1. define the problem;

2. specify the goals, the policy options or possible decisions, and the relevant economic concepts;

3. analyze the consequences of each of the policy options or decisions;

4. evaluate each of the options according to each goal; and

5. decide which of the alternatives is best in light of the evaluations and the relative importance of the different goals.

The first four steps are essentially asking for a careful definition of the costs and benefits of a series of alternatives. The fifth step asks for a decision based on the comparison of the costs and the benefits. One advantage of the approach is that it enables students to clearly identify the proper role for value judgments in step five. It also shows how

31

individuals with differing values, but with the same understanding of concepts and principles, can make different decisions.

WHAT ISN'T ECONOMIC EDUCATION?

Some materials and often what is actually taught in the classroom under the rubric of economics are not good economic education. Students are taught facts—or, even worse, opinions—which do not enable them to objectively analyze personal and societal economic problems. Many students spend time learning how to write a check, how to budget, and how to comparison shop. Some teachers devote time to memorizing facts and figures, studying the mechanisms of the stock market, differentiating between wants and needs, and learning that saving is "good." None of these is economics or economic education. Some are possible tools to use as activities to reinforce basic economic understanding or to provide the foundation for more sophisticated understandings to be developed later. Some may help students function as consumers. But they are not economics in and of themselves. Those teachers and those materials using these activities and going no farther—that is, not getting students to use concepts—are not contributing to students' understanding of how to apply the tools of economics to better understand the world and to reach objective, reasoned judgments.

WHAT QUESTIONS SHOULD TEACHERS
AND ADMINISTRATORS ASK?

A variety of print and audiovisual materials are produced by businesses, labor unions, think tanks, government agencies, and others. Some are excellent. Most are up to date, presented in attractive formats, and inexpensive or even free. Some, however, have a goal of promoting one particular point of view based on value judgments and not necessarily on sound economic analysis. Others emphasize memorization of facts and concepts.

The economic content of a curriculum should include some understanding of how our economy works and an introduction to the economic way of thinking. Will students understand how markets work, when markets fail, macroeconomic data, the general roles of monetary and fiscal policy, the importance of international trade, and the necessity of comparing costs and benefits in making decisions, and will they understand how to use those concepts?

32

Examples may help in evaluating objectivity. If the goals of a publication are to enhance understanding of the free enterprise system or to engender support of the American private enterprise system, or if the materials consistently argue against all regulation or consistently argue in favor of all regulation, or if they discuss environmental protection, minimum wage laws, or farm price supports without discussing the costs and benefits, teachers should be wary.

A university-based center for economic education can be called on for assistance in evaluating the accuracy, objectivity, and effectiveness of materials and more extensive programs. Teachers and administrators should take advantage of those opportunities. But in order to assist that evaluation process, the guidelines in Table 2.2 are provided.

Table 2.2 lists ten questions to ask when evaluating economic content. If the answers to all ten questions are positive, then the content of the material or program is likely to be of high quality. Teachers and administrators using these guidelines will find a wide variety of good materials to use in teaching economics in many different contexts. There exists a basic core of economic concepts, accepted by the vast majority of professionals. The *Framework* described earlier in this chapter represents that core. Teachers who select materials and programs fitting into that core and who have participated in effective economic education programs will be able to bring economics to their classrooms in the most efficient and effective manner possible.

TABLE 2.2
Questions to Ask

1. Do the materials cover concepts included in the Joint Council's *Framework* (described earlier in the chapter)?
2. Do the concepts fit into the curriculum in a fashion similar to that specified in an accepted scope and sequence?
3. Do the materials help students develop critical thinking skills?
4. After using the materials, can students apply the concepts to solve personal or societal problems and recognize the role of value judgments in that decision process?
5. Has the program been evaluated as to its effectiveness?
6. When the materials discuss policy recommendations or economic problems, are the costs and the benefits clearly included?
7. In the context of policy discussions, are value judgments clearly indicated?

TABLE 2.2 (Continued)

8. Are the materials focused on the teacher so that the teacher may continually reinforce the concepts and applications?

9. Does the opportunity for teacher education accompany the materials?

10. Does that teacher education provide sufficient classroom guidance?

REFERENCES

Boulding, K. E. (1969). Economic education: The stepchild too is father of the man. *Journal of Economic Education* 1(1):5–11.

Caldwell, J.; Dalgaard, B. R.; Highsmith, R. J.; Reinke, R.; Gilliard, J. V.; and Watts, M. (1988). *Economics: What and when—Scope and sequence guidelines, K–12.* New York: Joint Council on Economic Education.

Keynes, J. M. (1930). *The scope and method of political economy.* New York: Macmillan.

Saunders, P.; Bach, G. L.; Calderwood, J. D.; Hansen, W. L.; and Stein, H. (1984). *A framework for teaching the basic concepts.* 2d ed. New York: Joint Council on Economic Education.

Stigler, G. J. (1983). The case, if any, for economic literacy. *Journal of Economic Education* 14(3):60–66.

3. THE CASE FOR ECONOMIC EDUCATION IN THE SCHOOL CURRICULUM

by Steven Miller

In a typical issue, *Newsweek* listed some of the problems the Bush administration confronts: "the deficit, taxes, strategic-arms control, Third World debt, international terrorism, the drug war, education, the environment, . . . the medical-cost explosion [and] defense policy" (Barry & Morganthau, 1989, p. 13). This list might easily have been expanded to include additional items: two from Samuelson's (1989) column in the same issue—rising inflationary pressures and inadequate future electrical generating capacity (p. 45)—and two from other articles—America's continuing sluggishness in productivity growth and the problems of educating homeless children (Is America Working Smarter? 1989, p. 42; Can a Shelter Be a School? 1989, p. 51). The problems of the failing savings and loan banks, the social security system, international trade policy, and the entrenched underclass, among others, could be added.

Most of these national and international problems—for instance, the federal deficit, taxes, and rising medical costs—are plainly within the domain of economics. Perhaps less obviously, all of the other issues have economic dimensions or are issues where the concepts of the discipline can be usefully applied.

To take one example, defense policy is fundamentally a problem of deciding how many resources should be devoted to national defense and how those resources should be allocated. Moreover, policy makers must also determine how best to allocate defense resources to meet global security commitments. Since economics is the study of the allocation of scarce resources to alternative and competing ends, it is not surprising that the concepts of economics can and should be used in analyzing and clarifying the countless issues involved in defense policy.

That so many of the most crucial issues facing our society are economic is part of the reason why economic education must be included in the school curriculum. This chapter develops this case in detail. The

35

first section presents the case for economic education in general, beginning with a brief definition of economics and economic education. Next, an example is provided that specifies the various elements that must be included in economic education. The third section extends the argument for economic education in general to a specific curricular area by demonstrating that economic education both falls within the schools' mission of education for citizenship and is part of the "basics" in social studies education. Fourth, the present state of economics in the curriculum is examined, with particular attention given to the problems of the infusion of economics. Finally, it is argued that these problems are not inherent, that they can be overcome, and that the importance of economics justifies the effort to include economics as a substantial part of the curriculum.

ECONOMICS AND ECONOMIC EDUCATION

Understanding what is meant by economics and economic education is important in considering why economic education must be included in the curriculum. As noted above, a standard textbook definition of economics might be "the study of the allocation of scarce resources to alternative and competing ends." Others, emphasizing that the concepts and propositions from economics are widely applicable, simply define economics as the "science of making decisions." Miller (1988) has noted that "No matter the definition used, it is clear that the tools of the economist are useful whenever choices are to be made" (p. 8). As will be noted in the next section, the emphasis on economic reasoning is crucial, especially in view of the recent research in expert problem solving.

This view of economics embraces the standard economists' division of the discipline into positive and normative dimensions. Kennedy (1975) has given a fairly standard definition: "*Positive economics* is concerned with what is . . . . *Normative economics* takes as a starting point the results of positive economics and is concerned with what ought to be" (pp. 12–13). Thus, positive economics is an attempt to develop a science squarely within the positivist tradition. Economists attempt to build theory and generalizations founded on positive concepts grounded in research. These concepts and generalizations should be thought of as testable propositions and predictions, just as hypotheses in the hard sciences can be tested (Friedman, 1953). For example, economists are

36

willing to subject to scrutiny the idea that "at higher prices people want less of a given commodity, all other things being equal."

Normative economics emphasizes the use of economics in making decisions on issues based on the consequences of actions or policies in terms of the goals and values of the person making the decision. Given some set of desired outcomes and preferences (for instance, generally accepted social goals such as economic freedom or equity), one chooses the policy alternative that best promotes the desired results. Thus, the complete act of economic reasoning includes both positive and normative economics: the analysis of the issue and examination of probable consequences, and the valuing of the alternative outcomes in terms of personal and social goals.

The emphasis on reasoning in decision making in economics is reflected in the growing consensus concerning what constitutes economic education. Miller (1988, p. 4) saw similarities when reviewing definitions from three recent publications. Students must learn the appropriate *economic content,* *apply* this body of knowledge to problems, acquire the capacity to *analyze* new and unique problems, and use their analysis to make *reasoned decisions or judgments.*

Thus, the goal of economic education is more responsible and effective citizenship through helping students acquire the ability to use economics as independent decision makers confronting problems, personal and social, rather than merely helping them gain knowledge of the facts, concepts, and assumptions that comprise part of the discipline. It empowers students to understand their world, make reasoned decisions, and act appropriately on personal and social issues of significance.

THE CRITICAL ELEMENTS OF ECONOMIC EDUCATION: AN EXAMPLE

The energy crisis is precisely the sort of issue that economic educators believe should be addressed in the classroom and is used here partly because it is an excellent example of the difference between how experts and nonexperts view and solve problems. Recall that twice in the 1970s supply interruptions were followed by rationing, using lines at the gasoline pumps, purchase restrictions based on license plate numbers, and reduced gas station hours. World oil prices quadrupled (after adjusting for inflation) during the decade. Natural gas seemed to be in short supply as well: New customers were denied access to gas, and existing industrial and commercial users experienced supply interruptions during several harsh winters. The energy crisis was a major problem throughout the decade, contributing to sluggish economic performance and double digit inflation.

The following example illustrates how the problem of the energy crisis might have been examined in the classroom using a problem-solving approach that elaborates on a more familiar one from economic education (Saunders et al., 1984, pp. 6–7) by including some aspects of hypothesis formulation and testing familiar to social studies educators. It is important to note that alternative views of the energy crisis will be presented to help demonstrate how economists' views of this problem differed from the conventional wisdom of the time and to show that economic reasoning requires more than adherence to a particular decision-making model.

In this problem-solving model the students must

1. define the problem to be investigated,
2. identify the appropriate concepts for the analysis,
3. use these concepts to construct one or more hypotheses about the problem,
4. test these hypotheses by examining the available evidence,
5. suggest alternative policy options or actions,
6. explicitly state the criteria of judgment,
7. evaluate the relative merits of the consequences of the alternatives in terms of these criteria, and
8. decide which alternative best meets the criteria.

Consider just the first five steps in relation to the example of the energy crisis. Students might define the problem as "What should the United States do about the shortage of gasoline and natural gas?" They might identify relevant concepts for use in analysis—for instance, finite, renewable, and nonrenewable resources. Perhaps they would hypothesize that the energy crisis was occurring because oil and natural gas resources were finite and diminishing. The search for supporting evidence might include the lines at the gasoline pumps, the unavailability of natural gas, and the projections of future production and consumption.

Students might list alternative solutions that generally focus on conservation and alternative energy sources, several of which were, in fact, considered or implemented. Billions of dollars were spent on encouraging exotic energy alternatives and establishing the strategic petroleum reserve. Tax incentives were established to encourage the insulation of houses. People were exhorted to conserve—by using car pools, for instance—and the schools and media attempted to educate the public about the new era of energy scarcity (Weaver, 1981, pp. 16–17). Other methods, such as limiting purchases, reducing gas station hours, and rationing by license plate numbers, were also used. Policy makers seriously considered and planned for the possibility of invading the Middle East oil fields. These and other alternatives might be listed by the students as consistent with their hypothesis.

However, there is another, utterly different analysis based on economic theory that students might have used. The concepts include markets, supply, demand, price, and cartel. They might have hypothesized that prices were not being permitted to perform the essential functions of rationing available products and services among potential buyers and creating incentives to produce more and consume less. Their analysis would show that, at the equilibrium market price for oil products, the quantity buyers are willing and able to purchase equals the quantity sellers are willing to offer. Thus, for any product or service, including natural gas or gasoline, there is a price that will clear the market, eliminating any shortages. Furthermore, there was no signal of rising domestic prices to suppliers to produce more oil and natural gas.

Moreover, students might use economic theory to hypothesize that price controls and other government policies were, in effect, supporting OPEC. Cartels are unstable because in order to support higher prices, cartel members must abide by production quotas that are lower than potential output. An individual cartel member could benefit by cheating—that is, by cutting its price just a bit and selling all that it could produce. However, the pressure to cheat was reduced by U.S. government policies that destroyed the price incentives to produce and conserve and that actually subsidized imported oil and discouraged domestic production.

The shortages might be viewed as evidence of the effects of price controls. Students might also seek evidence to support the contention that OPEC was collapsing, such as indications that OPEC production quotas were being violated. An alternative that might emerge from this analysis is to simply remove the price controls.

Note that in both of the cases above the first five steps of the problem-solving model were followed. Yet clear differences emerge in the hypotheses, the concepts used, the analysis of the problem, and the interpretation of the evidence. Such differences are to be expected because economic reasoning is expert problem solving using the tools and methods of the economist. Teaching students to use a generalized decision-making model does not guarantee sound analysis if the appropriate concepts are not employed. Thus, the alternative of removing price controls, if analyzed from the hypothesis that dwindling finite resources were the problem, could not remedy the shortage since it was apparently due to the exhaustion of a nonrenewable resource. On the other hand, using economic theory, the conservation and alternative sources approaches could never remedy the shortages and would cost billions in subsidies.

To continue with the second case in our example, up to this point students have engaged in positive economics. However, economic decision making also requires the use of normative economics: the specification of the criteria and the evaluation of the relative merits of the consequences of the alternatives in terms of those criteria. Among the many criteria that might be used are economic freedom, economic efficiency, economic growth, price stability, and national security. In this example, students might conclude that energy alternatives, like the strategic petroleum reserve, might improve national security through greater energy independence. They might also judge that economic efficiency is better served through removing price controls.

It is important to emphasize that part of the decision-making process is weighing the trade-offs among desirable goals. It is rare that one alternative meets all of the criteria better than the other alternatives do. More often, one alternative is superior on some criteria and less successful on others. It is crucial for students to develop the skill to determine, for example, whether some amount of lost economic efficiency and economic freedom is worth some increase in economic equity or security. In addition, students will also see that individuals and groups will view the relative importance of these criteria differently. Indeed, by working in groups on problems such as the energy crisis, student discussions of the problem will probably mirror the clashes over these goals that are present in the larger society.

Thus, for effective economic education to take place, the curriculum must encompass all of these important steps in economic reasoning, including the teaching of the relevant economic concepts. It is not

40

sufficient to simply introduce economic concepts without applying the concepts as part of an explicit reasoning process. Nor is it sufficient to stress only a generalized process of reasoning without giving attention to appropriate economic concepts and how experts use these concepts to examine issues.

ECONOMIC EDUCATION, SOCIAL STUDIES EDUCATION, AND CITIZENSHIP

The preceding section demonstrates that economic education stands on its own as a critical component in education for effective citizenship. In this section, the case for economic education will be expanded by showing its relationship to social studies education and citizenship education, major aims of education that enjoy broad support. This is not to say that economics should not be included in other subjects—for instance, business education or science. However, as will be shown shortly, social studies has the explicit objective of improving citizenship, which cannot be accomplished without economic education. First, some key elements of citizenship education and some criteria for determining what is basic to the social studies are presented. Next, the energy crisis example of effective economic education will be used to demonstrate that economic education meets the key elements of citizenship education and the criteria of the basics in the social studies.

Promoting more effective citizenship has long been identified as an integral part of the mission of American public education, despite vigorous disagreements about what constitutes effective citizenship, the role of the schools in promoting it, and how best to achieve those ends once they are agreed on (Warren, 1988). These are among the continuing concerns of educational philosophers in general, and of social studies educators in particular (Pratte, 1988; Parker & Jarolimek, 1984). As Parker and Jarolimek (1984) have argued, education for citizenship is a special area of concern for the social studies:

> Nevertheless, among the family, the community, the church, the media, the ethnic group, the school, and the other agencies of citizenship education, it is the school that was created for the express purpose of developing citizens who would and could sustain the democratic experiment. Within the school, the social studies curriculum has been designated for the realization of this purpose. (p. 6)

41

Thus, it can be argued that citizenship education, however conceived, is an important part of the mission of education and a special responsibility of the social studies.

There are continuing disagreements about what constitutes citizenship or civic education. Parker and Jarolimek (1984) have argued that, at least in the social studies, the essential elements of citizenship education include (1) education to produce the informed citizen who has key knowledge of science, history, and the social sciences, including economic theories, systems, structures, and processes; (2) education to produce the skillful citizen who has skills in the gathering, organizing, and using of information in interpersonal relationships and social participation; and (3) education to produce the citizen who is committed to democratic values.

Economic education not only promotes each of these aspects of citizenship education, but also is indispensable to some. The example of the energy crisis and the issues cited in the introduction demonstrate why Jarolimek (1978) included economics among the key areas of knowledge for students. The energy crisis example also demonstrates the importance of economic reasoning in building the necessary skills of the citizen, including gathering, ordering, and using information. Wrestling with problems such as the energy crisis is an excellent way for students to increase their skills in interpersonal relations and their understanding of the value of participation in finding workable solutions in a pluralistic society. Finally, normative economics provides students with the crucial opportunity to weight and trade off values that are generally accepted as desirable in our society.

Economic education also is basic to the social studies. Jarolimek (1978) has offered the following criteria:

What is basic in the social studies are those values, skills, processes, experiences, or subject matter that:

1. teach the learners to participate in the common culture.
2. develop the learners' commitment to shared, general values.
3. develop the learners' functioning in a group.
4. increase the learners' capacity to engage in decision making.
5. develop the learners' willingness to live according to the norms that govern individual and group behavior.
6. prepare learners to engage in activities that are essential for societal continuity. (pp. 32–33)

As with citizenship education, economic education admirably fits these criteria. The economic system and the policy decisions that must be made in that system, such as those related to the energy crisis, are important elements of our common culture. As noted above, examining the relative importance of commonly held goals, including economic goals, is one important part of increasing students' understanding of and commitment to the shared values of the society. Group decision making about economic problems enhances both the skill of functioning in a group and the ability to make warranted decisions. By analyzing problems in terms of goals, students can come to the realization that policy decisions often represent the need to establish the relative primacy of certain values over others and that there is merit in the values established in our society. Finally, making decisions about economic problems, both personal and social, is fundamental to social continuity since participation in the economic system is an inescapable part of living.

Moreover, it is important to note that educators cannot meet all of the criteria of citizenship education and the basics of the social studies without including economic education. For instance, the research in problem solving and decision making indicates that such skills are not necessarily generic. Experts in a field solve problems differently from the uninitiated (Armento, 1986, p. 947). This strongly suggests that the skills necessary for economic decision making, skills that are basic to the social studies and essential for citizenship, must be learned through economic education.

Thus, economic education can be thought of as "basic" to social studies education in two ways. Economic education is basic to the social studies and an indispensable component of citizenship education, which is the primary focus of the social studies.

THE CURRENT STATE OF ECONOMICS IN THE CURRICULUM

Pratte (1988), noting the dismal state of civic education, has written:

> But there is nothing inconsistent or paradoxical about this state of affairs. It merely reflects the fact that civic education has been badly neglected in the public schools; it has not been at the heart of the curriculum, and hence its effort has been, at best, mixed, indirect, and tangential. (p. 304)

The experience of economics in the curriculum is a parallel one, as have been the results (at least as measured by student achievement scores on the *Test of Economic Literacy*, a test of basic economics).

It seems probable that the general absence of understanding of basic economic principles is due, in part, to the fact that economics simply has not been emphasized in the curriculum of enough school districts. Only about half of the states have an economics (or "free enterprise") requirement, and most implement it, at least in part, supposedly by infusion (Highsmith, 1989). However, as will be discussed in detail later, the present evidence strongly indicates that an infusion approach is less effective than is an economics course required of all students.

An important general problem affects economics in the curriculum, whether presented in a separate course or infused into other courses. Too often economics, as understood by many educators and presented to students in various courses, is really "consumer life skills," not economics. This distinction, while elementary, is both crucial and commonly overlooked. Courses and units of instruction labeled "economics" often focus on such topics as balancing a checkbook, comparison shopping, purchasing life insurance, and the like. Such courses or units are prevalent because teachers often do not have enough economics background to teach economic principles or to distinguish between economics and consumer life skills. Also, many teachers find consumer topics easier to teach and more "relevant" for students. The result is that there is much less economics in the curriculum and in classroom instruction than there appears to be.

Moreover, there are at least three major problems specific to the prevailing infusion approach. First, teachers of the courses wherein economics might be infused often do not do so, perhaps because they lack a basic understanding of economics and its relationship to the subject they teach (Miller, 1988, p. 21). Also, irrespective of the district curriculum, teachers tend to rely heavily on their textbooks, which often include little treatment of economics (Miller & Rose, 1983; Shaver, Davis & Helburn, 1979; Weiss, 1978).

Second, economics is not presented in a coordinated, building fashion. This is a reasonable inference from Armento's (1983) examination of economics curriculum guides drawn from schools with supposedly stronger economics programs. She found that "Concepts are dealt with at the introductory, definitional level—whether the guide is intended for the ninth or the twelfth grade. If this is the case, there must

44

be an assumption by curriculum builders that prior instruction in economic education has not occurred" (p. 26).

Third, this absence of a coordinated, building approach creates especially pernicious results for the economic understanding of students. One result is that critical economic concepts are simply never presented. Moreover, including all of the significant concepts in places where every student will have the opportunity to learn them does nothing to ensure the synthesizing of the conceptual learning into an integrated whole. Research by Walstad and Watts (1985) indicates that students who learn economics under the infusion approach are not likely to "acquire an overview of how individual concepts fit together in a meaningful whole" (p. 16). As Miller (1988) has noted:

> This has serious implications for economic education for citizenship given its focus on reasoned decisions on social problems and the value-laden nature of economic issues. Economic analysis of problems frequently requires the abilities to realize the implications of actions in one arena on results in another, and to evaluate the consequences of alternative actions. (p. 21)

Nonetheless, there are important reasons to improve the infusion approach. The first is the critical explanatory power of economics for other subjects, such as U.S. history. For instance, unionization can be thought of as attempting to oppose the monopsony in employment (one buyer) of the one company town with a countervailing monopoly over the supply of labor. Productivity and capital investment are critical concepts in understanding the Industrial Revolution (Miller, 1988, p. 19). Indeed, the failure to include economics in such courses as U.S. history results in serious misteaching (Miller & Rose, 1983).

Infusing economics can reorient the traditional emphasis from lower-level learning to problem solving and decision making. For instance, government classes often limit consideration of the economic regulating activity of the federal government to simply one item on a list of functions of the executive branch. However, economic education through infusion could emphasize the analysis of economic issues that agencies confront or the evaluation of government performance in macroeconomic policy. But this can be done only through economic education that requires students to use both positive and normative economics inherent in economic reasoning.

To summarize, the recent state of economics in the curriculum is not encouraging. Despite the number of states that require economics

45

instruction, too much of that instruction is about "practical economics" or "consumer life skills," rather than economics. The infusion approach, while prevalent, is less effective than a required course in economics. The failure to infuse economics where possible, the overreliance on textbooks, and the general lack of a comprehensive, coordinated economics curriculum combine to produce spotty, inconsistent, and fractured curricula that fail to provide students with an effective economic education. Nonetheless, an effective infusion of economic education in the curriculum presents the opportunity to correct serious errors and strengthen the courses where it might be infused.

SUMMARY

The problems of including economic education in the curriculum are not inherent. The crucial element is the recognition of its value and necessity to understanding and making warranted decisions about the problems that face our society and the planet, to enhancing citizenship education, to presenting a basic social studies program, and to improving courses where it is included.

However, that the problems are not inherent does not mean that they will be easily solved. Teachers, who often are the writers of the curriculum in school districts, must possess enough economic knowledge to recognize the opportunities to include it in the curriculum. There must be a willingness to focus on economic education, not on providing consumer life skills or simply on teaching economic concepts. The curriculum must be carefully crafted so that students will learn all of the important concepts of economics, be engaged in the process of economic reasoning, and understand the interrelationships of the discipline.

The effort is probably worth the cost. To return to the example of the energy crisis, in retrospect the analysis of the economics profession seems to have been largely correct. The removal of price controls ended the energy shortages. Gasoline rationing disappeared even as real prices fell to levels below those of the mid-1970s. Natural gas distributors began adding new customers. The OPEC cartel experienced increasing difficulty as individual members cheated on assigned quotas.

The costs to the U.S. economy of its energy policies of the seventies must surely be in the tens of billions of dollars due to lost economic efficiency, dislocations cause by inflation, lost economic growth, support of the OPEC cartel, and subsidization of alternatives that were not economically justified at the real prices of oil and natural gas. These costs are the price of economic illiteracy in our society. They are sure to be incurred again in new situations when an uninformed citizenry cannot participate effectively in the public policy process or, worse, can be led to support policies that do not really achieve their preferred outcomes.

REFERENCES

Armento, B. J. (1986). Research on teaching social studies. In *Second handbook of research on teaching*, ed. M. C. Wittrock, 942–51. New York: Macmillan.
———— (1983). A study of the basic economic concepts presented in DEEP curriculum guides, grades 7–12. *Journal of Economic Education* 14(3):22–27.
Barry, J., and Morganthau, T. (1989). The defense dilemma. *Newsweek*, 23 January, 13–18.
Can a shelter be a school? (1989). *Newsweek*, 23 January, 51.
Friedman, M. (1953). The methodology of positive economics. In *Essays in positive economics*, ed. M. Friedman. Chicago: University of Chicago Press.
Highsmith, R. J. (1989). *A survey of state mandates for economics instruction, 1989*. New York and Washington, D.C.: Joint Council on Economic Education and NFIB Foundation.
Is America working smarter? (1989). *Newsweek*, 23 January, 42.
Jarolimek, J. (1978). The basics in social studies: Implications for the preparation of teachers. In *Competency based teacher education: Professionalizing social studies teaching*, ed. D. Felder, 17–36. Washington, D.C.: National Council for the Social Studies.
Kennedy, P. (1975). *Macroeconomics*. Boston: Allyn and Bacon.
Miller, S. L. (1988). *Economic education for citizenship*. Bloomington, Ind.: ERIC Clearinghouse for Social Studies/Social Science Education, Foundation for Teaching Economics, and Social Studies Development Center.
Miller, S. L., and Rose, S. A. (1983). The great depression: A textbook case of problems with American history textbooks. *Theory and Research in Social Education* 11(1):25–39.
Parker, W., and Jarolimek, J. (1984). *Citizenship and the critical role of the social studies*. Boulder, Colo.: Social Science Education Consortium, ERIC Clearinghouse for Social Studies/Social Science Education, and National Council for the Social Studies.
Pratte, R. (1988). Civic education in a democracy. *Theory into Practice* 27(4):303–308.
Samuelson, R. (1989). What Bush should do. *Newsweek*, 23 January, 45.

Saunders, P.; Bach, G. L.; Calderwood, J. D.; Hansen, W. L.; and Stein, H. (1984). *A framework for teaching the basic concepts.* 2d ed. New York: Joint Council on Economic Education.

Shaver, J. P.; Davis, O. L.; and Helburn, S. W. (1979). The status of social studies education: Impressions from three N.S.F. studies. *Social Education* 43(2):150–53.

Walstad, W. B., and Watts, M. (1985). The current status of economics in the K–12 curriculum. In *Economics in the school curriculum, K–12,* ed. M. C. Schug, 14–15. Washington, D.C.: National Education Association and Joint Council on Economic Education.

Warren, D. (1988). Original intents: Public schools as civic education. *Theory into Practice* 27(4):243–49.

Weaver, K. (1981). Our energy predicament. In *Energy: Facing up to the problem, getting down to solutions,* 16–17. Washington, D.C.: National Geographic Society.

Weiss, I. R. (1978). *Report of the 1977 national survey of science, mathematics, and social studies education.* Research Triangle Park, N.C.: Research Triangle Institute.

4. DEEP: A PROCESS FOR CURRICULUM RENEWAL

by S. Stowell Symmes

DEEP is the process by which the network affiliates of the Joint Council on Economic Education help schools install economic education curricular programs. DEEP is therefore a means to an end rather than an end itself. In economic terms, DEEP is a process for producing economic education in schools so that students benefit by becoming more effective economic decision makers.

THE DEEP CURRICULUM CHANGE MODEL

Describing production processes as complex as DEEP is a challenging assignment fraught with pitfalls, but one that economic educators over the years have tried to accomplish by developing schematic models to explain how school districts should go about installing economic education programs within their K–12 curricular offerings. Although the Joint Council's network professionals may use different schematics to explain their work, all their models have a common core of essential elements: needs assessment; program planning; program implementation through curriculum development, including staff training and materials acquisition; program evaluation; and program maintenance.

Figure 4.1, used by the Joint Council since 1984 to depict DEEP, is an intentionally simplified graphic that shows linkages among these five major components and three subcomponents. It was developed as a better way to communicate the essential structure of DEEP to diverse audiences including uncommitted school administrators, teachers, donors, and others who might be interested in supporting the goals of economic education, but who have far less interest in the detailed

Abbejean Kehler, The Ohio State University, and Peter R. Moore, Rhode Island College, provided thoughtful and much appreciated comments on an earlier version of this chapter.

FIGURE 4.1
The Major Components of the DEEP Process

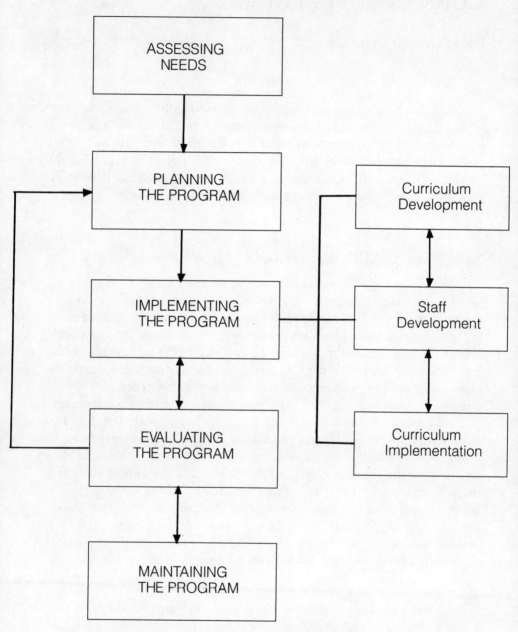

Source: Joint Council on Economic Education, 1989

processes of how the Joint Council network goes about doing that job. Details needed by local DEEP coordinators and network consultants were left to be specified in the *DEEP Handbook* (Kehler & Symmes, 1990).

Underlying this basic structure are five fundamental tenets shared by most economic educators which affect the way DEEP operates and determine its curriculum development goals. These tenets need to be made explicit because they determine the shape of the curriculum that economic educators are committed to install in schools.

1. Our society permits all its members to make decisions on economic matters; therefore, economic education must be provided to all students.

2. Economic education properly acquired equips people with the knowledge and reasoning skills that are necessary to understand and cope with the economic world in which they live.

3. Schools are the institutions best suited to deliver economic education to young people because schooling is required and economic education is too important to be left to chance.

4. Learning to be a more effective economic decision maker is a set of complex developmental tasks that can be best nurtured by students as they move through economics programs within a planned K–12 curriculum.

5. Skilled teachers with economics training are key elements in the process because they know how to take account of the special needs of all students and how to accommodate their different learning abilities, learning styles, and levels of maturation.

Significant implications for curriculum development derive from these common beliefs. Such beliefs imply that a range of grade levels should include economics programs, they suggest that a variety of curricula and instructional designs are needed to reach all students, and they assert that schools and their teachers are critical instruments for providing economic education to young people.

What Is a Curriculum?

Before moving ahead with an analysis of the DEEP processes designed to implement curriculum change, it will be helpful to have in mind a

51

common working definition of *curriculum*. Unfortunately, scholars in the field do not agree on what curriculum means. But without a workable definition, economic educators will find it difficult to know when an economic education curriculum is installed and will find it virtually impossible to measure its impact on students.

Is the curriculum a written guide or what the teacher does when the classroom door is closed? Glatthorn (1987) provides a useful definition for our purposes: "The curriculum is the plans made for guiding learning in schools, usually represented in retrievable documents of several levels of generality, and the implementation of those plans in the classroom; those experiences take place in a learning environment that also influences what is learned" (p. 1). For Glatthorn, curriculum includes both the plans for learning and the teaching of those plans. He does not think it sensible to separate curriculum from instruction. Most economic education guides prepared under the auspices of the Joint Council's network accept this view because they include both what is to be taught and how it is to be taught.

Furthermore, Glatthorn (1987) introduces a set of curriculum types that help sort out what it is that curriculum developers endeavor to implement and to be held accountable for in terms of the impact on students.

- The *recommended curriculum* is the ideal curriculum—what some scholar or committee thinks the curriculum should be. . . .

- The *written curriculum* is the curriculum embodied in the district's documents—its scope-and-sequence charts, its curriculum guides, its program of studies booklets. . . .

- The *taught curriculum* is what teachers actually teach in the classroom.

- The *supported curriculum* is defined by the resources you provide to support the curriculum—the staff, the time, the texts, the space, the training. . . .

- The *tested curriculum* is the curriculum you see when you look at unit tests and final examinations. It is the measured curriculum.

- The *learned curriculum* is the "bottom line" curriculum—what the students actually learn.

One of the tasks of curriculum leadership, obviously, is to use the right methods to bring the written, the taught, the supported, and the tested

52

curricula into closer alignment, so that the learned curriculum is maximized. (pp. 3–4)

Economic educators, as they help schools incorporate economic education into their curricula, deal with each type of curriculum at one time or another. In essence, DEEP processes should help schools align economic education curricula so that students learn what is recommended that they learn. The art of bringing more congruence among the recommended, taught, and learned economics curricula in schools is the real art of the economic educator.

How Is DEEP Different from Other Models?

What is it that economic educators do that is different from what other organizations do to try to change curriculum offerings in schools, and what do they do that is similar? In this regard, it is highly instructive to compare DEEP processes with those of noneconomic educators who engaged in various aspects of curriculum change in the 1970s.

Hahn (1976), using Havelock's framework for classifying studies of efforts to diffuse various innovations, categorized DEEP as a prototype of the Problem Solver (PS) model. The PS model is process oriented, rather than product oriented, and views diffusion primarily from the school system's perspective, rather than from the developer's perspective. In contrast, other subject-based curriculum projects of the 1960s—those in geography, sociology, government, history, and anthropology, known collectively as the new social studies projects—were classified by Hahn as prototypes of Havelock's research, development, diffusion, and adoption (RDDA) model. The RDDA model is product oriented and views diffusion from the developer's perspective.

The DEEP process begins when district personnel recognize a need to improve their economic education program for students. If they do not perceive a need, then no other steps in the process are taken. But if they do, a DEEP coordinator is appointed, plans are set forth, resources are committed, committees are organized, and needs assessments are conducted to determine requirements for curriculum change and teacher education. With the help of economic education consultants, local curriculum materials are reviewed and revised, and new teaching resources are examined, to be adopted or adapted at the discretion of local educators. This part of the process often runs concurrently with

53

teacher-training activities. With DEEP, curriculum implementation occurs when new economics programs become part of the regular curriculum once evaluation shows that new programs meet district needs. New materials adopted may or may not be programs produced by the Joint Council or its affiliates. As long as the instructional materials impart sound economic concepts, employ appropriate pedagogy, and serve the instructional goals of the district, the Joint Council's network can support their use.

By comparison, social studies projects using the RDDA model stressed the development of new curriculum products, usually a package of materials prepared by experts, which were then turned over to book publishers to disseminate. Much less thought was devoted to the diffusion phase or to helping potential adopters adapt the product to local conditions and local needs. Surveys sent by researchers to social studies teachers in several states in an effort to measure adoptions of these heavily funded, well-researched projects found very low levels of awareness and adoption even among teachers who were a targeted cohort for that innovative curriculum (Hahn, 1976). Interestingly, one study found that in-service training related to the materials significantly increased the user rate, yet few RDDA model projects related any teacher training to the instructional materials (p. 141). Another study concluded that "Evaluations demonstrating an innovation's effectiveness are important but not sufficient to guarantee adoption. Regardless of evaluation data, innovations will be adopted only if they further an objective that has high priority in the district" (p. 145). This finding supports both the critical importance of meshing with district curriculum priorities and the value of spending resources to shape that set of priorities, as has been done by economic educators through DEEP.

Is DEEP a Respectable Curriculum Change Model?

Reviews of several summaries of studies on various aspects of curriculum-building theory (Loucks-Horsley & Hergert, 1985; English, 1983; Hahn & Rushing, 1981; Hunkins, in Davis, 1976) and curriculum change practices (Glatthorn, 1987; Loucks-Horsley & Hergert, 1985) reveal that the underlying processes used in DEEP are supported by sufficient research findings to make DEEP respectable from the vantage point of both curriculum theory and practice. As noted above, Hahn (1976) found that DEEP fits the general PS model of curriculum diffusion, with its core premise that no curriculum change will take place unless the school is convinced that change is needed.

DEEP is also highly compatible with the Concerns-Based Adoption Model (CBAM), a research-based framework for school improvement developed by Loucks and Hall in the 1970s. CBAM has since been made a focal point of several publications and training seminars of the Association for Supervision and Curriculum Development (ASCD). *An Action Guide to School Improvement* (Loucks-Horsley & Hergert, 1985) outlines the seven-step CBAM process, which helps schools move systematically from "as it is now" to "as we'd like it to be." The seven steps employed by CBAM are remarkably similar to basic DEEP components.

Glatthorn, another curriculum change practitioner highly regarded by ASCD, advocates training local school personnel to implement curriculum change by using a consensus curriculum model (Glatthorn, 1987). Consensus curriculum is a process by which new curriculum areas can be installed by bringing objectives of the recommended, written, and taught curricula into closer congruence (p. 20). Heavy involvement of faculty members and examination of curriculum objectives and curriculum materials are hallmarks of the consensus model, clearly a process that fits well with DEEP processes used by economic educators to help schools infuse economics lessons and units into existing courses at all grade levels by having trained teachers use curricular materials they have selected.

These brief vignettes show that basic DEEP processes are highly compatible with the general curriculum development models espoused by leading curriculum theorists and practitioners outside the Joint Council network. Of course, finding that DEEP is a respectable curriculum change model does not assure that economic educators can successfully use it to implement a curriculum. What it does mean is that economic educators should not discard the process because they believe that DEEP is basically flawed or simply because it is a very difficult process to use. There is nothing fundamentally wrong with the DEEP curriculum change model. In fact, using DEEP processes may well be a major reason why economic education did not suffer the fate of social science curriculum projects of the 1960s, many of which did not make their way into the classroom in sufficient quantities to make a lasting impact on what students learn.

The scholars of the 1960's addressed their demands primarily to updating curriculum content, reorganizing curriculum elements, and introducing some innovative approaches to subject matter. In other words, they were concerned primarily with the development of materials rather than the procedures for creating curriculum or for introducing curriculum changes into schools. In their attention to specific content, the scholars ignored for the most part the technical aspects of implementation and maintenance. Perhaps because of these oversights, many of the innovations of the fifties and sixties failed to achieve maximum or even optimal utilization. (Hunkins, in Davis, 1976, p. 93)

Too often economic educators fail to remind themselves that all process models are merely tools for doing, not the reality of doing. They worry about details such as terminology, the order of steps to take, and proof that one recommended technique is superior to another in their concern to assure practitioners that their blueprints, if followed, will lead to success. And they should do no less. However, the reality of doing curriculum building in our schools has been, and always will be, an inexact science, primarily because doing it is such a complex set of activities, conducted in a political environment steeped in traditions and involving so many people with vested interests in the results that the best process model may not result in quality economic education programs for students every time. Economic educators must negotiate change; they cannot order it.

Admitting that curriculum building is an inexact science and that DEEP processes may not result in quality curriculum in every school district on a prescribed schedule should not lead to inaction. Economic educators cannot be so doctrinaire as to require complete proof that DEEP processes produce quality economic education before acting. They must act on faith in their mission, with insights and partial knowledge about how to achieve it, rather than proof, but they must act. It is precisely out of the actions–mistakes–trials cycle and the partial successes of today's professionals that a new generation of economic educators will emerge with the vision, talent, and technology to move closer to their goal.

Finally, it is incumbent upon economic educators to improve DEEP processes and not rest on their laurels. One of the most encouraging new documents in this regard is a set of recommendations prepared by the DEEP Planning Committee entitled *DEEP Enhancement Goals* (Moore et al., 1987). The report is a wonderfully pragmatic tool that suggests specific indicators to measure qualitative improvements in DEEP process components. It should be studied and embraced by the Joint Council's network as a framework for assuring that DEEP will become a more effective curriculum change system.

Is DEEP a Viable Curriculum Change Process?

It has been nearly 30 years since the National Task Force on Economic Education delivered its report (Committee for Economic Development, 1961) and sounded the clarion for expanding economic instruction in the nation's secondary schools. Just three years later, the Joint Council launched its five-year DEEP experiment in curriculum change to examine ways school districts could respond to the National Task Force (NTF) report. Other chapters in this volume review the historical record of DEEP and analyze the results from a variety of perspectives. Rather than duplicate those efforts, this chapter will provide readers with several macro-observations, looking back 25 years and contrasting what was then with what is today, regarding selected elements of the DEEP process: commitment to the goals of economic education, commitment to DEEP as a delivery mechanism, availability of curriculum development tools, availability of teacher-training opportunities, and measures of success.

COMMITMENT TO THE GOALS OF ECONOMIC EDUCATION

The NTF report served as a national needs assessment statement and a rationale for placing more economics in secondary school curricula. Although there was a brief reference to "experimental techniques underway at the elementary level that should be watched," curriculum change at the secondary level, not for kindergarten through grade 12, was the announced goal of the NTF report. Today the need for economic education across the curriculum is widely accepted.

At the time the report was issued, there were no nationally normed tests available to collect data to back up NTF assertions that students did not know enough economics to be good citizens. Today normed tests are available for several grade levels, and several national data bases on what students do or do not know about economics have been established.

57

These test instruments, used extensively at the district level to measure program impact in DEEP schools, are also used for basic research and evaluation to obtain data that can be used to increase commitments to economic education.

Twenty-five years ago there were few state mandates to include economics in the curriculum. Today 28 states give support to economic education as a curriculum priority.

In 1964 only three centers were established, and many of the 35 to 40 regional councils were little more than one-person operations, with several operating out of school district offices. Most DEEP services came directly to the schools from the Joint Council offices, and when these services stopped, commitments at the district level languished. It was evident that a strong servicing arm close to DEEP schools had to be created, or else recruiting new districts would be difficult, and maintaining curriculum and staff development gains would be less likely. One of the great achievements over the intervening 25 years has been the establishment of nearly 300 university-based centers for economic education and the increase in the number of well-managed affiliated councils. Without these agencies, the Joint Council could not hope to operate a curriculum change process such as DEEP.

COMMITMENT TO DELIVERING ECONOMIC EDUCATION THROUGH DEEP

Incentives for local school districts to make commitments to include more economics instruction in their curricular offerings have always been important, or else DEEP processes do not begin. Early on, it was determined that DEEP school districts themselves must bear the major burden of the costs of curriculum development within the scope of their state-directed responsibilities to provide quality education for students. Therefore, it was necessary for economic educators to provide enough incentives and support services to convince local schools to redirect curriculum priorities to include economic education. Purely as a process innovation, DEEP has been diffused to nearly 2,000 public school districts and scores of parochial and independent schools over the past 25 years. Over the same time span, more than 100 districts, after making initial commitments to DEEP, dropped from active participation for any number of reasons. Several have subsequently rejoined DEEP under new school leadership.

Incentives provided by Joint Council network affiliates to encourage school districts to join DEEP have been adjusted over the years to meet changing levels of available resources and to take into account the large differences in need between an urban New York City district with its 900,000 students and a rural Arapahoe, Nebraska, district with its 275 students. Data in Table 4.1 show that between 1984 and 1989, network incentives provided by the Joint Council, combined with state curriculum mandates in economics, resulted in large increases in the number of school district administrators willing to make written commitments to work with the Joint Council's network affiliates using the DEEP curriculum change model. In 1969 no states had written DEEP agreements; today 28 states have written agreements or letters of intent that spell out levels of commitment and responsibility. This in itself is a significant achievement. Economic educators are well aware that signing up does not mean an instant fix, but it does open the door for positive intervention to take place through the delivery of network services. And results from the Exemplary DEEP Awards Program described in Chapter 10 show that districtwide economic education programs can be installed in DEEP schools if the conditions are right. Peer competition among superintendents of schools will provide additional incentive for new districts to enroll and for those districts already enrolled to excel.

One of the most critical elements in moving farther ahead with DEEP

TABLE 4.1
Total Number of DEEP School Systems, 1983–89

FY	NUMBER
1983–84	725
1984–85	834
1985–86	1,057
1986–87	1,378
1987–88	1,662
1988–89	1,836

Source: Joint Council on Economic Education, Fall 1989.

Note: Fiscal year (FY) is July 1–June 30. DEEP school systems include public and parochial administrative districts and independent schools.

has always been the need to convince more members of the Joint Council network that the DEEP process is in fact a viable vehicle for delivering economic education to students in American schools. During the 1960s experimental phase, network organizations were not prominent players, except in a few instances, and in 1984 there was network resistance to a five-year plan for expansion and enhancement of economic education using DEEP processes. One of the main goals of that project was to provide both program and service incentives to get network support of DEEP. Table 4.2 shows the results of a variety of incentives directed at this objective. The data reflect a significant positive shift in network behavior toward delivering economic education through DEEP. It is equally evident that some states for a variety of reasons remain not so committed. Enrollment of DEEP districts has also grown so fast in some regions that service requirements have outstripped Joint Council network resources. It will be necessary for the Joint Council to put additional resources behind network building and new technology if quality services are to be rendered to a growing number of DEEP schools and hard-to-reach systems.

TABLE 4.2
Level of Statewide Commitment to DEEP, 1984 and 1989

CATEGORY	NUMBER OF STATES		PERCENTAGE OF STUDENTS SERVED	
	1984	1989	1984	1989
Excellent	5	22	17%	60%
Good	14	10	36	21
Fair	17	7	33	11
Poor	15	12	14	8

Source: Joint Council on Economic Education, 1989.

Note: Level of commitment was determined by the DEEP office executive director based on the following four criteria: (1) evidence of statewide DEEP expansion and enhancement plans, (2) evidence of DEEP support as shown by board of trustees' policy statements and council publications, (3) allocation of resources—both personnel and budget—to DEEP-related activities, and (4) acceptance of responsibility to provide the Joint Council with data on progress with regard to DEEP expansion. Number of states includes Washington, D.C.

AVAILABILITY OF QUALITY CURRICULUM DEVELOPMENT MATERIALS

In 1964 the only economic education curriculum development tools available were two small teachers' guides, one (Joint Council on Economic Education, 1964a) outlining the basic economic concepts set forth by the NTF report and a second (Joint Council on Economic Education, 1964b) giving suggestions for grade placement. The NTF report (Committee for Economic Development, 1961) had referred vaguely to Senesh's *Our Working World* experiments at the elementary level, but there were no prototype economics-focused curriculum guides at the elementary level and few curriculum publications in economics at the secondary level, except for economics textbooks that did not reflect instruction in the economic way of thinking espoused by the NTF report.

Chapter 20 reviews the evolution of DEEP curriculum materials production and projects future requirements. Here it is enough to assert that in 25 years there has been a tremendous qualitative improvement in curriculum-building resources available to DEEP schools and to give a few examples.

Among the most important is the *Master Curriculum Guide in Economics for the Nation's Schools* (MCG), published to provide DEEP school districts with a curriculum development tool that would be flexible, user friendly, and relatively inexpensive to assure widespread use. The MCG provides a framework for teaching basic economic concepts (Saunders et al., 1984), a ten-volume series of strategies guides for teaching economics at different grade levels and in various subject areas, and a unique scope and sequence document, *Economics: What and When* (Gilliard et al., 1988). This set of publications served to marry curriculum and instruction in economics by making available to teachers and curriculum development teams in local DEEP schools hundreds of ready-made, concept-driven, classroom-tested economics lessons, with permission given to incorporate MCG lessons into local guides. Although its benefits are difficult to measure, the MCG undoubtedly has had lasting impact on thousands of written and taught curricula, and after 12 years in print, it remains a very high impact program in terms of changing K–12 economic instruction. Over the years, economic educators have comprised one of the most successful groups of scholars in determining what to include and what not to include of their discipline in K–12 economic education curricula. Making such a determination is a requisite for successful curriculum development in any discipline.

Other high-impact curriculum development tools include a series of four award-winning television programs in economics for children—*Econ and Me* (primary), *Trade-Offs* (intermediate/middle), *Give & Take* (middle/junior high), and *Understanding Taxes* (senior high)—which are available to all schools on a public domain basis in most states; three nationally normed cognitive tests; two newsletters for teachers, *The Elementary Economist* and *The Senior Economist*; and a variety of specialized course guides targeted to students with special needs ranging from those at risk of dropping out of school to those capable of advanced placement work in economics. What other discipline can offer schools such easily accessible sets of concept-based materials along with curriculum management handbooks and staff development assistance? Of course, gaps do exist in some Joint Council economics curriculum programs, but compared to other disciplines vying for space in the school curriculum, economic educators stand tall regarding the availability of quality instructional materials that support the DEEP process.

TEACHERS TRAINED IN ECONOMIC EDUCATION

The Joint Council places the trained teacher using effective materials at the apex of its DEEP implementation model. Kehler (1989) warns that to ignore the teacher's role in disseminating curriculum risks failure to implement curriculum change even though the change is recommended by leading scholars or is ordered by a school administration or by state mandate. "Teachers possess the power to fail to consent, and thereby can negate all efforts to impose change from the outside" (p. 1). Furthermore, without trained teachers, the best written curriculum will not be transferred into taught curriculum. Loucks-Horsley (Forthcoming, n.d.) has conducted extensive research in the area of teacher development that is specific to curriculum implementation, and among her findings is the fact that teacher involvement in the decision to select the new curriculum and in the determination of how it is to be used is crucial to successful implementation (Loucks-Horsley & Hergert, 1985, p. 131). This implies that economic educators are right on track when they tie teacher in-service in economics to curriculum programs that are being considered for adoption by the schools.

Through the years, economic educators have improved the staff development component of the DEEP process. Joint Council network personnel have developed wide varieties of staff development programs, adjusting always to changing teacher preferences, including credit and noncredit programs and programs tailor made in response to district teachers' needs. Also, many staff development programs today are targeted to teams of teachers in single DEEP districts and are directly connected to helping teachers implement a particular set of teaching materials, either units or courses, rather than merely training teachers in economics content without reference to what would be done with that content in the classroom, as was commonly done in the past.

Economic educators do not yet have a good sense of how to target their training to build up a strong reservoir of teachers trained in economic education within the district. Local DEEP coordinators and Joint Council network field representatives must focus their staff development efforts by consciously planning to improve the base of teachers capable of delivering quality economic instruction within each curriculum program adopted by the district. Good examples of staff development targeted to achieve the critical mass necessary to make real change are found in Randolph, New Jersey, where the entire social studies department has strong economics background and in Carroll County, Maryland, where every sixth grade teacher has been trained to use *Trade-Offs*. Trained teachers greatly contributed to having these districts' economics curricula designated as exemplary DEEP programs (Joint Council on Economic Education, 1987, 1988, 1989).

MEASURES OF THE VIABILITY OF DEEP

Chapters 6, 7, and 8 of this volume review research and evaluation studies on DEEP. Indeed, DEEP is the most heavily evaluated curriculum change process in social science education (Brenneke et al., 1988; Brenneke & Soper, 1987; Brenneke & Soper, 1984; Buckles & Freeman, 1984; Symmes, 1981; Wentworth, Hansen & Hawke, 1977; Kim & Kratochvil, 1972; Grobman, 1970; Psychological Corporation, 1970; Joint Council on Economic Education, 1969; Maher, 1969). Although economic educators do not have proof in an absolute sense that DEEP works, in 25 short years marginal improvements have been made in every component of DEEP, and there are indicators that intervention through DEEP can change what schools teach to students about economics. Large numbers of school districts have made the initial commitment to include economics in their curricula using DEEP processes. And DEEP districts have reason, based on research findings, to believe that a commitment to DEEP will pay dividends.

Walstad and Soper (1988) concluded that DEEP is a significant predictor of economics achievement and contributes to gains in economic achievement. They acknowledge that the reasons for this effect are difficult to identify, but "DEEP participation probably helps teachers by giving them access to curriculum materials, consulting assistance and in-service education. These benefits, in turn, get incorporated into classroom instruction for students" (p. 255). In other words, DEEP processes create the environment for inclusion of taught economic education curricula. "An earlier study (Soper & Brenneke, 1981) concluded that DEEP school enrollment and its interaction with an economics course at the high school level is the single most important determinant of performance on the *Test of Economic Literacy* (TEL)" (p. 1). The fact that economic educators now have *Capstone: The Nation's High School Economics Course*, the *MCG Strategies for High School Economics Courses*, and the *Advanced Placement Instructional Package* (APIP) should mean that many more DEEP districts can take advantage of this research finding than could have done so in 1980.

Becker, Helmberger, and Thompson (1975) provided another indicator for believing in the viability of DEEP when they found, several years after DEEP servicing had halted, that the key variable in retaining economic education, as measured by student knowledge of economics in Minneapolis schools, was the concentration of DEEP teachers in one school within the district. This finding supports the view that targeted teacher training to assure concentrations of trained teachers within DEEP districts, rather than merely increasing numbers of teachers, should be recommended Joint Council network policy.

Another major evaluative indicator that DEEP is working is the results of the Exemplary DEEP Awards Program. Fifty-eight DEEP school districts have had their economic education programs evaluated and judged to be exemplary (Joint Council on Economic Education, 1987, 1988, 1989). The awards summaries serve as case studies of DEEP processes at work in real school districts. They reflect the power of DEEP as a process to install curriculum when there are both sufficient commitment at the district level and network services available to support and maintain the program. Chapters 10, 16, 17, and 18 in this volume describe several examples of DEEP programs and how they were installed.

CONCLUSIONS AND RECOMMENDATIONS

For 40 years economic educators have endeavored to increase the functional responsibility schools have for teaching students the basic economic concepts and thinking skills requisite to cope with their economic world. In the early years they did so solely through conducting workshops and courses and publishing instructional guides for teachers, on the belief that individual teachers, equipped with appropriate economic knowledge and pedagogical skills, could make a qualitative difference in the way students make economic decisions.

Twenty-five years ago DEEP was inaugurated as a curriculum change process designed to help school districts install and maintain multiple-grade-level economics curricula. DEEP is predicated on the belief that systematic instruction in economics based on explicit multiple-grade-level curriculum objectives is more likely to result in lasting improvement in student economic understanding than in merely conducting ad hoc workshops for teachers or simply publishing and disseminating instructional materials for teachers and students.

The Joint Council network is unique in that no other discipline-based organization has adopted a decentralized, school-based curriculum change process like DEEP as its vehicle for getting its mission accomplished. Indeed, other disciplines and competitive purveyors of economic education promote single publications or teacher-training programs as discrete elements, often as ends in themselves, panaceas, or blue-plate specials, rather than as tools to be used by professional educators in the process of helping school districts develop K–12 economics curricula for all students.

DEEP is flexible and can accommodate the wide diversity of traditions and school structures that are found in communities across this nation. By recommending flexible curriculum guidelines, economic educators are directive without being dogmatic. Furthermore, economic educators have found ways to hurdle the obstacles to change and now have economic education on the curriculum agendas of increasing numbers of school units and on the instructional agendas of increasing numbers of teachers. But they should not be complacent; they must continue to seek improvements in the way they work with schools and continue to upgrade the tools used to construct curriculum.

The following recommendations are actions to prepare economic educators for the twenty-first century and to move them closer to mission fulfillment:

- Convene a new National Task Force on Economic Education in the schools to reaffirm, modify, or deny the long-run mission of economic education and to outline the short-run goals to fulfill that mission.

- Continue to promote DEEP as the process for installing economic education in school curricula even though complete proof that DEEP is the best vehicle is not available. We have no proof that another vehicle will get us to our destination faster.

- Continue to encourage innovation within the network regarding DEEP processes. Among the unique strengths of the Joint Council are the autonomy and independence of its affiliate network which permit creative responses to problems.

- Establish training programs for network personnel in curriculum development to assure that center directors, field consultants, DEEP coordinators, and other satellite support staff have the skills necessary to help schools adopt curricula.

- Establish joint ventures with proponents of other school-based curriculum alignment models to test whether these well-defined general models are more efficient than DEEP as curriculum delivery systems.

- Revise and replenish selected curriculum development tools such as MCGs that have proven track records, reduce extraneous publications, and develop new materials to fill gaps in the recommended national economic education program.

- Expand targeted teacher training (TTT), linking staff development to specific curriculum programs and focusing teacher education within DEEP school districts to assure a critical mass of trained teachers who can deliver economic instruction to students.

- Invest heavily in the development of a professional core of executive-level economic educators, perhaps through the establishment of an academy associated with one of the Joint Council's affiliated centers, to assure that replacement personnel are available

66

for open positions within the network and to re-establish service arms in states where none now operates.

- Invest in the collection of multiple national measures of teacher knowledge of economics, student understanding of the economic way of thinking, and the aggregate level of curriculum change in economics.

REFERENCES

Becker, W. E., Jr.; Helmberger, J. D.; and Thompson, J. L. (1975). An evaluation of a Developmental Economic Education Project given limited data. *Journal of Economic Education* 6(2):120–25.

Brenneke, J. S.; Highsmith, R. J.; Soper, J. C.; Walstad, W. B.; and Watts, M. W. (1988). A research and evaluation agenda for DEEP and precollege economic education. *Journal of Economic Education* 19(1):5–13.

Brenneke, J. S., and Soper, J. C. (1987). A qualitative evaluation of an intensive DEEP. Paper presented at a meeting of the Eastern Economics Association, Philadelphia.

———— (1984). Evaluating DEEP and competing efforts: Three cross-sections. Paper presented at a meeting of the Western Economics Association, Las Vegas, Nevada.

Buckles, S., and Freeman, V. (1984). A longitudinal analysis of a Developmental Economic Education Program. *Journal of Economic Education* 15(1): 5–10.

Committee for Economic Development (1961). *Economic education in the schools: A report of the National Task Force on Economic Education.* New York: the Committee.

Davis, O. L., Jr., ed. (1976). *Perspectives on curriculum development 1776–1976.* Washington, D.C.: Association for Supervision and Curriculum Development.

English, F. W., ed. (1983). *Fundamental curriculum decisions.* Alexandria, Va.: Association for Supervision and Curriculum Development.

Gilliard, J. V.; Caldwell, J.; Dalgaard, B. R.; Highsmith, R. J.; Reinke, R.; and Watts, M. (1988). *Economics: What and when—Scope and sequence guidelines, K–12.* New York: Joint Council on Economic Education.

Glatthorn, A. A. (1987). *Curriculum renewal.* Alexandria, Va.: Association for Supervision and Curriculum Development.

Grobman, H. (1970). *Developmental curriculum projects: Decision points and processes.* Itasca, Ill.: F. E. Peacock Publishers.

Hahn, C. L. (1976). Research on the diffusion of social studies innovations. In

Review of research on social studies education, 1970–75, 137–51. Bulletin no. 49. Washington, D.C.: National Council for the Social Studies.

Hahn, C. L., and Rushing, F. W. (1981). Building an effective economic education program using principles of successful adoption and implementation. In *Economic education: Links to the social studies*, ed. S. S. Symmes, 28–41. Bulletin no. 65. Washington, D.C.: National Council for the Social Studies.

Joint Council on Economic Education (1987, 1988, 1989). *Annual DEEP awards, program summaries*. New York: the Joint Council.

———— (1969). *DEEP 1969: Perspectives on a 5-year experiment in curriculum change*. New York: the Joint Council.

———— (1964a). *Teacher's guide to DEEP Part One: Economic ideas and concepts*. New York: the Joint Council.

———— (1964b). *Teacher's guide to DEEP Part Two: Suggestions for grade placement and development of economic ideas and concepts*. New York: the Joint Council.

Kehler, A. (1989). Response to DEEP: A process for curriculum renewal. Paper presented at the Cleveland DEEP Conference, May.

Kehler, A., and Symmes, S. S., eds. (1990). *DEEP Handbook*. New York: Joint Council on Economic Education.

Kim, Y., and Kratochvil, D. W. (1972). *Developmental Economic Education Program: Product development report no. 16*. Palo Alto, Calif.: American Institute for Research.

Leet, D. (1985). The Developmental Economic Education Program (DEEP): A strategy for achieving economic literacy. *Social Studies Review* (California Council for the Social Studies) 24(2):8–12.

Loucks-Horsley, S. (Forthcoming). Managing change: An integral part of staff development. In *Handbook for staff development*. Oxford, Ohio: National Staff Development Council.

———— (n.d.). At last: Some good news from a study of school improvement. Andover, Mass.: Regional Laboratory for Education Improvement of the Northeast and Islands. Typescript.

Loucks-Horsley, S., and Hergert, L. F. (1985). *An action guide to school improvement*. Alexandria, Va.: Association for Supervision and Curriculum Development.

Maher, J. (1969). DEEP: Strengthening economics in the schools. *American Economic Review* 59(2):230–38.

Moore, P.; Caldwell, J.; Dick, J.; Harrington, P.; Kehler, A.; and Leet, D. (1987). *DEEP enhancement goals: A DEEP planning committee report*. New York: Joint Council on Economic Education.

Psychological Corporation (1970). *A report of evaluation of the Developmental Economic Education Program*. New York: Joint Council on Economic Education.

Saunders, P.; Bach, G. L.; Calderwood, J. D.; Hansen, W. L.; and Stein, H. (1984). *A framework for teaching the basic concepts*. 2d ed. New York: Joint Council on Economic Education.

Soper, J. C., and Brenneke, J. S. (1981). The Test of Economic Literacy and an evaluation of the DEEP system. *Journal of Economic Education* 12(1):1–14.

Symmes, S. S., ed. (1981). *Economic education: Links to the social studies*. Bulletin no. 65. Washington, D.C.: National Council for the Social Studies.

Walstad, W. B., and Soper, J. C. (1988). A report card on the economic literacy of U.S. high school students. *American Economic Review* 78(2):251–56.

———— (1982). A model of economic learning in the high schools. *Journal of Economic Education* 13(1):40–54.

———— (1969). *DEEP handbook for curriculum change: Guidelines and appendices*. New York: Joint Council on Economic Education.

Wentworth, D. R.; Hansen, W. L.; and Hawke, S. H., eds. (1977). *Perspectives on economic education*. Washington, D.C.: Joint Council on Economic Education, National Council for the Social Studies, and Social Science Education Consortium, Inc.

5. RECOMMENDATIONS FOR TEACHER EDUCATION IN THE CONTEXT OF THE REFORM MOVEMENT

by Henry J. Hermanowicz

> If an unfriendly foreign power had attempted to impose on America the mediocre educational performance that exists today, we might well have viewed it as an act of war. As it stands, we have allowed this to happen to ourselves. We have even squandered the gains in student achievement made in the wake of the Sputnik challenge. Moreover, we have dismantled essential support systems which helped make those gains possible. We have, in effect, been committing an act of unthinking, unilateral educational disarmament. (National Commission on Excellence in Education, 1983, p. 5)

BACKGROUND

And so the provocative rhetoric of one of the opening paragraphs of a commission report calling for major reform of our schools captured the attention of the nation. The language of the report was deliberately alarmist in nature, and it struck a sensitive chord. With wide media coverage, the report commanded the attention of not only ordinary citizens but also governors, legislators, business leaders, and educators with the realization that the most powerful nation in the world had allowed its system of public schooling to become unprepared and inadequate as it moved toward the twenty-first century. Even the title of the short report, *A Nation at Risk: The Imperative for Educational Reform*, was designed to shock readers out of any false sense of complacency that may have existed in American society about the quality of its schools.

Among the findings of the report were startling concerns such as the following: Some 23 million American adults were functionally illiterate in terms of the simplest tests of everyday reading, writing, and comprehension. Many 17-year-olds, it was claimed, could not perform

70

any higher-order intellectual skills other than those of a very basic nature. Out of this new generation, for example, nearly 40 percent could not draw inferences from written material; only one-third could solve a mathematics problem involving several steps, and only one-fifth could write a persuasive essay.

The remedies offered in the report were related to four aspects of the educational process—*content, expectations, time,* and *teaching*—along with the necessity for greater leadership and fiscal support of the schools. In the area of content, the report recommended strengthening state and local high school graduation requirements with minimums for all students in five basic areas: (1) four years of English, (2) three years of mathematics, (3) three years of science, (4) three years of social studies, and (5) a half-year of computer science. No mention of obligatory study in economics was offered in *A Nation at Risk* with the exception that, among other emphases, social studies programs should focus on helping students "understand the fundamentals of how our economic system works and how our political system functions" (National Commission on Excellence in Education, 1983, p. 26).

That single statement hardly represented a clarion call to revitalize economic education. Nevertheless, the overall impact of the total report was very significant. Perhaps just as consequential as the report itself, with its dramatic analysis of the deficiencies of public secondary education in the United States, was its incredible timing. A number of other major reports or studies which had been in the works were also released in 1983 and throughout 1984. This "wave" of reports reinforced the conviction that our schools, both elementary and secondary, were in serious trouble—trouble that could not be corrected with minor repair or adjustment.

The reports that quickly followed *A Nation at Risk* included three notable books, each supported by important, influential sponsors: John I. Goodlad's (1984) *A Place Called School: Prospects for the Future*; Ernest L. Boyer's (1983) *High Schools: A Report on Secondary Education in America*; and Theodore R. Sizer's (1984) *Horace's Compromise: The Dilemma of the American High School*. In addition, there were early and significant studies from key organizations including the National Science Board Commission on Precollege Education in Mathematics, Science, and Technology (1983); the Business Higher Education Forum (1983); the Task Force on Education for Economic Growth of the Education Commission of the States (1983); the Twentieth Century Fund (1983);

71

the Southern Regional Education Board (1983); the College Board (1983); and the Council of Chief State School Officers (1984).

Public reactions were as dramatic as some of the reports. Within the social, political, and economic framework of feeling that we were losing our competitive edge with other industrial nations were general concerns about lowered measured average achievement of students, about poor comparisons of achievement between U.S. students and students in other countries, about previous declines in SAT scores, and about educational programs that generally appeared to be shortchanging our children and thus our future as a nation. In less than two years more than 30 national studies were addressing the need for reform of our schools. This, in turn, was accompanied by the appointment of over 250 state committees or commissions to recommend and push numerous reform efforts.

The initial actions taken in response to such concerns and this so-called "first wave" of reports were to increase state regulations/ requirements and to establish mandatory testing programs for both students and prospective teachers (and sometimes in-service teachers as well). Virtually all of the states increased the number of academic courses required for a high school diploma, and many states also established obligatory testing programs for all students, sometimes tied to school graduation, grade promotion, or required remedial instruction. Over 40 states subsequently established examinations tied in some manner to teacher certification. This was all part of the national and state effort to demonstrate deliberate and quick corrective action as well as greater public accountability for improvement of our schools.

Increasing academic requirements, strengthening regulations, and instituting mandatory testing programs were characterized by many as the "quick fix" approach to educational improvement. While such efforts had their positive effects, they hardly touched on the major reforms suggested in the analyses offered in the studies by Goodlad, Boyer, and Sizer previously cited. Furthermore, those of us concerned with the level of general economic literacy in the United States felt that economic education in the schools and in teacher preparation was getting short shrift in the process. How can individuals in a democratic society make critical judgments and wise decisions as consumers and as citizens in a world replete with economic information if they lack basic economic understandings? In this day and age, how can one even read a newspaper with intelligent insight without some basic knowledge of economics? And how can our next generation gain basic economic literacy through our system of schooling if we give very little attention to economic education and if a vast majority of our teachers lack fundamental knowledge of economics themselves? These kinds of questions were left unanswered in the opening reform efforts and persist.

THE JOINT COUNCIL ON ECONOMIC EDUCATION'S COMMITTEE ON TEACHER EDUCATION

Under the foregoing circumstances, the Joint Council on Economic Education was obligated to take stock of its own position regarding the appropriate role of economic education in (1) the preparation of teachers and (2) state mandates for economic instruction. The first item is the subject of this chapter. State mandates are dealt with in other parts of this volume. It was rather evident that additional reports were calling for major changes in the preparation of teachers, and it was imperative for the Joint Council to develop a set of recommendations about the economic education of prospective teachers since its last official document addressing such issues dated back to 1966.

Therefore, a resolution was passed by the Joint Council's Board of Trustees in December 1983, and shortly thereafter Louis Gerstner, Jr., chairman of the Joint Council and then also chairman and CEO of American Express, appointed a special 13-member Committee on Teacher Education. The committee's principal task was to develop a general policy statement with recommendations for the essential economic education of teachers. Such a policy statement had to be concise, clear, and reasonable in view of the fact that over 1,200 diverse institutions of higher education in the United States conducted programs for the preparation of teachers. Furthermore, such matters as program accreditation and teacher certification involved a complexity of important vested interest groups and agencies.

The 13-member committee was chaired by the author of this chapter and included such critically important contributors as Lee Hansen, professor of economics at the University of Wisconsin; Tom Shannon, executive director of the National School Boards Association; Frances Haley, executive director of the National Council for the Social Studies; Bill Monat, then chancellor of the Illinois Board of Regents; Lee McMurrin, then superintendent of the Milwaukee Public Schools; and James Tobin, Nobel laureate and Sterling Professor of Economics at Yale

University. (The composition of the full committee is identified in Joint Council on Economic Education, 1985.)

RECOMMENDATIONS

The Joint Council's committee deliberated over the kinds of recommendations for economic education that should be basic to the preparation of teachers. The major curricular components of all teacher preparation programs include general education and academic specialization as well as professional education. Therefore, it was necessary to address the issues of what fundamental requirements in economic education should reside in those three curricular components of collegiate programs for preparing all, as well as specialized, teachers. In addition, because business education, home economics, social studies, and economics teachers per se deal with economic content in greater depth than do teachers of other subject matter fields or elementary school teachers, it was necessary to address the issue of their special needs. And, finally, because the vast majority of the states moved to mandatory examinations tied to teacher certification requirements, it was necessary to address the general requirements of economic knowledge that should be included in such testing programs for teachers.

The committee condensed its report to nine very basic recommendations: four that dealt with the general education and/or academic specialization of prospective teachers, two that dealt with professional education, and three that dealt with required testing programs for teachers. These basic recommendations were as follows:

A. The General Education and Academic Specialization of Prospective Teachers

1. All prospective elementary and secondary school teachers should be required to complete at least one basic course or preferably the principles sequence in economics as part of their general education program in college.

2. All prospective teachers of social studies, business education, and home economics should be required to take additional economics instruction beyond that required of all teachers. At least nine semester hour credits of coursework including macro- and micro-economics and an advanced course in economics should constitute their collegiate program of academic specialization.

74

3. All prospective teachers of secondary school economics should be required to take additional coursework in economics, completing the equivalent of a field of concentration in economics. This amounts to at least 18 semester hour credits of coursework.
4. All prospective teachers of advanced placement courses in economics or of economics for gifted students should complete the equivalent of a major in economics (at least 30 semester hours).

B. For the Professional Education of Prospective Teachers
5. All professional education programs for elementary school teachers should include instruction in the pedagogical treatment of economics. This instruction should be included in both their methods courses and their clinical experience.
6. All professional education programs for secondary school teachers in social studies, business education, home economics, and economics should include instruction in the pedagogical treatment of economics. This instruction should be included in both their methods courses and their clinical experience, with more intensive exposure for those who plan to teach economics.

C. For States with Certification Tests
7. All required teacher examinations for prospective elementary teachers should contain an adequate number of questions to assess economic literacy.
8. All required teacher examinations for prospective secondary teachers in social studies, business education, home economics and economics should contain an adequate number of examination items to assess their understanding of economics.
9. All required teacher examinations for prospective secondary school teachers of economics courses should assess the breadth and depth of their knowledge of economics. (Joint Council on Economic Education, 1985, p. 8)

The foregoing recommendations and a report were transmitted in July 1985 to John A. Georges, chairman of the Joint Council's Board of Trustees and CEO of the International Paper Company, and were subsequently adopted.

The Joint Council's report and recommendations preceded the report of what was to be the most significant national study on changing teacher education in the United States. This was the report issued by the Carnegie Forum on Education and the Economy entitled *A Nation Prepared: Teachers for the 21st Century* (Task Force on Teaching as a Profession, 1986). Three implicit goals seem to underlie the recommendations of the Carnegie task force: (1) to overhaul (rather than simply improve) present curricula for preparing teachers in the United States, (2) to convert teaching from an occupation to a bona fide profession, and (3) to provide the kind of educational conditions whereby teachers would become the major players in the substantive transformation of the schools and their instructional programs.

To bring this revolution about, the Carnegie task force proposed the following interrelated major steps as crucial in changing national educational policies:

1. Create a National Board for Professional Teaching Standards, organized with a regional and state membership structure, to establish high standards for what teachers need to know and be able to do, and to certify teachers who meet that standard.
2. Restructure schools to provide a professional environment for teaching, freeing them (teachers) to decide how best to meet state and local goals for children while holding them accountable for student progress.
3. Restructure the teaching force, and introduce a new category of Lead Teachers with the proven ability to provide active leadership in the redesign of the schools and in helping their colleagues to uphold high standards of learning and teaching.
4. Require a bachelor's degree in the arts and sciences as a prerequisite for the professional study of teaching.
5. Develop a new professional curriculum in graduate schools of education leading to a Master in Teaching degree, based on systematic knowledge of teaching and including internships and residencies in the schools.
6. Mobilize the nation's resources to prepare minority youngsters for teaching careers.
7. Relate incentives for teachers to school-wide student performance, and provide schools with the technology, services, and staff essential to teacher productivity.
8. Make teachers' salaries and career opportunities competitive with those in other professions. (Task Force on Teaching as a Profession, 1986, p. 3).

CRITICAL NEED

There is sufficient evidence to indicate that the basic recommendations offered by the Joint Council's committee for the economic education of teachers represented a critical need and that such recommendations would fit into the framework of the Carnegie task

76

force report. For example, in a study supported by the National Endowment for the Humanities, the Southern Regional Education Board conducted an analysis of over 6,000 transcripts of students completing teacher preparation programs, as well as of arts and science majors. The study involved 17 colleges and universities throughout 14 states including several "flagship" institutions. The findings indicated that 75 percent of the teacher candidates never took a single course in economics in completing their degree requirements, while 59 percent of arts and science graduates never had a single economics course (Galambos, Cornett & Spitler, 1985, p. 32). Even prospective teachers concentrating in the social sciences took only an average of four semester hours of study in economics as part of their total collegiate program (Galambos, Cornett & Spitler, 1985, p. 59).

Such data are particularly alarming when it is realized that some of the same states included in the transcript study also mandate instruction in economics within the public schools. In short, economics instruction is required in certain states without any assurance that the teachers of economics will have had adequate preparation in the discipline itself. In fact, in 1985–86, 27 states (now 28 states) mandated some form of economics instruction (Brennan, 1986). Yet many of the same states did not specify formal study in economics in their teacher preparation program approval regulations or their requirements for teacher certification.

In addition to the foregoing revelations, a study of economic literacy, utilizing the results of over 8,000 students taking the *Test of Economic Literacy* in 1986, proved to be equally alarming (Walstad & Soper, 1988). The analysis made by Walstad and Soper of the test results clearly indicated that high school students generally were failing in basic knowledge of economics. We are in fact creating a population of economic illiterates during a period when the schools are supposed to be undergoing major qualitative academic improvement. Much needs to be done. But requiring formal instruction in economics in our schools by teachers well prepared in the discipline would be a major step to correct such problems.

PRE-SERVICE AND IN-SERVICE TEACHER EDUCATION

It is serious enough to realize that our high school graduates are failing in measures of basic economic literacy. It is unconscionable, however, to continue, without correction, programs and practices that produce teachers who themselves have insufficient knowledge in economics, whether they are obligated to teach that subject matter field or not. We simply have to change the fundamental way we prepare teachers. In addition, however, it is imperative that practicing teachers of social studies in the elementary grades, as well as middle and secondary school teachers of subject matter with economic content, be given assistance with economic concepts, knowledge, instructional procedures, and materials as part of their in-service education. This is why the in-service training efforts, instructional materials, and curriculum activities associated with DEEP are critically important. DEEP represents a comprehensive approach to improving economic education, while allowing adaptability of such measures to the particular needs of the teachers, their students, and their local school districts. Unquestionably, the improvement of economic education in our schools must involve deliberate efforts in both pre-service and in-service teacher education.

CONTINUED FERMENT

Past efforts at educational reform seem to have come and gone like fashion styles. Indeed, many pundits were predicting that the national concerns and reform efforts begun in the first half of the eighties to improve the schools would have died down by now. They have not. Additional reports and national projects have emerged in what have been characterized as subsequent "waves," and, if anything, efforts to reform the quality of our schools have intensified and certainly will continue through the next decade. Even the language of the more recent reports emphasizes the need for a major "transformation" or a basic "restructuring" of our schools. [See, for example, California Commission on the Teaching Profession (1985), The Holmes Group (1986), Task Force on Teaching as a Profession (1986), National Governors' Association (1986), National Research Council (1989), National Center on Education and the Economy (1989), and American Association for the Advancement of Science (1989).]

Rather than simple regulatory changes, the issues are shifting to the need for very fundamental changes in such areas as curriculum design, strategies of instruction, instructional staff differentiation, and the wise, effective use of technology. Additional central issues focus on the need for greater emphases on the higher cognitive development of learners, on more critical thinking and active forms of inquiry by students, and on subject matter content that is intellectually richer. Such changes, along with a concomitant transformation of the preparation, licensure, advanced certification, and central involvement of teachers exercising leadership roles in the substantive overhaul of schooling, are moving to center stage.

Do such efforts represent a pretentious, overambitious, and un-realizable dream? Some argue that such is the case. But deliberate, major renovation of public education clearly has become a national priority closely associated with our future progress or stagnation in a dramatically changing global economy. Economic education will have to play a central role in that process. At the heart of such initiatives must be major efforts at improving the economic education of prospective as well as in-service teachers. Otherwise, we will be perpetuating problems of national economic illiteracy—problems that our nation can ill afford as it moves toward the twenty-first century.

REFERENCES

American Association for the Advancement of Science (1989). *Science for all Americans.* Waldorf, Md.: AAAS.

Boyer, E. L. (1983). *High schools: A report on secondary education in America.* New York: Harper & Row.

Brennan, D. C. (1986). *A survey of state mandates for economics instruction: 1985–86.* New York: Joint Council on Economic Education.

Business Higher Education Forum (1983). *America's competitive challenge: The need for a national response.* Washington, D.C.: the Forum.

California Commission on the Teaching Profession (1985). *Who will teach our children: A strategy for improving California's schools.* Sacramento: the Commission.

College Board (1983). *Academic preparation for college: What students need to know and be able to do.* New York: College Entrance Examination Board.

Council of Chief State School Officers (1984). *Staffing the nation's schools: A national emergency.* Washington, D.C.: the Council.

Galambos, E. C.; Cornett, L. M.; and Spitler, H. D. (1985). *An analysis of transcripts of teachers and arts and science graduates.* Atlanta: Southern Regional Education Board.

Goodlad, J. I. (1984). *A place called school: Prospects for the future.* New York: McGraw-Hill.

The Holmes Group (1986). *Tomorrow's teachers: A report of the Holmes Group.* East Lansing, Mich.: The Holmes Group, Inc.

Joint Council on Economic Education (1985). *Economic education for future elementary and secondary teachers: Basic recommendations.* New York: the Joint Council.

National Center on Education and the Economy (1989). *To secure our future: The federal role in education.* Rochester, N.Y.: the National Center.

National Commission on Excellence in Education (1983). *A nation at risk: The imperative for educational reform.* Washington, D.C.: U.S. Government Printing Office.

National Governors' Association (1986). *Time for results: The governors' 1991 report on education.* Washington, D.C.: the Association.

National Research Council (1989). *Everybody counts: A report to the nation on the future of mathematics education.* Washington, D.C.: National Academy Press.

National Science Board Commission on Precollege Education in Mathematics, Science, and Technology (1983). *Educating Americans for the 21st century.* Washington, D.C.: National Science Foundation.

Sizer, T. R. (1984). *Horace's compromise: The dilemma of the American high school.* Boston: Houghton Mifflin.

Southern Regional Education Board (1983). *Meeting the need for quality: Action in the South.* Atlanta: the Board.

Task Force on Education for Economic Growth (1983). *Action for excellence: A comprehensive plan to improve our nation's schools.* Denver: Education Commission of the States.

Task Force on Teaching as a Profession (1986). *A nation prepared: Teachers for the 21st century.* New York: Carnegie Forum on Education and the Economy.

Twentieth Century Fund (1983). *Report of the task force on federal elementary and secondary education policy.* New York: the Fund.

Walstad, W. B., and Soper, J. C. (1988). A report card on the economic literacy of U.S. high school students. *American Economic Review* 78(2):251–56.

6. RESEARCH ON DEEP: THE FIRST 25 YEARS

by Michael Watts

It is useful to discuss the history of DEEP, and the related research on its effectiveness, in terms of the three historical stages of the program that have been announced by the Joint Council on Economic Education. Accordingly, the first section of this chapter discusses the experimental stage, which ran from 1964 to 1967; the second section discusses the Cooperating Schools Program of 1968–83; and the third section covers the expansion and enhancement phase, which took us from 1984 to 1990. I have also added a fourth section, summarizing my own impressions of what the historical experience with DEEP has to say about the prospects and problems facing DEEP—and, for that matter, most other kinds of precollege economic education programs—in the decade of the 1990s.

STAGE 1 (1964–67): AN EXPERIMENT IN DEVELOPMENTAL CURRICULUM METHODS

DEEP was originally announced in 1964 as an experimental teaching program involving 29 school systems from around the United States. Three model schools [in Contra Costa (California), Minneapolis, and Pittsburgh] were identified in 1964; the remaining 26 pilot schools were selected from 1964 to 1966. These schools were chosen for both geographic and organizational diversity and were provided substantial financial and in-kind subsidies. This first phase of DEEP was evaluated in several published and unpublished reports.

S. Stowell Symmes and Robert J. Highsmith at the Joint Council on Economic Education provided copies of several reports and some of the data cited here. George Vredeveld, David A. Dieterle, and Stow Symmes offered helpful comments on a draft version of the chapter.

The Psychological Corporation prepared two reports on DEEP for the Joint Council during this period. The first (1968) concluded that the project was promising in terms of offering unique benefits for participating schools, encouraging development and use of new instructional materials and curriculum planning, and demonstrating effective administration of a national project involving independent school districts. The second (1970) was able to evaluate more districts at later stages of their implementation plans and supported the conclusions of the first report in identifying promising aspects of DEEP. It also identified several important problems facing DEEP, including

- the importance of providing state and local support for DEEP through the council and center networks.
- wide differences in the extent of support for DEEP by participating districts.
- limited classroom use of the many instructional and curriculum materials developed for DEEP.
- a tendency by districts and the Joint Council to underestimate the resources required to produce materials and the number of years needed to effectively implement DEEP in school systems.
- the need to develop administrative support for DEEP within school systems and offer effective in-service programs for teachers. (pp. iii–v)

These findings were consistent with those in two reports discussed by Maher (1969), which also provided new information. Maher reported on teachers' gains in economic understanding resulting from in-service courses provided in some DEEP programs and concluded that such training could achieve gains as large as those observed in regular university course work in economics. He also noted positive results from the first longitudinal study of a DEEP system (Minneapolis) and from testing on economic learning in history and other social studies courses in another DEEP system (Pittsburgh). Results from Contra Costa were, however, at least partly unfavorable.

Maher, Saunders, Hollenbeck, and other representatives from the Joint Council and various DEEP school systems published a collection of articles in the monograph *DEEP 1969: Perspectives on a 5-Year Experiment in Curriculum Change* (Joint Council on Economic Education, 1969). This volume, together with *DEEP Handbook for*

Curriculum Change/Guidelines (Symmes, 1969) and *Economics in the Curriculum: Developmental Economic Education Program* (Joint Council on Economic Education, 1970), marked the end of the first phase of DEEP. At that point, promising opportunities and important problems to be met in improving and expanding the program had been identified. On balance, most impartial observers found much of value in the DEEP idea and process. For example, Grobman (1970) prominently featured DEEP in her book on developmental curriculum projects and pointed out that DEEP was based on several key assumptions:

> Curriculum diversity is desirable. Curriculum improvement is a local concern. Some outside stimulus and resources are needed if economics education is to be expanded at the local level. Local school personnel—primarily teachers—can develop and evaluate materials. Local systems know how to plan for materials development and dissemination. Once materials are prepared, they will be used by the system sponsoring their preparation. Teacher training is a major facet of curriculum-improvement efforts. Community involvement is essential in change. And major curriculum development and dissemination can be accomplished in three years with relatively small funds and limited personnel. (p. 24)

Grobman then concluded the following:

> During the course of its program, the JCEE learned that some of these assumptions were valid and others were not. Some school systems were better geared to curriculum development and change than others. For some, the JCEE contribution served as seed money, and stimulated far greater local contributions; for others, it did not. Despite some dramatic successes in terms of quality of new materials prepared under the DEEP aegis, numbers of teachers trained in economics, and students actually using the new materials profitably, it became obvious that some circumstances were more compatible with the effective development and dissemination of materials and teacher preparation, and that certain procedures for materials development and implementation were more appropriate than others. Thus, to a considerable extent, the DEEP project changed its focus to an exploration of various processes for curriculum development and dissemination and to the development of effective prototypes for such curriculum development and change. (p. 24)

Near the end of the experimental phase of DEEP, the Joint Council announced its Cooperating Schools Program for DEEP, sometimes promoted as a program of "economics teaching for the 1970s." The diffusion and dissemination policy was adopted in 1967 and marked a further decentralization of DEEP in that state councils and local centers became responsible for recruiting school systems for the program. Expected progress and problems with this approach were discussed in a report on DEEP by Kim and Kratochvil (1972), published in a series of 21 such reports on promising educational products funded by the U.S. Office of Education. Apart from detailing the new dissemination phase of DEEP, however, the Kim and Kratochvil report is very similar to the earlier studies conducted by the Psychological Corporation.

STAGE 2 (1968–83): THE COOPERATING SCHOOLS PROGRAM

In the dissemination phase, several hundred school systems "joined" DEEP by identifying a DEEP coordinator for the district, whose name was forwarded to the Joint Council on a one-page form signed by an economic educator from a state group affiliated with the Joint Council. This form also included a statement of understanding, indicating that the school system was, or would be, "engaged in a program of curriculum development in economic education [involving] plans for effective coordination, in-service education, materials development and K–12 experimentation."

The extremely decentralized nature of DEEP in this stage was reflected in the structure and/or findings of most research conducted on DEEP in this period. For example, in a study of secondary curriculum guides developed by individual DEEP school districts, Armento (1983) questioned the plans reflected in these documents for a truly sequential and comprehensive program of economic education. She noted that

the concepts in the study guides tend to be primarily definitional in nature and are fairly similar across the grade levels. Except for the different conceptual emphasis at the 10th and 12th grade levels, one would have a difficult time telling the appropriate grade level by looking at the type of generalization provided. It appears from an examination of these 43 guides that concepts are dealt with primarily at the introductory, definitional level—whether the guide is intended for 9th or 12th grade. . . . [T]here must be an assumption by curriculum builders that prior instruction in economic education has not occurred. (pp. 26–27)

Two longitudinal studies conducted on progress in individual school systems during this period were also published in the *Journal of Economic*

Education. Becker, Helmberger, and Thompson (1975) found the following in the Minneapolis school system:

> The termination of DEEP appears to have had a significant negative effect on student learning of economics [and] suggest[s] that a "pump-priming" type of program may not be sufficient to maintain high levels of student learning. After the initial training of teachers and developmentary work is terminated, it may still be necessary to continue with programs specific to the school district being serviced. Continuing programs must allow teachers to update themselves as well as the student materials the teacher is using. (p. 124)

Buckles and Freeman (1984) found that "a traditional DEEP project can result in significant increases in levels of economic understanding throughout the elementary and secondary curriculum" (p. 5), using data from one Missouri school district. Student testing was done in this district from 1977 to 1980, and despite the positive general conclusions of this report, the authors also warned that "increased understanding may not always occur during the first or second year [of intervention]" (p. 10).

The first of only a few rigorous quantitative studies involving large numbers of school districts was also published in this stage of DEEP. A study by Soper and Brenneke (1981) used data from the sample of students participating in the national norming of the first edition of the *Test of Economic Literacy* (TEL). They found that

> students who were enrolled in DEEP Cooperating School Systems, and had had instruction in economics scored substantially higher than other students. Students in DEEP schools who were not exposed to economics instruction per se scored relatively lower, other things remaining the same. (p. 12)

They suggested that this result might occur because some DEEP schools are only "paper participants." However, a major limitation of this study was that no data were available on student IQ or achievement test scores or on many other important demographic, economic, and structural characteristics of different school systems in the study, including effective DEEP status as noted above. Recognizing this, the authors called for collection of more extensive data relating to these issues.

In a subsequent study by Walstad and Soper (1982), which included an IQ-proxy variable with a new data base, a stronger statement on the

85

impact of DEEP could be made. This study involved students who had not participated in the original TEL norming and included attitudinal as well as cognitive outputs. After analyzing these data, Walstad and Soper concluded:

> Students enrolled in DEEP schools showed significantly more economic understanding than students in non-DEEP schools. The DEEP students also enjoyed economics more than non-DEEP students and held more sophisticated attitudes toward economic issues. These positive but relatively weak effects in both the cognitive and affective domains may provide initial justification for the substantial resources which have been devoted to trying to improve economics instruction in the DEEP schools. (p. 52)

The Walstad-Soper and Soper-Brenneke findings were challenged by Luker (1984) who used incremental and partial R^2 values to evaluate what proportions of total and residual variance the DEEP variable explained in a multiple regression model. Although the DEEP variable was statistically significant, when entered as the last variable in the regression equation, Luker judged its contribution in explaining either measure of variance to be "trivial." Responses by the authors of the two original papers (Soper & Brenneke, 1984; Walstad & Soper, 1984) criticized Luker's statistical procedures as inappropriate and rejected his criticism of modeling and estimation procedures used in the earlier studies.

The last large-scale study on Stage 2 DEEP districts was conducted by Watts (1985, 1986), using a stratified random sample of schools. In this report on over 200 classes in 79 districts from around the state of Indiana, it was possible to control for a variety of school district economic and structural characteristics (enrollment size, assessed valuation per student, and proportion of students receiving federally paid "free lunches"), as well as student IQ/aptitude scores and some background variables for the students' social studies or economics teachers. Results were estimated in four grade levels (5, 8, 11, and 12) where all students were required to take a social studies course. In three grades the DEEP variable exhibited a negative influence on student pretest scores—twice significantly; on posttest equations investigating student learning, the DEEP variable was only significant once (positively). Watts concluded that these less favorable results on the DEEP variable, compared to the earlier studies noted above, probably resulted from a systematic relationship between DEEP status and other school system characteristics. An important limitation of this study, however, is that it did not use nationally normed test instruments.

STAGE 3(1984–90): DEEP EXPANSION AND ENHANCEMENT

In January of 1984 the Joint Council announced a programmatic and fund-raising campaign designed to take DEEP into school districts reaching 70 percent of the nation's precollege students. Lou Gerstner, Jr., then chairman and CEO of American Express and chairman of the Joint Council's Executive Committee (now chairman of RJR/Nabisco, Inc.), played a leading role in establishing this target level of students and the related fund-raising goals—$7 million by 1990 at the Joint Council, with a major portion of those funds passed through to state councils and local centers for regional and local expansion efforts. A fair degree of controversy within the national network of state councils and college and university centers for economic education was generated by these decisions, most visibly at an open session of the Joint Council/National Association of Economic Educators (NAEE) meetings held in San Antonio, Texas, in 1983.

While there was no real debate about the benefits of something like a DEEP program in areas where schools and strong councils/centers were committed to such an approach, many questioned whether the Joint Council and its network were large and strong enough, in terms of both financial and personnel resources, to deliver such results. The $7 million target budget was viewed by many as greatly out of line (i.e., too low) with the goals for student and school district contacts. Others complained that the schools themselves were too pressed by competing demands in these same resource areas, and by competing demands for curriculum time and in-service training, to make the expansion plans realistic. Complaints about the average quality of existing DEEP schools and the unglamorous image of both the DEEP concept and (especially) the acronym were also expressed.

Partly in response to these criticisms, some significant changes were made in the overall design of the expansion effort. For a time there was discussion of raising the Joint Council's fund-raising goal to $11 million, but in later years the official target was still reported as $7 million. A DEEP Planning Committee of Joint Council and NAEE representatives was established in 1984, and one of its most significant acts in shaping the expansion and enhancement phase, as well as the basic structure of DEEP itself and later research on the program, was to create a new classification system for DEEP school districts. Previously, the only measure available to or from the Joint Council concerning a district's status in DEEP was a "yes or no" binary, where all districts that had the one-page agreement for cooperating school status on file were counted as DEEP, and all others as non-DEEP. Clearly, not all schools in DEEP had equally effective programs in economic education, and some non-DEEP schools had better economic education programs than did some DEEP programs. That was all consistent with, and part of the basic problem to consider in, the Stage 2 research discussed in the last section.

The new classification system was, by necessity, still fairly simplistic in design and inexpensive to compile and update. It established a "formal" and "informal" distinction and among the formal districts recognized "initiating," "implementing," and "sustaining" categories of schools. The criteria for each of these categories were identified and distributed in the document shown in Table 6.1, but the fundamental departure in all of this was to make state council directors responsible for providing these ratings and to ask them to update this information annually. It was expected that in most states the council directors would do this in cooperation with the local center directors who, typically, have the greatest amount of regular contact with teachers and administrators from the individual school districts. Ideally, over time a district would move smoothly up the scale from informal to formal sustaining DEEP and stay there, but it is well known that many districts go through cycles of increasing and decreasing interest, activity, and training in economic education (and other things, too, of course).

Several measures and reports on the success of the expansion and enhancement stage are now available, although it is still premature to speak of a truly final accounting and assessment. The number of public and private school districts in DEEP, at all classification levels, rose to 1,739 by the end of 1988, up from just over 800 districts at the outset of this phase. The rate at which new districts were being added was still strong, with almost 300 "joining" during the 1987–88 academic year. Estimated student enrollments in all DEEP districts stood at 15.8 million in December of 1988, and more than 840,000 teachers worked in these districts. (These data are taken from Joint Council reports dated December 1988 and February 1989. Note that it is not claimed that all

TABLE 6.1
Criteria for and Characteristics of DEEP School Systems

INFORMAL DEEP SCHOOL SYSTEMS	FORMAL DEEP SCHOOL SYSTEMS		
Cooperating Stage	Initial Planning Stage	Implementation Stage	Sustaining and Improving Stage
Minimum Criteria	Minimum Criteria	Additional Minimum Criteria	Additional Minimum Criteria
1. Recognition of need for economic education by some school administrators and teachers.	1. Recognition of need for economic education by school administrators.	1. Districtwide implementation of program development in process (i.e., K–12, 9–12).	1. Districtwide curriculum in use by appropriate teachers (i.e., K–6, economics, business ed).
2. Involvement in program activities with JCEE/NAEE network.	2. Acceptance of DEEP process—systematic curriculum change.	2. Pilot programs, as needed, completed.	2. In-service procedures provided for new teachers.
3. Activity reports submitted as needed.	3. Involvement with JCEE/NAEE network according to signed formal contractual agreement.	3. Faculty members have completed initial in-service training and are concentrating upon formal curriculum.	3. Planned in-service for all teachers for updating and renewing.
	4. Designated coordinator or person assigned.		
Characteristics	5. Multiple grade level view of program development, systemwide.	*Characteristics*	*Characteristics*
Program activities seen as independent events that meet defined curriculum development needs of school system or individual teachers. Each activity planned using basic DEEP process; no required, long-term plan relates each event in terms of multiple grade level education. Planning, teacher education, curriculum development, and evaluation applicable to each activity.	6. Program reports submitted on annual basis with projections for future plans.	Goals from initial formal stage being implemented.	Planned change has occurred and school district seeks JCEE/NAEE consultation as needed for dynamic, living economic education curriculum.
	Characteristics		
	Program activities seen as part of long-term plan leading to multiple grade level program of economic education. DEEP processes apply to each activity, but also directed at changes in total economic education program offered. "Macro" measures (changes in student knowledge, teacher competence, and curriculum materials) examined on 3- to 5-year basis for school system.		

students in a DEEP district are receiving instruction in economics.) About $4 million for DEEP expansion had been awarded to the Joint Council through 1988 from 37 corporate, foundation, and individual donors. Although this represents only about 60 percent of the official fund-raising goal set for DEEP expansion and enhancement from 1984 to 1990, and roughly 50 percent of the goal of involving school districts that serve 70 percent of the nation's precollege students (census reports show about 45 million such students in all U.S. schools in 1986), this basic counting up suggests that substantial growth did occur. Clearly, the Joint Council and its national network appear to have been more focused and active at the precollege level than they had been for many years prior to the expansion and enhancement stage. That general conclusion holds up under more careful analysis of these data, but as in earlier stages such questioning does raise several reasons for a more cautious and restrained view of DEEP's current effectiveness and impact.

The growth in DEEP associated with the expansion and enhancement stage is, as noted above, significant and impressive, but not as impressive as the "raw" numbers might indicate for several reasons. First, as any economist must point out, because more extensive and regular procedures were set up to count DEEP schools and because some small grants, awards, and other incentives were established to encourage DEEP recruitment and enrollments, part of the growth reflects that improved reporting and those incentives. Second, much of the growth in DEEP is concentrated in the informal and formal initiating categories described earlier. Unfortunately, hard estimates of that mix are not yet available at the national level, but even a pattern highly skewed to the lower levels of achievement and participation would not, per se, constitute a basic criticism of the DEEP expansion effort or policies. To the contrary, it is exactly the pattern one would expect to see, and the policies economists would be likely to recommend, in the early stages of such an initiative. The pattern is only worrisome if schools stay in the informal and initiating stages. It is also a legitimate concern to note that the program costs of moving districts into the more advanced categories are likely to be higher than the costs of attracting them into the program were.

There is also some reason to worry that state council and center directors may overstate the number of districts they are actually servicing and may overstate the "qualitative" level at which the districts are functioning just to make their own efforts look better. But the financial and professional incentives for them to do so are usually quite limited, and the national Joint Council network is still small enough that many other colleagues at the local, state, and national levels are generally aware of the level and quality of each state's operations. Of course, as the DEEP program grows, and if more substantial incentives are provided to those who are responsible for both generating and reporting these data, such qualifications will become more important to consider. Under those circumstances more explicit forms of monitoring and cross-checking may be warranted.

Some of the most simple, but dramatic evaluation measures currently reported by the Joint Council in fund-raising and public relations releases, comparing DEEP and non-DEEP systems, are similarly open to qualification on closer inspection. For example, scores on individual test items from various editions of the TEL and other standardized tests have frequently been released with comparative data on the percentages of correct responses in DEEP and non-DEEP schools. Invariably, students in DEEP schools are shown to have better scores on these items, and that is a comforting and accurate observation as far as it goes. Unfortunately, that is not very far.

To see the potential problem with such measures, it is important to know that the school districts in the norming samples for these exams are not chosen at random. Instead, state council and local center directors are asked to help recruit DEEP and non-DEEP schools from their service areas, and, thus, stronger DEEP districts may well be more likely to participate than are other districts. Furthermore, in classes where no formal economics instruction is occurring, teachers who see the pretest and become concerned that their students will "embarrass" themselves, the teacher, and/or the school may be more likely to drop out of the posttest sample, especially if they know that their district is ostensibly engaged in an economic education program such as DEEP. Such sample selection issues are known to affect evaluation results in many other areas of both economics and education research. The empirical procedures to correct for such effects are relatively new and thus far have been used in only one economic education study, as reported below.

What all of this suggests is not that such simple comparisons can't be used at all—after all, it is probably better news that DEEP students have higher scores on these items than it would be if their scores were lower. Nor does it suggest that the standardized tests are bad instruments, or even that the overall norming data are particularly suspect. Truly random norming groups are rarely available for tests like these, even for the best known national achievement and aptitude tests. But it is crucial to remember that the DEEP/non-DEEP comparisons based on individual items from such exams do not meet the standards for careful academic research. Overall scores on an exam—and, even better, pre-post differences for two exams while controlling for differences in students' innate and socioeconomic differences—are far more important to use in evaluating DEEP and similar kinds of programs.

The only extensive evaluations of the national DEEP effort conducted during the expansion and enhancement stage are built around the second edition of the *Test of Economic Literacy* (see Soper & Walstad, 1987, 1988; Walstad & Soper, 1988a, 1988b). In these publications focusing on pretest, posttest, and posttest minus pretest scores as output measures, and controlling for student IQ levels and other student, teacher, and school district characteristics, the authors made this general finding:

> The DEEP variable is a significant predictor of economics achievement and contributes to gains in economic knowledge. Students in DEEP districts, which provide teacher in-service education . . . and which build economics into the curriculum, score 1.6 points higher [on the 46-item TEL] than students in non-DEEP districts. . . . [W]hen the pre-test variable is included . . . there is still a 1.4 difference in favor of students in DEEP districts.
>
> . . . The results clearly indicate that the more education in economics a teacher has, the better the students do and the higher the level of achievement. Teachers need to be encouraged to take more coursework in the ever changing field of economics if they are to stay current. One way to do this would be for a school district to make a stronger commitment to economic education through DEEP. (Walstad & Soper, 1988a, p. 255)

Yet again, however, these favorable conclusions require a considerable amount of elaboration and qualification. For one thing, this evaluation was limited to the formal implementing and sustaining categories of DEEP districts, which makes its message more limited and refined than were those of the earlier studies from the experimental and cooperating schools stages. This is a reasonable and desirable distinction to make, of course, and one that was simply not available in the earlier studies. But it also means that these findings are directly applicable only to the DEEP districts in the two highest categories of the program.

Becker and Walstad (1990) have also shown that the positive finding in the Walstad and Soper (1988a) report quoted above is linked to sample selection problems and that "[i]t appears that the DEEP designation does not contribute to student learning of economics after adjusting for sample selection bias" (p. 7). Instead, two of the active components of DEEP—a capstone course in economics and the number of economics courses teachers have completed—show even greater effect on student learning than Walstad and Soper had estimated. Apparently, then, what is most important in this national sample of over 5,000 students from more than 200 high schools is not how a DEEP district is labeled, or even whether the district is formally in or out of DEEP, but how active it is in getting students and teachers to complete economics course work or in hiring teachers who already have such training.

Another national data base that offers the promise of evaluating the expansion and enhancement stage of DEEP was collected by the Joint Council during the 1986–87 school year, with funding from the Pew Freedom Trust, Inc. TEL scores were collected for over 3,300 high school seniors (a slightly smaller group than was used in the TEL norming sample) from 121 schools. But the strength of this new data set is that it offers much more extensive background information on students and their teachers, schools, and school districts and that a follow-up survey of the students is planned, which will provide longitudinal information on these students' career and/or educational choices after high school. It will obviously be fascinating to see whether differences in their level of economic understanding translate into other kinds of behavioral differences.

Over 40 potential researchers at conferences held at Princeton University in the summers of 1987 and 1988 were introduced to this data set and to new empirical research techniques that are especially appropriate for use with such survey-based data. Thus far, however, the only published report from this source deals with basic descriptive statistics on the first set of in-school data (Baumol & Highsmith, 1988). This article offers no direct evaluation of DEEP, but the complete report of the survey responses does indicate that 47 percent of the 111 school districts included in the data base were "members" of DEEP. Moreover, among students who had completed an economics course, TEL scores were significantly higher in DEEP districts than in other districts. Among students who had not taken an economics course, the TEL scores were also higher in DEEP districts, but that difference was small and not statistically significant. That pattern is, of course, reminiscent of Soper and Brenneke's (1981) findings cited earlier.

One statewide evaluation of a unique DEEP expansion and enhancement effort, which featured cooperative efforts involving the state council network and the Junior Achievement (JA) program in the state, was conducted in Michigan. This experimental approach was funded by a grant from the W. K. Kellogg Foundation, which also provided for an "outside" evaluation report by Selection Research, Inc. (1988), of Lincoln, Nebraska. The evaluation process involved student testing and telephone surveys of key professional and administrative personnel from schools, the Michigan council network, and JA. Student testing showed significant gains in pre- and posttest scores in grades 9 and 12, but not in grade 6. In all three grades, posttest scores for the students tested (731 in total) were significantly higher than were national norming data for students in the same grades who had received no formal instruction on economics. Unfortunately, it is not noted whether such differences were also present for pretest scores from these students or whether the difference in the posttest minus pretest scores is significantly higher than the gains reported for the national norming sample.

The telephone surveys in Michigan suggested that, much as reported in the Psychological Corporation's reports on the first experimental stage of DEEP in the late 1960s, real progress was made in calling attention to economic education efforts in the participating school districts and in expanding the use of instructional materials and in-service training in economics. More specific to this project were findings that the cooperation with JA and the use of part-time "certified DEEP trainers" could, with sufficient coordination and sufficient time, be effective. And even in terms of student outcomes, the Michigan project provided further evidence (supporting the Buckles and Freeman study cited earlier) that benefits from DEEP are likely to be larger and more significant in the second or third year of an intensive intervention program than in the first year. Like all of the DEEP projects and stages described earlier, the continued success of this Michigan experiment seems likely to depend on the continued availability of funding and personnel resources to sustain the commitment to the goals of economic education and economic literacy. It is, of course, a near certainty that the funds to support that commitment will not continue to come from any one foundation, and probably not from any group of foundations and private sponsors over time.

As Michael MacDowell and Peter Harrington point out elsewhere in this volume, without stronger state and local support for DEEP and economic education in the schools, particularly from state and local public education agencies, both expansion and enhancement efforts are likely to have decidedly limited and temporary results. At the national level today there continues to be enough support to fund exciting and frequently effective demonstration or model programs, but not enough commitment to guarantee consistent, stable, widespread, and routine results. A one-time injection of $5 million, $7 million, or even $11 million is, quite literally, only a token down payment when weighed against any goal like reaching 70 percent of the nation's precollege students, or even the teachers of that number of students.

FUTURE DEEP

For two decades DEEP has been shown to be, both in theory and in practice, a promising and potentially powerful process by which to achieve major revisions and improvements in the K–12 curriculum. At the same time, many of the features that make it attractive to classroom teachers and school system administrators may result in inherent problems that must be resolved to make the program truly effective. A decentralized, voluntary, infusion-based program for economic education would be expected to work better if most teachers are well trained, and currently trained, in economics; if they are aware of many quality teaching materials on economics they feel they can use confidently with their students; and if they feel there is time available in the curriculum for increased instruction in basic economic concepts. In fact, national and state surveys show that this is generally not the case (see Walstad & Watts, 1985).

The somewhat mixed research and evaluation results on DEEP to date (which are perhaps better described as simply hard to pin down) stem largely from the voluntary nature of the program and from recent researchers' ability to better control for key components of DEEP, like teacher training and a district's current level of achievement in, and commitment to, the program. For example, counting only implementing or sustaining districts as DEEP districts makes it more likely that positive and significant results will be discovered. On the other hand, carefully controlling for teacher training in the same regression equation where a DEEP binary variable is specified makes it less likely that the coefficient on the direct indicator of DEEP participation will be positive and significant. Long-term controlled experiments involving DEEP and non-DEEP districts have not been completed and are not currently underway, but at this point in the research history they might well tell us more than additional large-scale, cross-sectional "snapshots."

Moving into the 1990s, the lessons of the past 25 years seem to be telling us that

- DEEP can work if enough people in and around the school district want it to.
- DEEP requires a continuing commitment of resources to work—when resources disappear, so do student and teacher test results.
- capstone courses in economics are a particularly effective way to get significant gains in student test scores and usually are more reliable than a K–12 infusion approach; but it is not at all clear that a one-semester or one-year course in economics at any grade level is sufficient to guarantee a satisfactory level of economic understanding or literacy.

The major barriers to DEEP and other economic education programs in the schools include

- the overcrowded curriculum, which is jammed with traditional academic course work and a variety of "social problem intervention" sessions or courses (e.g., drug/sex/AIDS education).
- perceptions that economics is, though important, a difficult, dry, and overly technical subject for precollege students and the teacher.
- limited training in economics among precollege teachers and administrators and among parents of most school-age children, which restricts both the supply of and the demand for more systematic economic education programs.
- "competition" from more established educational groups which promote the virtues of such programs as social studies/citizenship education, traditional history and government courses, or global/geography education to the exclusion of economics course work and infusion material (including space in state or local curriculum guidelines).
- the negative probusiness and apologist/propaganda image that some educators have of economic education (see Watts, 1987).
- the sometimes drab and dreary image of DEEP itself, and of other economic education programs.

- the lack of a clearer, more comprehensive statement on the private and social benefits of economic education.

On the other hand, the historical successes of DEEP offer clear evidence of programmatic strength and a substantial resource base. Some problems featured prominently in earlier assessments, such as the limited quality and quantity of good K–12 instructional materials, have been largely overcome. A few of the remaining barriers may also be eliminated, given the proper levels of leadership, creativity, and, of course, future funding. But most of those obstacles look to be highly resistent to any quick-fix solutions, so what we may need most are the kind of resolve that took Churchill's England through its time of toil and tears and the good sense to celebrate the victories that do come our way during the struggle. Of course, the economic wisdom to look for activities where additional benefits exceed additional costs will also help.

REFERENCES

Armento, B. J. (1983). A study of the basic economic concepts presented in DEEP curriculum guides, grades 7–12. *Journal of Economic Education* 14(3):22–27.

Baumol, W. J., and Highsmith, R. J. (1988). Variables affecting success in economic education: Preliminary findings from a new data base. *American Economic Review* 78(2):257–62.

Becker, W. E., Jr.; Helmberger, J. D.; and Thompson, J. L. (1975). An evaluation of a Developmental Economic Education Project given limited data. *Journal of Economic Education* 6(2):120–25.

Becker, W. E., and Walstad, W. B. (1990). Data loss from pretest to posttest as a sample selection problem. *Review of Economics and Statistics* 72(1):184–88.

Buckles, S., and Freeman, V. (1984). A longitudinal analysis of a Developmental Economic Education Program. *Journal of Economic Education* 15(1):5–10.

Grobman, H. (1970). *Developmental curriculum projects: Decision points and processes*. Itasca, Ill.: F. E. Peacock Publishers.

Joint Council on Economic Education (1970). *Economics in the curriculum: Developmental Economic Education Program*. New York: the Joint Council.

———— (1969). *DEEP 1969: Perspectives on a 5-year experiment in curriculum change*. New York: the Joint Council.

Kim, Y., and Kratochvil, D. W. (1972). *Developmental Economic Education Program: Product development report no. 16*. Palo Alto, Calif.: American Institute for Research.

Luker, W. A. (1984). DEEP revisited. *Journal of Economic Education* 15(2):111–18.

Maher, J. (1969). DEEP: Strengthening economics in the schools. *American Economic Review* 59(2):230–38.

Psychological Corporation (1970). *A report of the evaluation of the Developmental Economic Education Program.* New York: Joint Council on Economic Education.

——— (1968). *A report of the first-year evaluation of the Developmental Economic Education Program.* New York: Joint Council on Economic Education.

Selection Research, Inc. (1988). *Project DEEP: End-of-project evaluation report.* Lincoln, Nebr.: Selection Research, Inc.

Soper, J. C., and Brenneke, J. S. (1984). DEEP revisited: Another reply. *Journal of Economic Education* 15(2):123.

——— (1981). The Test of Economic Literacy and an evaluation of the DEEP system. *Journal of Economic Education* 12(1):1–14.

Soper, J. C., and Walstad, W. B. (1988). What is high school economics? Posttest knowledge, attitudes, and course content. *Journal of Economic Education* 19(1):37–51.

——— (1987). *Test of Economic Literacy: Examiner's manual.* 2d ed. New York: Joint Council on Economic Education.

Symmes, S. S., ed. (1969). *DEEP handbook for curriculum change/Guidelines.* New York: Joint Council on Economic Education.

Walstad, W. B., and Soper, J. C. (1988a). A report card on the economic literacy of U.S. high school students. *American Economic Review* 78(2):251–56.

——— (1988b). What is high school economics? TEL revision and pretest findings. *Journal of Economic Education* 19(1):24–36.

——— (1984). DEEP revisited: A reply. *Journal of Economic Education* 15(2):119–22.

——— (1982). A model of economics learning in the high schools. *Journal of Economic Education* 13(1):40–54.

Walstad, W. B., and Watts, M. (1985). Teaching economics in the schools: A review of survey findings. *Journal of Economic Education* 16(2):135–45.

Watts, M. (1987). Ideology, textbooks, and the teaching of economics. *Theory into Practice* 26(3):190–97.

——— (1986). Empirical evidence on economic literacy in the schools. In *Economics education: Research and development issues,* ed. S. Hodkinson and D. Whitehead, 196–215. London and New York: Longman Group, Ltd.

——— (1985). A statewide assessment of precollege economic understanding and DEEP. *Journal of Economic Education* 16(3):22–35. [See also errata, 16(4):286.]

7. ECONOMIC LITERACY IN SENIOR HIGH SCHOOLS

by William B. Walstad and John C. Soper

High school plays an important role in the lives of students. It is at this stage in their education that students consolidate the learnings of elementary and middle schools and prepare either for more intensive study at the college level or for entry into the job market. Economics can and should be taught at these grade levels because students are capable of understanding basic economic concepts and how economic systems work. A knowledge of economics is also essential for answering economic questions and making decisions in one's life roles as consumer, worker, and voting citizen.

But knowing that economics can and should be taught in high schools is insufficient. We need more information about what students know, what concepts students understand, and how to improve the teaching of this vital subject. Obtaining information to answer these questions requires careful study and analysis of national data so that any conclusions drawn will serve as a guide to the development of effective economics education among high school students. This need is all the more pressing because more states have recognized the value of teaching economics to high school students and are including the subject in the curriculum (Highsmith, 1989). Teachers are also under pressure because they must now teach a subject for which their knowledge or their access to quality instructional materials may be limited (Walstad & Watts, 1985).

Fortunately, there is emerging a body of research that contains direct implications for the teaching and learning of economics at the precollege level (Dawson, 1977; Miller, 1987; Becker, Greene & Rosen, 1990; Schug & Walstad, forthcoming). One factor contributing to the growth of research, especially since 1985, was the preparation of a research agenda for DEEP and precollege economic education (Brenneke et al., 1988). This agenda outlined the need for the development of new test instruments or the revision of existing instruments and called for the collection of national data sets that can be used by researchers. It also suggested areas for quantitative and qualitative studies and identified ways to enlist more people in the research and evaluation process. Although the agenda is not without criticism (Hansen, 1988; Saunders, 1988), a number of the suggestions have been undertaken by the Joint Council on Economic Education that have aided in building a greater knowledge base about economic education in elementary and secondary schools.

This chapter describes basic findings from one of the first steps in the agenda process: the revision of the *Test of Economic Literacy* (Soper & Walstad, 1987). The norming data from the 8,205 students who took this test provide base line data about senior high school students' knowledge of economics from an overall perspective and across major economic concepts. Further comparisons are made by breaking down the data by the type of course to determine how much economics is taught to students in a separate course or through infusion in social studies or consumer economics courses. The chapter also compares the level of student performance across concepts with responses to teacher surveys asking what concepts are being taught in the classroom to identify areas of success or failure in the economic education of students. Finally, the chapter suggests actions that teachers and school administrators can take to improve the economic education of students in senior high school.

MEASURING ECONOMIC LITERACY

There is no exact definition of what it means for high school students or adults to be economically literate. As a starting point, George Stigler (1970), winner of the 1982 Nobel Prize in Economics, offers an authoritative definition:

Economic literacy is knowledge of theories which are held by professional economists. Time will eventually reveal that some of those theories are wrong and all are incomplete, but at any one time there is a best scientific view and this best must be the basis for any appraisal of literacy. (p. 83)

This definition, however, does not tell us how to measure economic literacy. We still have to decide what theories to select to test for student knowledge and what group of economists we should sample to determine the "best scientific view." We also need to know how detailed the

100

assessment of economic knowledge should be. In other words, there needs to be an operational definition for the measurement of economic literacy.

In his discussion of economic literacy, Hansen (1977) concluded that there was no definition that provided a useful basis for measuring the construct. Ideally what is sought, according to Hansen, is a measure that would show that the "level of economic literacy has observable consequences in people's behavior and in their beliefs about the economic system" (p. 62). None of the existing instruments fulfills that expectation, although test scores and opinion surveys often serve as proxy measures. Hansen criticizes the use of test scores because they simply reflect the mastery of economics obtained through course work. Instead, he prefers opinion surveys, and in his chapter on economic literacy (Hansen, 1977) he shows how opinion surveys can be interpreted to provide evidence about the level of economic literacy among adults.

For the current debate over school reform, however, standardized test scores from secondary students rather than surveys of adult opinion may be of more value. In fact, most of the discussion in the campaign for literacy in various subjects has focused on what students know about the subject, be it history, geography, science, or mathematics. Although questions may be raised about what level of test performance constitutes mastery of the material, test scores provide an indication of the relative achievement of students. A test of economic understanding also seems more consistent with Stigler's view of economic literacy as "knowledge of theories which are held by professional economists." With this thought in mind, we can now discuss the development of the *Test of Economic Literacy* (TEL).

THE TEST OF ECONOMIC LITERACY

In 1977 a national task force report was issued that identified the economic understandings essential for the high school graduate. The report was developed by a national committee of prominent economists and was published as *A Framework for Teaching Economics: Basic Concepts* (Hansen et al., 1977). This publication described a concept structure of the economics discipline and identified those economic concepts that should be or might be taught at the secondary level. It also served as the content validity document for the first edition of the TEL (Soper, 1979).

Content Validity of the TEL

The *Framework* was revised in 1984 to incorporate changes in the structure of the economics discipline and to reorganize the presentation of the basic concepts (Saunders et al., 1984). The basic difference between the old and the new versions was the change in the fundamental economic and macroeconomic concepts listings. Also, more emphasis was placed on international concepts and less emphasis on economic goals in the new version. The *Framework* revision invalidated the first TEL as a measure of student economic understanding. The national norms for the original TEL were also almost a decade old and were suspect as indicators of economic achievement. So the TEL was revised in 1985 by a national committee of economists, high school economics teachers, and test experts following standard test development procedures to establish content validity and reliability.[1]

As shown in Table 7.1, the second edition of the TEL consists of two 46-item forms. Test items are well distributed across four concept clusters. Approximately 26 to 30 percent of the questions on each form cover fundamental economic, microeconomic, or macroeconomic concepts. About 15 to 17 percent of the questions also focus on international concepts. Thus, given the *Framework* as a content guide, a case can be made that the TEL is a content-valid measure of the economic understanding of high school students.

Although not reported in Table 7.1, items were also classified by cognitive level, using a slightly modified form of Bloom's *Taxonomy of Educational Objectives* (Bloom et al., 1956). There are 17 percent of the questions at the knowledge level, 28 to 30 percent at the comprehension level, and 22 percent at the application level. At the two highest levels, 22 to 24 percent of the questions were classified at the analysis level, and the remaining 9 percent were placed at the evaluation level. The synthesis level of Bloom's *Taxonomy* was omitted because it is difficult to use a multiple choice format to assess such characteristics as originality or creativity.

Several other considerations were addressed to make certain the test met high standards. The test was kept to a reasonable length so that it could be administered in a 40- to 50-minute class period. Also, all items on the test were reviewed by a reading specialist to make certain that they were appropriate for high school students. This reading analysis was made more difficult because, as with other sciences, there is a specialized vocabulary in economics. Finding substitute terms for such concepts as

TABLE 7.1
The TEL Content Matrix

CONTENT CATEGORIES	NUMBER AND PERCENTAGE OF ITEMS BY FORM			
	A	%	B	%
Fundamental Economic Concepts	12	26.0	12	26.1
1. Scarcity	2		2	
2. Opportunity costs/trade-offs	3		2	
3. Productivity	2		2	
4. Economic systems	1		1	
5. Economic institutions & incentives	2		4	
6. Exchange, money & interdependence	2		1	
Microeconomic Economic Concepts	13	28.3	13	28.3
7. Markets & prices	2		1	
8. Supply & demand	4		4	
9. Competition & market structure	2		3	
10. Income distribution	2		2	
11. Market failures	2		1	
12. Role of government	1		2	
Macroeconomic Economic Concepts	13	28.3	14	30.4
13. Gross national product	1		2	
14. Aggregate supply	1		1	
15. Aggregate demand	2		2	
16. Unemployment	1		1	
17. Inflation & deflation	2		2	
18. Monetary policy	3		3	
19. Fiscal policy	3		3	
International Economic Concepts	8	17.4	7	15.2
20. Comparative advantage/barriers to trade	3		3	
21. Balance of payments & exchange rates	3		2	
22. International growth & stability	2		2	
Total Number of Questions	46	100.0	46	100.0

Source: Soper and Walstad (1987, pp. 5–6, Tables 3 & 4).

"opportunity cost" or "gross national product" was not possible. Knowledge of these concepts and others was viewed as part of the knowledge that should be possessed by economically literate graduates of high schools.

TEL Reliability, Construct Validity, and Knowledge

The TEL was normed with 8,205 students in the spring of 1986. Form A was administered to 4,235 students, and Form B was administered to 3,970 students. As shown in Table 7.2, the Cronbach alpha reliability was .87 for Form A and .88 for Form B. Reliability is estimated on an increasing scale from .00 to 1.00. These estimates indicate, therefore, that items on the test are providing an internally consistent measure of economic understanding. Most standardized achievement tests report reliability estimates in the range of .85–.95, so the TEL meets this measurement standard.

TABLE 7.2
Aggregate Statistics for the TEL

MEAN	FORM A			FORM B		
	Score	% Correct	N	Score	% Correct	N
Overall	22.06	48	4,235	22.18	48	3,970
(std. dev.)	(8.33)			(8.64)		
With economics	23.33	51	3,153	23.92	52	2,765
(std. dev.)	(8.45)			(8.85)		
Without economics	18.37	40	1,082	18.01	39	1,205
(std. dev.)	(6.71)			(6.64)		
Cronbach alpha	.87			.88		

Source: Soper and Walstad (1987, p. 12, Table 5).

Table 7.2 also presents overall data for students in the norming sample *with* and *without* economic instruction. For the *with economics* groups, the 3,153 students who took Form A had a mean score of 23.33 points. The 2,765 students who took Form B had a mean score of 23.92. In contrast, for the *without economics* students, the 1,082 who took Form A had a mean score of 18.37, and the 1,205 students who took Form B had a mean score of 18.01. These data indicate that there are significant differences in economic understanding on the TEL for students with and without economics. The differences of +4.96 points on Form A and +5.91 points on Form B suggest that economic instruction increases TEL scores 27 to 33 percent when scores are computed using the mean scores of students without economics as the starting level. These differences also provide initial evidence of the construct validity of the TEL.

A less impressive, but still accurate, way to view the scores is to calculate the average percentage of items correct out of the 46 possible items. The overall percentage correct for all students on both forms was 48 percent. On Form A, students with economics scored 51 percent correct, and students without economics scored 40 percent correct, for an 11 percent difference. On Form B, students with economics scored 52 percent correct, and students without economics had 39 percent correct, for a 13 percent difference. On both forms there is a sizable spread in the percentages correct.

There is, of course, a mixed message when looking at the differences in performance. On the one hand, instruction makes a difference in what students know about economics. Both percentage increases are large relative to the *without economics* score as the starting base (27–33 percent) or relative to the total possible score (11–13 percent). On the other hand, the final level of performance is relatively low. Even after economics instruction, students can answer only about half the questions on either form of the test. Although some consideration should be given to the fact that the test is designed as an achievement and not a mastery test, the final level of achievement seems inadequate for students graduating from senior high school. This result raises questions about the economic literacy in the nation's senior high school students and the quality of the economic education students receive.

Relative Performance on the TEL

The data can also be examined to identify the areas of relative strength and weakness in student knowledge of economic concepts based on results from the two 46-item forms. To simplify the exposition, however, items on each form are combined. Because 15 items are common to each form, these common items are counted only once to produce one 77-item test instead of one 92-item test. This arrangement provides the benefit of more item information, but it does not distort the analysis. As a review of the scores in Table 7.2 shows, student performance on Form A and that on Form B were almost equivalent. The analysis of the combined form test of 77 items is found in Table 7.3.

The combined item data can be studied from an overall perspective, across broad concept clusters, and across the 22 *Framework* concept categories. The average percentages correct are 51 percent for students with economics and 40 percent for students without economics. These results are similar to the separate form results in Table 7.2. The percentages correct for the four major *Framework* concept clusters show that those students with economics have higher performance levels on the fundamental economic concepts (57 percent) and the microeconomic concepts (55 percent) than they do on the macroeconomic concepts (45 percent) and the international concepts (45 percent). The data tend to confirm earlier speculations about the comparative weakness of student learning in the macroeconomic and international economic areas, compared to performance in the fundamental and microeconomic areas (Soper & Brenneke, 1981; Walstad & Soper, 1988a).

The data in Table 7.3 also show which of the specific concepts within each broad concept cluster present more or less difficulty to students with economics in the norming sample. Comparing the percentages correct for specific concepts to the average percentage correct of 51 percent (with economics), such concepts as economic systems (75 percent), economic institutions and incentives (61 percent), exchange, money, and interdependence (65 percent), supply and demand (61 percent), and unemployment (63 percent) are concepts where student performance is well above average (60 percent). The scores on the concepts of scarcity (54 percent), markets and prices (55 percent), competition and market structure (59 percent), gross national product (56 percent), and aggregate demand (53 percent) were above average, while the scores on the concept areas of opportunity cost/trade-offs (51 percent), productivity (51 percent), income distribution (51 percent), and role of government (52 percent) were at or near average performance levels. However, scores for aggregate supply (44 percent), fiscal policy (46 percent), comparative advantage/barriers to trade (48 percent), balance of payments and exchange rates (44 percent), and international growth and stability (43 percent) were below average. Finally, scores for the concepts of market failures (39 percent), inflation and deflation (34 percent), and monetary policy (36 percent) were well below average (<40 percent).

TABLE 7.3
TEL With and Without Economics Data
(Percentage Correct on the Combined TEL)

NO. OF ITEMS	CONCEPTS	WITHOUT ECONOMICS (N=2,287)	WITH ECONOMICS (N=5,918)
77	All items	40%	51%
20	Fundamental	44	57
22	Microeconomics	42	55
23	Macroeconomics	34	45
12	International	36	45
3	Scarcity	32	54
5	Opportunity cost/trade-offs	40	51
3	Productivity	40	51
1	Economic systems	57	75
5	Economic institutions & incentives	49	61
3	Exchange, money & interdependence	52	65
2	Markets & prices	41	55
7	Supply & demand	49	61
4	Competition & market structure	48	59
3	Income distribution	41	51
3	Market failures	33	39
3	Role of government	38	52
2	Gross national product	42	56
2	Aggregate supply	31	44
3	Aggregate demand	42	53
2	Unemployment	51	63
4	Inflation & deflation	25	34
5	Monetary policy	28	36
5	Fiscal policy	35	46
5	Comparative advantage/barriers to trade	36	48
4	Balance of payments & exchange rates	38	44
3	International growth & stability	34	43

Source: Soper and Walstad (1988, p. 46, Table 7).

One implication of this analysis is that teachers of economics courses who wish to improve the performance of their students might focus on those concepts or concept clusters noted above where students had the weakest level of performance. In the macroeconomics cluster, inflation and deflation, monetary policy, aggregate supply, and fiscal policy appear to be areas of relatively weak student understanding. Attention to these concepts may improve student understanding of macroeconomics. In addition, comparative advantage/barriers to trade, balance of payments and exchange rates, and economic growth, which constitute the international cluster, are concepts with relatively low levels of achievement. In the microeconomics cluster, only the concept of market failures reveals comparatively weak student understanding. If teachers focus classwork and provide more instruction in these low achievement areas, they may be able to raise overall knowledge by significant amounts and provide a foundation for improved economic literacy.

Another implication of these student test results is that developers of instructional materials need to focus attention and effort on the macroeconomics and international clusters. Evidence of this need is found in the *Framework* (Saunders et al., 1984, p. 70). The classification table of student activities found in various strategies volumes of the *Master Curriculum Guide* series, published by the Joint Council on Economic Education, shows that out of 89 total activities at the secondary level, only 6 (or 6.7 percent) dealt with macroeconomic concepts and only 5 (or 5.6 percent) focused on international economic concepts. The authors of the *Framework* also concluded their monograph with this statement: "we would like to encourage educators to develop more activities in macroeconomics and in international economics" (Saunders et al., 1984, p. 71).

Pre- and Posttest Samples

Although it may be tempting to make comparisons of the differences between students with and without economics, this comparison is only a first step in any analysis, and it should be viewed with caution. The *with* and *without* groups are different samples, and there may be significant background differences on such variables as grade level, intelligence, or income, among others.[2] To overcome this problem and yet keep the analysis as uncomplicated as possible, data from a sample of norming students who had taken the TEL at the beginning of the 1986 spring semester (a pretest) and the same group of students who had taken the TEL at the end of the semester (a posttest) were matched. As shown in Table 7.4, there were 3,199 matched cases.

What the matched data reveal, which is masked in the *with* and *without* data in Table 7.3 and in the overall data in Table 7.4, is that the percentage correct on the posttest varies substantially for students. How much economics students learn over a semester depends on the type of course taken. To illustrate this point, students were classified as taking one of three courses based on information from a teacher survey. Of the matched sample, 47 percent took an economics course, 18 percent attended a consumer economics course, and 35 percent were enrolled in a social studies course.[3] On the posttest, economics students, as might be expected, scored the highest—52 percent correct on the TEL. Social studies students got about 42 percent of the TEL items correct. Students in consumer economics courses scored the lowest, with 40 percent correct. These levels of achievement, however, even for the economics students, would be considered as failing under most grading standards.

The other problem is the change in percentage correct from pre- to posttest. Only students in an economics course show a significant change (7.5 percent). This gain is not very impressive, and it makes one wonder what is being taught. The majority of this improvement can be attributed to greater understanding of fundamental items (+11 percent), compared with the other concept categories (+6–7 percent). Consumer economics and social studies students show essentially no change in economic understanding. In fact, the data suggest that the indirect method of teaching economics by infusing it in consumer economics and social studies courses may not work.

The analysis of the posttest data by concept cluster confirms the overall conclusion drawn from Table 7.3. For all course types, the best scores are on fundamental and microeconomic items, and the worst are on macroeconomic and international items. Economics students, for example, were 58 percent correct on fundamental items and 56 percent correct on microeconomic items, compared with 47 percent correct on macroeconomic items and 48 percent correct on international economic items. Thus, students show about 6–10 percent more understanding of fundamental and microeconomic concepts than they do of macroeconomic and international economic concepts. The students' lower levels of knowledge of macroeconomics and international economics directly contribute to their poor performance on the overall test and raise

TABLE 7.4
Pre- and Posttest Data by Course Type
(Percentage Correct on the Combined TEL)

COURSE & ITEMS	PRETEST	POSTTEST	CHANGE
Overall [3,199 cases]			
All items (77)*	43.2%	46.5%	3.2%
Fundamental (20)	45.3	51.7	6.3
Microeconomics (22)	47.4	49.8	2.5
Macroeconomics (23)	39.0	40.8	1.9
International (12)	40.4	42.6	2.1
Economics [1,499 cases]			
All items	44.9	52.4	7.5
Fundamental	47.0	58.4	11.4
Microeconomics	48.6	55.5	6.9
Macroeconomics	41.0	46.5	5.5
International	42.2	47.9	5.7
Consumer economics [579 cases]			
All items	40.3	40.1	−0.2
Fundamental	42.9	45.6	2.7
Microeconomics	44.5	43.4	−1.1
Macroeconomics	35.9	33.6	−2.3
International	36.7	37.6	0.9
Social studies [1,121 cases]			
All items	42.5	42.1	−0.5
Fundamental	44.3	45.9	1.6
Microeconomics	47.1	45.8	−1.3
Macroeconomics	37.8	37.1	−0.7
International	39.9	38.4	−1.5

*Number of items is in parentheses.

Source: Adapted from Walstad and Soper (1988b, p. 252, Table 1).

questions about whether the concepts in these clusters are being taught by teachers.[4]

What the matched data indicate is that having students take a separate economics course may be the only reliable way of guaranteeing that

110

students receive an economic education. This decision, however, is not without controversy for there is opposition to separate (elective or mandated) courses in a crowded curriculum. Even with a separate course in economics, exposure to macroeconomic or international economic concepts appears limited. This finding is unsettling because students are showing the worst levels of achievement in the areas that are most debated in the news media and in Congress.

Teacher Survey Results

As a part of the norming process, teachers administering the TEL to their students were also asked to complete survey questionnaires. These questionnaires asked teachers to report information about their professional background, the characteristics of their school and economics courses, and their teaching practices. For the sake of brevity, the analysis is restricted to teacher responses to one item, which asked teachers to check off those economic concepts they currently teach. Table 7.5 provides a summary of teacher responses to this question broken down by (1) economics course teachers, (2) consumer economics course teachers, and (3) social studies course teachers.

TABLE 7.5
Concepts Currently Being Taught
(TEL Teacher Responses in Percentages)

CONCEPTS	ECONOMICS TEACHERS (N=94)	CONSUMER ECONOMICS TEACHERS (N=41)	SOCIAL STUDIES TEACHERS (N=53)
All concepts	76.9%	53.7%	39.1%
Fundamental	79.4	56.1	36.3
Microeconomics	77.2	59.6	39.2
Macroeconomics	82.3	59.5	48.3
International	54.8	15.9	24.6
Left all blank	3.2	9.8	37.7

Source: Soper and Walstad (1988, p. 47, Table 8).

Inspection of the data reveals significant differences in the percentage of concepts covered by teachers in the three courses. As might be expected, economics teachers have the highest average percentage of

111

coverage of concepts at 76.9 percent versus 53.7 percent for consumer economics teachers and 39.1 percent for social studies teachers. Obviously, economics teachers report teaching more concepts, and, consequently, we should expect economics students to outperform social studies and consumer economics students, as found in Table 7.4.

Within the concept clusters, fundamental economic items and microeconomic items were the clusters where students showed the best levels of performance, irrespective of the type of course. It would not be surprising then that the reported coverage of these clusters would be above average: 77–79 percent for economics teachers, 56–60 percent for consumer economics teachers, and 36–39 percent for social studies teachers. In contrast, the level of achievement on international concepts in Table 7.4 was low. Data in Table 7.5 suggest the reason why performance on international concepts is so poor. Those concepts are ones teachers report emphasizing the least, irrespective of course type (55 percent for economics, 16 percent for consumer economics, and 25 percent for social studies teachers).

Ironically, the macroeconomic cluster receives the largest percentage of coverage: 82 percent of economics teachers, 60 percent of consumer economics teachers, and 48 percent of social studies teachers report coverage of macroeconomic concepts. But, as found in Tables 7.3 and 7.4, macroeconomics is the area of the weakest performance by students. Thus, teachers may think they are teaching macroeconomic concepts, but apparently the knowledge is not being conveyed to students. Whether this problem is due to the level of teacher understanding of macroeconomics, poor classroom materials, or the complexities of the topic is difficult to decipher, but the marked contrast in teacher responses and student scores suggests a problem with instruction in macroeconomics.

At the bottom of the table is the percentage of questionnaires where the respondent left the entire question blank. Only 3.2 percent of the economics teachers and 9.8 percent of the consumer economics teachers left all items blank. The reason that 37.7 percent of the social studies teachers left all items blank was that they were told not to complete the part of the survey that contained this question if they did not teach any economics in their courses. Slightly over 32 percent of the teachers stated that they did not teach any economics in their courses and did not complete this question, so only about 5 percent of the social studies teachers who completed the entire survey did not respond to this

112

question. What these percentages indicate is that about one-third of the social studies teachers who are teaching courses in government or U.S. history are not conscious of providing any instruction in basic economic concepts. The other two-thirds of the teachers are providing some economics instruction, but only on selected concepts. As with the data in Table 7.4, these percentages suggest that there may be severe problems with reliance on economic instruction through an infusion approach. Students may receive no instruction or only sporadic exposure to economic concepts if they happen to take social studies courses from teachers who choose not to include much economics in their classes.

CONCLUSION

Several conclusions can be drawn from the discussion and data presented that have implications for economic education in senior high schools.

- There is no exact definition of what it means to be economically literate, but one authoritative definition suggests that it is "knowledge of theories which are held by professional economists."

- Standardized achievement tests in economics provide proxy measures of economic literacy.

- The *Test of Economic Literacy* (TEL) is a valid and reliable test of student understanding of basic economic concepts that are recommended for instruction in high school.

- The economic knowledge of high school students is low: 51 percent correct on the TEL for students *with* some economics and 40 percent correct for students *without* economics.

- Only direct instruction in economics courses appears to make a significant contribution to student economic understanding when compared with indirect instruction in social studies and consumer economics courses.

- Students in all courses show the worst levels of understanding of macroeconomic and international economic concepts, the very areas of most discussion among many elected officials and the news media.

113

- Teachers in all courses report the most concept coverage of macroeconomics, but this coverage is not reflected in student performance, suggesting that teachers are not doing an adequate job with instruction in this area.

- The reason students do poorly on international economics is that teachers in all courses pay the least attention to that concept cluster.

- More curriculum materials on macroeconomics and international economics are needed, and more intensive teacher training in these areas should help improve economic understanding among high school students.

- Teachers, curriculum developers, administrators, and economic educators must work together to improve the condition of economic education in senior high schools.

NOTES

1. Members of the test development committee included William Carlson (Guilford High School, Ill.), John Morton (Homewood-Flossmoor High School, Ill.), Michael Watts (Purdue University), and the authors. Members of the national advisory committee included G. L. Bach (Stanford University), William Baumol (Princeton and New York universities), William Becker (Indiana University), Rendigs Fels (Vanderbilt University), Kalman Goldberg (Bradley University), W. Lee Hansen (University of Wisconsin), Robert Highsmith (Joint Council on Economic Education), Karen Horn (Cleveland Federal Reserve Bank), Herbert Neil, Jr. (Financial and Economic Strategies Corporation), and James Tobin (Yale University). For a description of the test development work, see Soper and Walstad (1987).

2. See Walstad and Soper (1982, 1988b & 1989) for studies that use multiple regression techniques to control for background differences. The results confirm the basic findings reported here about the effectiveness of an economics course and the relative ineffectiveness of courses in consumer economics and social studies.

3. The course titles that were given for "economics" courses were economics, free enterprise, applied economics, economic history, economics/government, and comparative economic systems. Course titles used for the "consumer economics" designation were consumer economics, marketing/sales management, business economics, home economics, agricultural economics, business math, and law. For the "social studies" designation, course titles were U.S.

history, world history, government, social studies, geography, psychology, contemporary America, local history, and social problems.

4. More detailed data on performance on each of the 22 *Framework* concepts for the students in an economics course are found in Walstad and Soper (1988b, p. 253). These results were similar to those in Table 7.3 and are not reported here.

REFERENCES

Becker, W.; Greene, W.; and Rosen, S. (1990). Research in high school economic education. *American Economic Review: Proceedings* 80(2):14–22.

Bloom, B. S., ed., et al. (1956). *Taxonomy of educational objectives: The classification of educational goals, Handbook I: Cognitive domain.* New York: McKay.

Brenneke, J. S.; Highsmith, R. J.; Soper, J. C.; Walstad, W. B.; and Watts, M. (1988). A research and evaluation agenda for DEEP and precollege economic education. *Journal of Economic Education* 19(1):5–13.

Dawson, G. G. (1977). Research in economic education at the precollege level. In *Perspectives on economic education,* ed. D. R. Wentworth, W. L. Hansen, and S. H. Hawke, 85–104. New York: Joint Council on Economic Education.

Hansen, W. L. (1988). A research and evaluation agenda for DEEP and precollege economic education: A comment. *Journal of Economic Education* 19(1):15–17.

_____ (1977). The state of economic literacy. In *Perspectives on economic education,* ed. D. R. Wentworth, W. L. Hansen, and S. H. Hawke, 61–79. New York: Joint Council on Economic Education.

Hansen, W. L.; Bach, G. L.; Calderwood, J. D.; and Saunders, P. (1977). *A framework for teaching economics: Basic concepts.* New York: Joint Council on Economic Education.

Highsmith, R. J. (1989). *A survey of state mandates for economics instruction, 1989.* New York and Washington, D.C.: Joint Council on Economic Education and NFIB Foundation.

Miller, S. (1987). This issue: Developing economic literacy. *Theory into Practice* 26:162. See also the other articles on economic literacy in this issue.

Saunders, P. (1988). A research and evaluation agenda for DEEP and precollege economic education: A comment. *Journal of Economic Education* 19(1):17–19.

Saunders, P.; Bach, G. L.; Calderwood, J. D.; Hansen, W. L.; and Stein, H. (1984). *A framework for teaching the basic concepts.* 2d ed. New York: Joint Council on Economic Education.

Schug, M., and Walstad, W. B. (forthcoming). Teaching and learning economics. In *Handbook of research on social studies teaching and learning*, ed. J. P. Shaver. Washington, D.C.: National Council for the Social Studies.

Soper, J. C. (1979). *Test of Economic Literacy: Discussion guide and rationale*. New York: Joint Council on Economic Education.

Soper, J. C., and Brenneke, J. S. (1981). The Test of Economic Literacy and an evaluation of the DEEP system. *Journal of Economic Education* 12(1):1–14.

Soper, J. C., and Walstad, W. B. (1988). What is high school economics? Posttest knowledge, attitudes, and course content. *Journal of Economic Education* 19(1):37–51.

———— (1987). *Test of Economic Literacy: Examiner's manual*. 2d ed. New York: Joint Council on Economic Education.

Stigler, G. J. (1970). The case, if any, for economic education. *Journal of Economic Education* 1:77–84.

Walstad, W. B., and Soper, J. C. (1989). What is high school economics? Factors contributing to student achievement and attitude. *Journal of Economic Education* 20(1):23–38.

———— (1988a). What is high school economics? TEL revision and pretest findings. *Journal of Economic Education* 19(1):24–36.

———— (1988b). A report card on the economic literacy of U.S. high school students. *American Economic Review* 78(2):251–56.

———— (1982). A model of economics learning in the high schools. *Journal of Economic Education* 13(1):40–54.

Walstad, W. B., and Watts, M. W. (1985). Teaching economics in the schools: A review of survey findings. *Journal of Economic Education* 16(2):135–46.

8. ECONOMIC KNOWLEDGE IN JUNIOR HIGH AND ELEMENTARY SCHOOLS

by John C. Soper and William B. Walstad

The acquisition of economic knowledge by junior high and elementary school students has been something of a mystery, with relatively little hard evidence available on what economics these students actually know.[1] Although formal economics courses are rare at these grades, there is ample *a priori* argumentation to support the need for such formal instruction.

Students in junior high school and even in elementary school are mature enough to have learned significant amounts of economics and are at an age at which economics is becoming a more obvious and important part of their lives. Consumer expenditures by students at these grade levels are already large and growing. Clearly they are making economic decisions every time they make purchases in the marketplace. Moreover, growing numbers of students, by the time they enter high school, perform some kind of paid work and are therefore entering the economic mainstream as producers (and even as taxpayers, although they cannot yet vote to determine how those tax dollars will be spent). It is also an unfortunate fact that all too many of these students truncate their formal education at, or shortly after, the junior high level. The absence of a sound economic education for the growing numbers of pre-high-school dropouts bodes ill for the future of the American economy and its labor force. Thus, there is a strong case for formal economic education well before students enter high school. Deferring such an education to the eleventh or twelfth grade capstone course misses far too many of our youth and denies even those few who take this upper-level course many years of relevant and important economic education.[2]

But arguments about the *need* for economics teaching at the junior high and elementary grades are not sufficient. We need to know something about what economics students at these grade levels know, what they can learn, and what they are taught. The purpose of this chapter is to outline the answers to these vital educational questions and

117

to provide guidance in the development of more effective economic education for students at this age. The generation, analysis, and interpretation of hard evidence become essential in answering these questions and in beginning to solve the mystery of pre-high-school economic education.

In this chapter, we describe the basic findings from the analysis of a large national sample of eighth and ninth graders who took the *Test of Economic Knowledge* (TEK) (Walstad & Soper, 1987), a cognitive test instrument designed to measure economic achievement of students at these grade levels. The norm data from the 6,887 students who took this test provide base line information about junior high school students' knowledge of economics, both from an overall perspective and across major economic concepts or concept clusters. We are also able to compare student knowledge by type of course to determine how much economics is taught to students in a separate economics course, compared to economic instruction through infusion in social studies (or other) courses. We are also able to compare levels of student performance across concepts with responses to teacher surveys asking what economic concepts are being taught at these grade levels to identify areas of relative strength or weakness in the economic knowledge of these students. Careful review of such national data is an essential first step in the process of improving the economic education of early adolescents in our schools. This analysis also provides the basis for some suggested actions that teachers, school administrators, and economics curriculum and materials developers can take to effect educational improvements.

At the end of the chapter, we briefly discuss the *Basic Economics Test* (BET) (Walstad & Robson, 1990). This achievement test assesses the performance of fifth and sixth graders and provides information about how intermediate elementary students, with and without economic instruction, perform on test questions. Although it is possible to use other methods to measure the economic knowledge of students (see Chapter 7), we base the results reported in this chapter on the BET and the TEK, both objective tests of student economic achievement.

THE TEST OF ECONOMIC KNOWLEDGE

The *Test of Economic Knowledge* was developed in 1986 by a national committee composed of economists, classroom teachers, and test and reading experts.[3] This committee worked nearly a year on the development of the test, following standard test-development procedures (Gronlund, 1981) to establish content validity and reliability. The TEK consists of two 39-item forms, with individual test items distributed across four major concept clusters. Table 8.1 displays the content schema used for the final, published version of each form of the TEK.

Content Validity of the TEK

Table 8.1 shows the distribution of items broken down according to the economic concepts listed in *A Framework for Teaching the Basic Concepts* (Saunders et al., 1984), the content validity document for the test. By major concept cluster, 26 percent of the items are classified as fundamental concepts, 33 percent as microeconomic concepts, 28 percent as macroeconomic concepts, and 13 percent as international concepts.

Items on the TEK were also classified by cognitive category, using essentially the first three categories from Bloom's *Taxonomy of Educational Objectives* (1956). Depending on the form, 33 percent of the items on the TEK are in the knowledge category, 31–36 percent in the comprehension category, and 31–36 percent in the application and "higher" categories. For the most part, few (or no) items on the TEK were included in the analysis, synthesis, and evaluation categories because the test development committee members concluded that little, if any, economic instruction takes place in these categories of Bloom's *Taxonomy* in the eighth and ninth grades.

These 39-item forms provide good content coverage of the *Framework* concepts (Saunders et al., 1984), are at a junior high school reading level,[4] and can be completed by most students in a standard 40- to 50-minute class period. Given the exhaustive test development, field testing, and norm generation, we can argue that the TEK is a valid measure of eighth and ninth grade understanding of basic economics.

TEK Reliability and Construct Validity

The TEK was normed with a national student sample of 6,887 eighth and ninth graders in the winter of 1987. The norm data were collected from 91 middle, junior high, and senior high schools across the nation. Table 8.2 reports the summary statistics generated from the norming, where 3,230 students took Form A and 3,657 students took Form B. The Cronbach alpha reliability was 0.82 for Form A and 0.85 for Form B.

TABLE 8.1
The TEK Content Matrix

CONTENT CATEGORIES	NUMBER AND PERCENTAGE OF ITEMS BY FORM			
	A	%	B	%
Fundamental Economic Concepts	10	25.6	10	25.6
1. Scarcity	2		2	
2. Opportunity cost/trade-offs	2		2	
3. Productivity	1		1	
4. Economic systems	2		2	
5. Economic institutions & incentives	1		2	
6. Exchange, money & interdependence	2		1	
Microeconomic Economic Concepts	13	33.3	13	33.3
7. Markets & prices	2		2	
8. Supply & demand	5		5	
9. Competition & market structure	1		1	
10. Income distribution	2		1	
11. Market failures	1		1	
12. Role of government	2		3	
Macroeconomic Economic Concepts	11	28.2	11	28.2
13. Gross national product	1		1	
14. Aggregate supply	0		0	
15. Aggregate demand	1		1	
16. Unemployment	2		2	
17. Inflation & deflation	3		3	
18. Monetary policy	1		2	
19. Fiscal policy	3		2	
International Economic Concepts	5	12.8	5	12.8
20. Comparative advantage/barriers to trade	4		4	
21. Balance of payments & exchange rates	0		0	
22. International growth & stability	1		1	
Total Number of Questions	39	100.0	39	100.0

Source: Soper and Walstad (1987, pp. 5–6).

TABLE 8.2
Aggregate Statistics for the TEK

MEAN	FORM A			FORM B		
	Score	% Correct	N	Score	% Correct	N
Overall	17.52	44.9	3,230	18.61	47.7	3,657
(std. dev.)	(6.71)			(7.29)		
With economics	19.67	50.4	1,138	20.79	53.3	1,268
(std. dev.)	(7.08)			(7.62)		
Without economics	16.35	41.9	2,092	17.47	44.8	2,389
(std. dev.)	(6.20)			(6.84)		
Cronbach alpha	.82			.85		

Source: Walstad and Soper (1987, p. 10, Table 5).

These reliability estimates indicate that the test items are providing an internally consistent measure of economic understanding.

Table 8.2 also presents overall data for students in the norming sample *with* and *without* economic instruction. For Form A 35.2 percent of the students had economic instruction, and for Form B 34.7 percent had economic instruction. For the *with economics* students, the 1,138 who took Form A had a mean score of 19.7, and the 1,268 who took Form B had a mean score of 20.8. By comparison, for the *without economics* students, the 2,092 who took Form A had a mean score of 16.4, while the 2,389 who took Form B had a mean score of 17.5. These data indicate that there are significant differences in economic knowledge, as measured by the TEK, for students with and without economic instruction. The differences of +3.3 points on Form A and +3.3 points on Form B suggest that economic instruction increases TEK scores 19 to 20 percent when scores are computed using the mean scores of students without economics as the base. These differences also provide evidence of the construct validity of the TEK.

Another way to look at differences in economic knowledge is to calculate the average percentage correct out of the 39 possible items. On Form A the overall percentage correct was 44.9 percent, and on Form B

47.7 percent. On Form A students with economic instruction scored 50.4 percent correct, while students without economics scored 41.9 percent correct, for a difference of about 8.5 percent. On Form B the *with economics* students scored 53.3 percent correct, while the *without economics* students scored 44.8 percent correct, for a difference of about 8.5 percent.

The percentage differences show the eighth and ninth grade students *can* and *do* learn some economics when they are exposed to formal economic instruction. But the differences are not very spectacular, especially when compared to the 11–13 percent difference reported at the senior high school level (see Chapter 7). The test data suggest that economic instruction at these grade levels, when it does occur, is relatively weak. They also suggest the possibility of large up-side gains in economic knowledge if instruction at these grade levels is enhanced.

Relative Performance on the TEK

The TEK norming data can also be examined to identify areas of relative strength and weakness in student knowledge of economic concepts and of the major concept clusters. To enable such analysis, Table 8.3 presents the percentage correct, by concept and by concept cluster, for students with and without economic instruction. To simplify the analysis, the table percentages are based on the 58-item, combined form of the TEK, where the 20 "anchor items" (i.e., those items common to each form) are each counted only once. Overall, students with economics scored 51 percent correct, while students without economics scored 43 percent correct. The percentages correct for each of the four major concept clusters on the *Framework* (Saunders et al., 1984) show that students with economics have higher-than-average performance levels on fundamental economic concepts (53 percent), microeconomic concepts (54 percent), and international economic concepts (52 percent) and lower-than-average performance levels on macroeconomic concepts (47 percent). As with the senior high school case, we again find evidence of relative weakness in the area of macroeconomic knowledge (see Chapter 7). For students without economic instruction, the relative lack of knowledge of macroeconomics is quite obvious, in that they score only 38 percent correct.

While the test data seem to suggest that students, with or without economics, show relatively better levels of performance on international

122

TABLE 8.3
TEK With and Without Economics Data
(Percentage Correct on the Combined TEK)

NO. OF ITEMS	CONCEPTS	WITHOUT ECONOMICS (N=4,481)	WITH ECONOMICS (N=2,406)
58	All items	43%	51%
15	Fundamental	42	53
20	Microeconomics	47	54
16	Macroeconomics	38	47
7	International	45	52
2	Scarcity	40	53
3	Opportunity cost/trade-offs	31	41
1	Productivity	43	47
4	Economic systems	46	56
3	Economic institutions & incentives	45	57
2	Exchange, money & interdependence	50	59
4	Market & prices	47	56
8	Supply & demand	47	53
1	Competition & market structure	48	59
3	Income distribution	49	58
1	Market failures	42	46
3	Role of government	45	49
2	Gross national product	34	51
2	Aggregate demand	32	38
2	Unemployment	44	54
5	Inflation & deflation	42	51
2	Monetary policy	35	44
3	Fiscal policy	35	42
6	Comparative advantage/barriers to trade	47	54
0	Balance of payments & exchange rates		
1	International growth & stability	37	43

Source: Walstad and Soper (1987, Tables 10–13).

items, compared with the other clusters, this conclusion is highly suspect for several reasons. First, there were only 7 international items on the test, compared with 16 macro, 20 micro, and 15 fundamental items. Second, questions on balance of payments and exchange rates were not included because the test development committee concluded that these concepts were given little or no emphasis at the junior high level (see Table 8.4).

The data in Table 8.3 also give a rough indication of the specific economic concepts within each broad concept cluster that present more or less difficulty for students with economic instruction. Comparing the percentages correct for specific concepts to the overall percentage correct of 51 percent, student performance is above average on such concepts as scarcity (53 percent), economic systems (56 percent), economic institutions and incentives (57 percent), exchange, money, and interdependence (59 percent), markets and prices (56 percent), competition and market structure (59 percent), income distribution (58 percent), unemployment (54 percent), and comparative advantage and barriers to trade (54 percent). Scores were at or near the overall average for the specific concepts of supply and demand (53 percent), the role of government (49 percent), gross national product (51 percent), and inflation and deflation (51 percent). Finally, for the specific concepts of opportunity cost and trade-offs (41 percent), productivity (47 percent), market failures (46 percent), aggregate demand (38 percent), monetary policy (44 percent), fiscal policy (42 percent), and international growth and stability (43 percent), scores were below average.[5]

One conclusion from the above analysis is that teachers who wish to improve the performance of their students might focus attention and instruction on those concepts or major concept clusters where students have the weakest levels of performance. For the eighth and ninth grades, this means more emphasis on the macroeconomics cluster, and especially on the concepts of aggregate demand, monetary policy, and fiscal policy. Another conclusion from the above analysis is that textbook authors and developers of curriculum and instructional materials need to focus their efforts on macroeconomics at these (and other) grade levels.

Teacher Survey Results

One likely reason for these differential performance levels by concept and by concept cluster is that teachers nof the tested students actually teach some of the concepts, but not others. In other words, if many students did not receive instruction dealing with certain concepts, it is likely that their performance on test questions from these concept areas would be poor.

As a part of the posttest norming process, teachers administering the TEK to their students were also asked to complete a survey questionnaire. This questionnaire asked teachers to report information about their professional background, the characteristics of their school and economics courses or units, and their teaching practices. The analysis here is restricted to teacher survey responses on one item, which asked teachers to check off those economic concepts they currently teach. Table 8.4 provides a summary of teacher responses to this question broken down by (1) economics course teachers and (2) social studies course teachers.

Close inspection of this table reveals sharp differences in the concept coverage reported by teachers of economics courses relative to teachers of social studies courses. For instance, 50.5 percent of economics teachers cover concepts in the fundamental cluster, while only 35.1 percent of social studies teachers report teaching in this area. For the microeconomics cluster, 52.3 percent of economics teachers provide some coverage, but only 40 percent of social studies teachers do likewise. The largest differential emerges in the macroeconomics cluster where 56.6 percent of economics teachers cover this area, but only 32 percent of

TABLE 8.4
Concepts Currently Being Taught
(TEK Teacher Responses in Percentages)

CONCEPTS	ECONOMICS TEACHERS (N=36)	SOCIAL STUDIES TEACHERS (N=77)
Fundamental	50.5%	35.1%
Microeconomics	52.3	40.0
Macroeconomics	56.6	32.0
International	18.8	14.0

Source: Walstad and Soper (1987), teacher survey data.

social studies teachers report some coverage. For the international cluster, the difference is smaller—18.8 percent for economics teachers versus 14 percent for social studies teachers.

We may also compare the concept teachings of the eighth and ninth grade economics teachers with those of the eleventh and twelfth grade economics teachers who were surveyed in connection with the national norming of the *Test of Economic Literacy* (see Chapter 7, Table 7.5). By major concept cluster, 79.4 percent of the 94 high school economics teachers surveyed reported teaching concepts in the fundamental cluster, compared to only 50.5 percent of the 36 teachers in the TEK survey. For microeconomics, 77.2 percent of the high school teachers provided coverage, whereas only 52.3 percent of the junior high school teachers did. For macroeconomics, the comparative figures are 82.3 percent for high school teachers and 56.6 percent for junior high school teachers. Finally, in the international cluster, the high school percentage is 54.8 percent, while at the lower grades it is only 18.8 percent. In short, much less concept teaching is reported by economics teachers at the eighth and ninth grades, compared to economics teachers at the eleventh and twelfth grades.

THE BASIC ECONOMICS TEST

The *Basic Economics Test*, first published in 1981 (Chizmar & Halinski, 1981), was designed as a measure of the economic understanding of intermediate elementary students. By 1988 there was a need to revise the BET for four reasons. First, over time the achievement norms had become dated and more suspect as indicators of the relative achievement of students. Second, a second edition of the test was needed to incorporate the new outline of economic concepts presented in the revision of the *Framework* (Saunders et al., 1984). Third, the first edition of the BET was designed for grades four through six; however, consultations with reading experts and elementary teachers suggested that the original test was difficult for most fourth graders and that the test should be revised to focus just on the fifth and sixth grades. Fourth, many of the test items were in need of revision to improve clarity and to improve content assessment.

The second edition of the *Basic Economics Test* (Walstad & Robson, 1990) began with the work of a national committee of test experts, economists, and classroom teachers. The committee drew items from the first edition of the BET and rewrote those items to conform to content specifications as outlined in the *Framework* (Saunders et al., 1984). The test development committee also created new items in those content areas where there were no existing questions or where existing questions were weak. Drafts of the test were then field tested and the results reviewed by a national advisory committee of economists and educators. Also, a reading specialist suggested revisions to improve the readability of items. Several reading assessments showed the reading level to be at the fifth-sixth grade level. Finally, a psychometric consultant provided advice on improving the psychometric properties of the text.[6]

The final version of the second edition of the BET consists of two 29-item forms, with 11 items common to each form. As shown in Table 8.5, for Forms A and B there is excellent coverage (over 40 percent of the items) of the fundamental and microeconomic concept clusters of the *Framework* (Saunders et al., 1984). Only a few items (6.9 percent) are included on the test to cover macroeconomic and international economic concepts. The reason that fundamental and microeconomic items are given more weight on the test is that it was the opinion of the committee members and experts involved in the test construction that concepts in these clusters would more likely be taught than would concepts in the macroeconomic and international areas. Further support for this content weighting can be found in *Economics: What and When* (Gilliard et al., 1988), a recommended scope and sequence for economic education, and in survey data on the concept teaching of elementary teachers reported by Watts (1987). Thus, the BET appears to be a content-valid measure of the economic knowledge of fifth and sixth grade students.

BET Reliability and Construct Validity

After the test development work, the BET was normed in the spring of 1989 based on data collected from 9,182 students in 188 elementary and middle schools nationwide. The aggregate statistics for the two forms of the test are reported in Table 8.6. The 4,584 students who took Form A got 58.0 percent of the items correct, while the 4,598 students who took Form B got 61.1 percent of the items correct, indicating that Form A is slightly more difficult for students.

The reliability of Form A is slightly higher (.82), compared to the reliability of Form B (.79). This result was not unexpected because the

TABLE 8.5
The BET Content Matrix

CONTENT CATEGORIES	NUMBER AND PERCENTAGE OF ITEMS BY FORM			
	A	%	B	%
Fundamental Economic Concepts	13	44.8	12	41.4
1. Scarcity	2		2	
2. Opportunity cost/trade-offs	2		2	
3. Productivity	3		2	
4. Economic systems	1		1	
5. Economic institutions & incentives	2		2	
6. Exchange, money & interdependence	3		3	
Microeconomic Economic Concepts	12	41.4	13	44.8
7. Markets & prices	1		2	
8. Supply & demand	6		6	
9. Competition & market structure	1		1	
10. Income distribution	1		1	
11. Market failures	1		1	
12. Role of government	2		2	
Macroeconomic Economic Concepts	2	6.9	2	6.9
13. Gross national product	0		0	
14. Aggregate supply	0		0	
15. Aggregate demand	0		0	
16. Unemployment	1		1	
17. Inflation & deflation	1		1	
18. Monetary policy	0		0	
19. Fiscal policy	0		0	
International Economic Concepts	2	6.9	2	6.9
20. Comparative advantage/barriers to trade	2		2	
21. Balance of payments & exchange rates	0		0	
22. International growth & stability	0		0	
Total Number of Questions	29	100.0	29	100.0

Source: Walstad and Robson (1990, pp. 4–5, Tables 3 and 4).

TABLE 8.6
Aggregate Statistics for the BET

MEAN	FORM A			FORM B		
	Score	% Correct	N	Score	% Correct	N
Overall	16.82	58.0	4,584	17.74	61.1	4,598
(std. dev.)	(5.52)			(4.99)		
With economics	18.48	63.7	1,699	18.88	65.1	1,240
(std. dev.)	(5.64)			(5.31)		
Without economics	15.84	54.6	2,885	17.32	59.7	3,358
(std. dev.)	(5.21)			(4.80)		
Cronbach alpha	.82			.79		

Source: Walstad and Robson (1990, p. 11).

slightly greater difficulty of Form A may mean that it has slightly more discriminating items, which affect reliability. The reliability estimates for the BET are also somewhat lower than those for the TEK and the *Test of Economic Literacy* (TEL) (Soper & Walstad, 1987). This difference is most likely due to test length, which affects reliability; there are only 29 items, compared to 39 items on the TEK and 46 items on the TEL. The alphas, therefore, indicate that the BET is a reliable measure.

The BET possesses construct validity, as shown by the comparison of performance of students with and without economic instruction. This difference is greatest for Form A, the more reliable and difficult form. Students in the *with economics* group taking Form A had a mean score of 18.48, while the *without economics* group had a score of 15.84, for a score difference of +2.64 points. On Form B, students with economics had a score of 18.88, while students without economics had a score of 17.32, for a score difference of +1.56 points. The change suggests that economic instruction increases BET scores by about 9 to 17 percent when scores are computed using the mean scores of students without economics as the base.

The alternative way to view the scores is to compare the percentage correct for each group. On Form A the percentage correct for students with economics was 63.7 percent, compared to 54.6 percent for those without economics, or a change of 9.1 percent. The percentages correct on Form B were 65.1 percent for students with economics and 59.7 percent for those without economics, for a difference of 5.4 percent. With either form, there is a significant difference in performance: Intermediate elementary students can learn basic economic concepts.

Although the absolute score and percentage correct differences for students with and without economics are smaller relative to those reported for the TEK and the TEL, it should be remembered that the time and intensity of economic instruction are less at the intermediate elementary level. Some students may have had only a week of instruction, whereas other students may have been exposed to a concentrated economic unit for five weeks. The aggregate data reported in Table 8.6 mask the propensity of the BET to measure achievement differences in economics because the norming sample of the *with economics* group contains a mix of students, some with a little and some with a great deal of economic instruction. This mixture, especially if it is more heavily weighted with students who have only limited economics exposure, will tend to blur the score comparison between those students with and without economics.[7]

Relative Performance on the BET

As with the TEK data, the BET data can be used to study the relative performance of students in different concept clusters and across different concepts. To undertake the analysis and for simplicity, item data on the two forms are combined. This change produces a test of 47 unique items because the 11 items that are common to each form are used just once in the analysis. Items are then categorized by concept cluster and concept category, and the average percentage correct is calculated. The final results are reported in Table 8.7.

The percentages must be viewed with caution because the average percentages depend on the number and types of items within a cluster or concept category. The performance comparison is also more difficult to make with the BET than with the TEK and the TEL because there are fewer items on which to judge category performance. What can be concluded about the concept clusters is that the *with economics* data basically show that there is only a very slight difference between student performance on the 20 items in the fundamental cluster and on the 20 items in the microeconomic cluster (66 percent versus 65 percent correct) and student performance overall (66 percent correct). This result

TABLE 8.7
BET With and Without Economics Data
(Percentage Correct on the Combined BET)

NO. OF ITEMS	CONCEPTS	WITHOUT ECONOMICS (N=2,939)	WITH ECONOMICS (N=6,243)
47	All items	66%	59%
20	Fundamental	66	55
20	Microeconomics	65	60
4	Macroeconomics	71	66
3	International	63	58
3	Scarcity	63	50
3	Opportunity cost/trade-offs	47	26
4	Productivity	76	68
1	Economic systems	49	38
4	Economic institutions & incentives	71	66
5	Exchange, money & interdependence	69	61
3	Market & prices	73	70
11	Supply & demand	64	58
1	Competition & market structure	43	35
1	Income distribution	60	56
1	Market failures	67	63
3	Role of government	72	68
0	Gross national product	—	—
0	Aggregate supply	—	—
0	Aggregate demand	—	—
2	Unemployment	85	81
2	Inflation & deflation	57	51
0	Monetary policy	—	—
0	Fiscal policy	—	—
3	Comparative advantage/barriers to trade	63	58
0	Balance of payments & exchange rates	—	—
0	Economic growth	—	—

Source: Walstad and Robson (1990, pp. 14–15, Tables 9–10).

is consistent with findings for the TEK and the TEL. No conclusion can be drawn about performance in the other clusters because there are so few items in the macroeconomic area (four items) and the international area (three items).

Further breakdowns by concept indicate that the weakest areas of student understanding within the two clusters are opportunity cost and trade-offs (47 percent), economic systems (49 percent), and competition and market structure (43 percent). However, it is also difficult to judge the relative performance here because there is only one item measuring each of the last two concept areas. Yet the poor level of performance on opportunity cost is not too surprising. This economic concept is difficult to grasp, and it may be that many teachers do not teach it to students despite the emphasis given to it by economic educators (Walstad & Watts, 1985). In addition, the fact that students without economic instruction show worse performance on fundamental items, compared with microeconomic items (55 percent versus 60 percent correct), may be due in large part to poor performance on opportunity cost items (26 percent), whereas that performance improves (47 percent) after instruction and the gap between fundamental and microeconomic clusters vanishes.

CONCLUSIONS

This study of economics teaching and learning at the junior high and elementary grade levels is based on two large national samples of students, one junior high school group taking the TEK and one intermediate elementary group taking the BET. In addition, for the TEK sample both students and their teachers provided rich data to subclassify the test results, and the teachers completed a lengthy survey questionnaire on the nature of their background, their school, and their teaching practices.

By clustering student responses to the items on the TEK around major concept clusters, we were able to identify areas of relative strength and weakness in student economic knowledge. Students were weakest in the macroeconomics area, a finding consistent with past research on students at the high school level. The survey responses of a significant sample of junior high school teachers of economics and social studies present indications suggestive of why students perform differently in the two kinds of courses.

132

The results on the BET indicate that elementary students can and do learn economics. The amount that students learn may not be all that great, in part because of the limited amount of instruction. But students show basic understanding of a wide range of fundamental and microeconomic concepts and some knowledge of a few macroeconomic and international economic ideas. The new base line data for both the BET and the TEK should contribute to our understanding of the process of economic learning in American elementary and junior high schools.

Our work on the development of these two pre-high-school test instruments and our analysis of the data generated in their national norming lead us to some recommendations:

- Considerably more economics can be learned by pre-high-school students than they are currently learning. This is due primarily to the fact that students at these grade levels receive little or no economic instruction. There are powerful reasons to conclude that *more economics ought to be taught at these grade levels.*

- At the eighth and ninth grade levels, there is evidence that students learn less in the macroeconomics area than in the fundamental and microeconomics areas. This appears to be because teachers place less emphasis on macroeconomics, as do curriculum and materials developers at these grade levels. Relatively large gains in macroeconomics knowledge are likely to result from efforts to *give more teaching emphasis to macroeconomic concepts.*

- At the intermediate elementary grade levels, students can and do learn economics, but the amount of economic instruction at the fifth and sixth grade levels appears to be small on average, and highly variable. If teachers devote more time to economic instruction, student economic learning will increase, particularly in the fundamental and microeconomic concept clusters. We believe that *intermediate elementary teachers ought to include more economic instruction in their courses of study,* primarily because of the developmental nature of economic learning.

- From a curriculum design standpoint, teachers at the pre-high-school grade levels are most likely to employ the infusion approach to economic education; stand-alone economic instruction is rare at these grade levels. Therefore, *curriculum developers and instructional materials producers (e.g., textbook publishers) ought to infuse more*

133

economics into the standard social studies curriculum because this appears to be the most likely place for economic instruction to occur.

NOTES

1. Precursor studies at the upper elementary and middle school grade levels are few in number and often lacking in substantial quantitative evidence on student learning (see Buckles & Freeman, 1983, 1984; Chizmar et al., 1985; Highsmith, 1974; Kourilsky, 1987; MacDowell et al., 1977; O'Brien & Ingels, 1987; Schober, 1984; Schug, 1983; and Watts, 1985). None of the previous studies focused on student learning of major groups or clusters of economic concepts.

2. For students who receive an economic education *only* through the capstone high school course, economics often comes across as extremely difficult. This should surprise no one—think of what it would be like if all mathematics education was postponed until the junior or senior year in high school. Math literacy would be described as "abysmal," "totally inadequate," or "frightening." It is difficult to argue that mathematics learning is developmental throughout the curriculum, but that economic learning is not. (See Chapter 9.)

3. The test development committee consisted of Joanne Ariff (Charlotte Wood Intermediate School, Danville, Calif.), Ronald A. Banaszak (Foundation for Teaching Economics [FTE], San Francisco), Jody Wara (Vacaville High School, Calif.), Michael W. Watts (Purdue University), and the authors. The national advisory committee consisted of William R. Allen (UCLA), Ronald A. Banaszak (FTE), Paul Heyne (University of Washington), Robert Highsmith (Joint Council on Economic Education), Phillip Saunders (Indiana University), and John Scadding (Federal Reserve Bank of San Francisco). For a more complete description of the test development work, see Walstad and Soper (1987).

4. A reading specialist, Dr. Roger Bruning, of the University of Nebraska–Lincoln, provided a detailed reading analysis of the TEK, with several suggestions for changes to make the test more readable at the eighth and ninth grade levels. A copy editor at the Joint Council on Economic Education also reviewed the test for economic content, grammar, readability, and sentence structure.

5. Caution should be exercised in drawing too firm a conclusion about concept performance, given the limited number of items for each concept category.

6. The test development committee included Marsha Foley (Indianapolis Public Schools), Jo Ellen Hubbard (Harcourt Elementary School, Indianapolis),

John Hail (Indiana–Purdue University at Indianapolis), Denise Robson and William Walstad (both of the University of Nebraska–Lincoln), and Michael Watts (Purdue University). The national advisory committee consisted of Beverly Armento (Georgia State University), Mary Bolenbaugh (Ithan Elementary School, Bryn Mawr, Pa.), Robert Highsmith (Joint Council on Economic Education), Marilyn Kourilsky (UCLA), Mary McFarland (Parkway School District, Mo.), and Mark Schug (University of Wisconsin–Milwaukee). The reading specialist was Dr. Roger Bruning, and the psychometric consultant was Steven Wise (both of the University of Nebraska–Lincoln). A further explanation of the test features and development is found in Walstad and Robson (1990).

7. The classification of students with and without economics was based on student response to this statement: "Mark whether you've had lessons or a unit on economics in school. ___Yes ___No ___Don't Know." Students who marked Yes were treated as with economics. The use of teacher data to make the distinction produced similar, but less distinct results, compared to student responses. For further discussion, see Walstad and Robson (1990).

REFERENCES

Bloom, B. S., ed., et al. (1956). *Taxonomy of educational objectives: The classification of educational goals, Handbook I: Cognitive domain.* New York: McKay.

Buckles, S., and Freeman, V. (1984). A longitudinal analysis of a Developmental Economics Education Program. *Journal of Economic Education* 15(1):5–10.

_____ (1983). Male-female differences in the stock and flow of economic knowledge. *Review of Economics and Statistics* 65(2):355–58.

Chizmar, J. F., and Halinski, R. S. (1981). *Basic Economics Test: Examiner's manual.* New York: Joint Council on Economic Education.

Chizmar, J. F.; McCarney, B. J.; Halinski, R. S.; and Racich, M. J. (1985). "Give & Take," economics achievement, and basic skills development. *Journal of Economic Education* 16(2):99–110.

Gilliard, J. V.; Caldwell, J.; Dalgaard, B. R.; Highsmith, R. J.; Reinke, R.; and Watts, M. (1988). *Economics: What and when—Scope and sequence guidelines, K–12.* New York: Joint Council on Economic Education.

Gronlund, N. E. (1981). *Measurement and evaluation in teaching.* 4th ed. New York: Macmillan.

Highsmith, R. J. (1974). A study to measure the impact of in-service institutes on the students of teachers who have participated. *Journal of Economic Education* 5(2):77–81.

Kourilsky, M. L. (1987). Children's learning of economics: The imperative and the hurdles. *Theory into Practice* 26(3):198–205.

MacDowell, M. A.; Senn, P. R.; and Soper, J. C. (1977). Does sex really matter? *Journal of Economic Education* 9(1):28–33.

O'Brien, M. U., and Ingels, S. J. (1987). The economic values inventory. *Journal of Economic Education* 18(1):7–18.

Saunders, P.; Bach, G. L.; Calderwood, J. D.; Hansen, W. L.; and Stein, H. (1984). *A framework for teaching the basic concepts.* 2d ed. New York: Joint Council on Economic Education.

Schober, H. M. (1984). An analysis of the impact of teacher training in economics. *Theory and Research in Social Education* 12(1):1–12.

Schug, M. C. (1983). The development of economic thinking in children and adolescents. *Social Education* 47(2):141–45.

Soper, J. C., and Walstad, W. B. (1988). What is high school economics? Posttest knowledge, attitudes, and course content. *Journal of Economic Education* 19(1):37–51.

———— (1987). *Test of Economic Literacy: Examiner's manual.* 2d ed. New York: Joint Council on Economic Education.

Walstad, W. B., and Robson, D. (1990). *Basic Economics Test: Examiner's manual.* 2d ed. New York: Joint Council on Economic Education.

Walstad, W. B., and Soper, J. C. (1987). *Test of Economic Knowledge: Examiner's manual.* New York: Joint Council on Economic Education.

Walstad, W. B., and Watts, M. (1985). Teaching economics in the schools: A review of survey findings. *Journal of Economic Education* 16(2):135–45.

Watts, M. (1987). Survey data on pre-college scope-and-sequence issues. *Journal of Economic Education* 18(1):71–91.

———— (1985). A statewide assessment of precollege economic understanding and DEEP. *Journal of Economic Education* 16(3):225–35.

9. THE DEVELOPMENT OF STUDENTS' ECONOMIC THOUGHT: IMPLICATIONS FOR INSTRUCTION

by Mark C. Schug

How does the economic world appear to a child? The answer may surprise some adults. To many children, the owner of a good is the person who is nearest to it. A parent at the grocery checkout is participating in an odd ritual of exchanging dollars and coins. The price of a toy depends on how big or little it may be. Studies of children's thinking about the economic world reveal patterns that are starkly different from economists' thinking. Research also shows that children improve their economic understanding with formal instruction and with increasing maturity. Special training for elementary teachers enhances the economic understanding of young people.

DEVELOPMENTAL STUDIES

There is a growing body of research concerning how children think about economic problems. The following paragraphs describe examples of studies of children's thinking about economic concepts and how children's economic thinking can be influenced through instruction. The importance of this research is found in the clues it reveals that can help teachers and curriculum leaders develop educational experiences that are appropriate for students.

About 25 studies have been reported on the development of children's thinking about economic concepts. For the purpose of this chapter, I have selected studies that investigate children's thinking about traditional economic concepts. While this criterion was not always easy to apply, I have included studies dealing with fundamental economic ideas including profit, ownership, and price. I have excluded other studies that deal more with such topics as attitudes toward rich and poor and toward unemployment.

The methodology of these studies is similar. It usually involves posing situations that illustrate economic ideas to children and interviewing them about their understanding or explanation of the situation. The interviews are often accompanied by props such as money or by play shops to help stimulate the children's thinking. Another characteristic of these studies is their non-American origin. About half involve interviews with European children.

Ownership

The notion of private property is fundamental to understanding the operation of any economic system. Private ownership tends to promote two important social goals: encouraging individuals to take care of material possessions and making individuals accountable for their own actions.

Few studies have focused on the idea of ownership. Danziger (1958) investigated ownership of means of production by asking 41 Australian children between five and eight years of age about "the boss." In his study, the youngest children considered the boss to be someone who helps and gives advice, and the oldest children defined the boss as the owner, stating that one becomes the boss of a company by purchasing or inheriting it.

Berti, Bombi, and Lis (1982) offer more recent and elaborate insights into ideas about ownership. They interviewed 120 Italian students from 4 to 5 years old up to 12 to 14 years old. They asked the students, for example, who owned their home, the bus, the factories, and the farms and how ownership was acquired. They found consistent patterns in the emergence of the idea of ownership. The following is an example of the students' responses about who owns property.

Level 1: Students identify the owner as the person found in spatial contact with the object. For example, the owner of the bus is the passenger. Students cannot explain how one becomes an owner.

Level 2: Students identify the owner as the one who controls or directs the production of the good or service. The bus driver is the owner. The worker owns the factory, and the farmhand owns the fields. Students explain that the owner acquired the production means by purchasing it or by working with it—for example, by driving the bus or working the field.

Level 3: Students identify the owner as one who not only directly uses the producing means, but also controls its use by others. In addition to purchasing the means of production, the factory owner may also have acquired the factory by building it.

Level 4: Students distinguish between the owner and the employee. The boss is the owner.

Level 5: Students recognize a hierarchy of command with the owner at the top and the boss in an intermediate position between owner and worker.

Berti, Bombi, and Lis also inquired about the purpose or use of the means of production. They found that the following sequence was typical:

Level 1: Students do not understand the productive function. They have no idea of what happens in a factory. For the bus, the idea of providing a public service is not present.

Level 2: Students know that means of production such as factories and farms produce goods and services, but they fail to understand that the desire to earn a profit is an incentive for production.

Level 3: Students are aware of the selling of goods and services for payment, but do not see the connection between selling and revenue earned by the owner. They recognize that factory goods are sold, but tend to think that the boss must work at another job to obtain money for himself and his employees.

Level 4: With encouragement, students recognize the connection between the production of goods and services and the buying and selling of goods and services.

Level 5: Students spontaneously describe the relationship between the production of goods and services and the buying and selling of goods and services. Students state that this is how the owner and the employees make a living.

Profit

Strauss (1952) interviewed 66 students ranging in age from 4 1/2 to 11. He used transactions at a store to investigate the students' understanding of fundamental ideas, including the value of coins, the meaning of a transaction, and the concept of profit.

Strauss concluded that there are nine stages in students' thinking. Children at stage one (median age 5.4 years) can identify nickels, but have trouble naming other coins. Children understand that money is used to buy things, but they tend to see exchange as a ritual or a custom: We use money to exchange for goods because that is the way we do it or because it would be wrong to do it any other way. At stage three (median age 6.3) a personal motive—an early notion of profit—also enters in: The storekeeper is interested in making money or in getting rich. At stage five (median age 7.10), the exchange system extends beyond the store. The children understand not only that producers must pay workers, but also that producers must spend money to buy raw materials. At stage eight (median age 9.9) there is a much clearer understanding of profit. Students realize that storekeepers sell goods for more money than they buy them for and that this is fair and agreed on. Shopkeepers are entitled to their profits. Furth (1978) modified Strauss's original work by combining some of the overlapping categories and reducing his nine categories to five.

Danziger (1958) focused on questions involving rich and poor, money, what employers are, and how employers achieve their positions. His report is not as detailed as Strauss's work, but his findings are similar. For example, he describes two stages of thinking about the idea of exchange. The first is that a transaction is a ritual that serves no real purpose. The second stage occurs when the student understands that an exchange is a reciprocal relationship. Danziger did not find an understanding of profit emerging until age eight.

Jahoda (1979) investigated the notion of profit in the context of shop transactions and banking. He interviewed 120 working-class Scottish students between the ages of 6 and 12. He worked with a simple notion of profit—a merchant must buy products for sale at less than the selling price. He developed a role play of a shop wherein the student took the role of the shopkeeper and the experimenters played the roles of customers and suppliers. The shop used a system of play money. Goods were arranged on a counter with prices clearly marked. It was arranged that the second shop customer would exhaust the stock of supplies so that the shopkeeper would need to purchase additional supplies. The student needed to order new supplies and to pay for them with play money. The student had three opportunities to consider the relationship between selling price and buying price. When the student consistently understood that the buying price paid by the merchant was less than the selling price, he or she was considered to understand the idea of profit. When the prices for buying and selling were the same, it was judged that the student did not understand the idea of profit. A combination of responses was considered to be transitional. Next, the students were asked questions, including the following samples:

- What happens to the money in the till at the end of the day/week?
- From where does the shop get its goods? Does the shopkeeper have to pay for them?
- If so, does the shopkeeper pay more than, less than, or the same as the customer does?
- From where does the shopkeeper get the money to pay for the goods?

Findings from the interviews can be explained by examining the following four categories of reasoning that have emerged from the study:

1. *No grasp of any system.* In this case, transactions were seen as mainly rituals. The following interview sequence between an experimenter and a subject is an example:

   E: What do you do when you buy something?
   S: Give the shoplady money.
   E: What does she do with it?
   S: Gives the money back.
   E: Is it the same money?
   S: Yes.

2. *Two unconnected systems.* Here, students realized that a shop has to pay for its goods, but did not understand that the money came from consumers. They often stated that the money came from the government or from jobs. The reasoning was confused.

3. *Two integrated systems.* From age ten, there was an increasing awareness that there was a difference between selling price and buying price.

   E: What happens to the money at the end of the day?
   S: I think it gets counted out. I don't think they give it out till the end of the week.

141

E: Who do they give it out to?
S: They pay the people who've been serving.
E: Do they give it all out?
S: They keep some to buy more stuff for the shop.
E: Does the shop pay the same for the things?
S: I think they get them cheaper. If they got them at the same price, they wouldn't be making anything.

4. *The role of the employer.* Before students understand the integration of the two systems, the role of the employer is unclear. Many students, even after they understand profit, do not have a clear picture. For example, when asked where managers get their money, a student might respond by saying that they have another job.

Jahoda stresses an important point in his work. It was his impression from this study that a large majority of the students were not just repeating something that they had learned in school or at home. They were faced with questions that were new to them, and they were trying to fit together information they had in order to produce answers. In other words, they were attempting to "construct" their understanding of social events.

It also appears that the concept of profit is a difficult one for students. A clear shift toward understanding profit, which is fundamental to understanding how a market system works, does not occur until around age 11. Although it is premature to draw firm conclusions from this study, the introduction of the concept of profit much below age 11 needs to be investigated.

In a later study, Jahoda (1981) extended his work to include students' understanding of the bank. In this study, he interviewed 96 students aged 11 through 15 who were from schools classified as working class or middle class. Based on the interview data, Jahoda identified five levels of thinking.

1. *No knowledge of interest.* These students reasoned that money placed in the bank neither increased nor decreased. The bank is a safe place to keep or store your money. You get back precisely what you gave the bank.

2. *Interest on deposits only.* The responses here suggested that if you left your money in the bank for a period of time, you could earn

interest. Some students began to understand that the bank uses the money in various ways, and some connected uses to the interest that banks charge.

3. *Interest is paid on both loans and deposits, but deposits are stressed.* There was some recognition that the same principle that applied to the bank—paying interest on deposits—also applied to the bank customers—paying interest on loans.

4. *Interest is the same on deposits and loans.* Students at this level are beginning to realize that the bank has to make a profit and are close to understanding that banks make a profit from loans.

5. *Interest charged for loans is more than interest paid on deposits.* Here, the subjects understand banks must charge more for the use of money as loans than they pay on customers' deposits to make a profit.

Jahoda concludes that students tend to view the principles regulating bank transactions as the same as those between friends: If you borrow something, you return the same. Anything else would not be "fair." Only gradually do students begin to recognize the need for a bank to make a profit. He notes further that these findings illustrate how difficult it is for students to begin to separate their views of personal arrangements from the more impersonal arrangements of society.

Price

Burris (1976) posed questions to preschool children about the price of objects: why things may cost a little and why they may cost a lot. The responses of the children were distinct, suggesting a stagelike progression. The youngest children in the study stated that price or, in Burris's terms, exchange value was determined entirely by the object's physical characteristics. A diamond does not cost very much, for example, because it is so tiny. A book costs more than a wristwatch because it is bigger. The second type of response suggested that value was determined by function. An object's value is determined by its usefulness. A wristwatch costs more than a book because you can tell time. A bicycle costs more than a doll because you can go places on a bike. The third type of response reflected the type, quantity, or cost of inputs. Raw materials and labor were frequently cited.

Schug and Birkey (1985) followed up on an earlier study (Schug, 1983) to learn how students six to nine years old understand several basic economic concepts including scarcity, choice, opportunity cost, monetary value, and price. After interviewing 70 students from an urban preschool and two nearby elementary schools, they placed the students' responses into two categories—unreflective and emerging. These categories were influenced by the work of Jean Piaget. Unreflective reasoning was characterized by ideas that were judged to be highly literal or tautological. Unreflective responses were often based on physical properties of the object or process being discussed. Also included were responses where the student was unable to reason beyond a simple yes or no response. Emerging reasoning was considered to represent an advance in thinking. Examples included understanding the viewpoint of another in a concrete context. Responses in this category were less literal and showed more flexible thinking.

Similarly to the work of Burris, students' ideas about price were investigated by asking the students to name some things that cost a lot of money and to explain why those things cost so much. Next, they were asked what things were inexpensive and why those cost so little.

1. Unreflective responses suggested that size determined price: Big things—like houses and cars—were expensive and small things like candy and gum—were cheap. A second common response was a simple tautology such as "a new phone [costs a lot] because of the price tag."

2. Emerging responses mentioned factors of production such as labor or tools or stressed the function of the product or work performed by the product as criteria that make an item expensive or inexpensive. For example, "a pencil costs a little because it doesn't take that much to put it together." Function was reflected in this statement: "A refrigerator [costs a lot] because it's cold and you can really put your food in there and make it cold."

This study suggested that students' understanding of economic concepts follows a developmental pattern, although the overall pattern varies for some concepts. That is, concepts such as scarcity develop more quickly than do others such as choice, opportunity cost, and monetary value. The development of students' economic thinking apparently varies somewhat by concept and may depend to some extent on students' experiences.

Research by Tan and Stacy (1981) fits well with the conclusions from several of the studies discussed thus far. They interviewed 120 Malaysian Chinese students aged 6 to 15 about such concepts as selling, savings, banking, and gambling. Patterns of reasoning that emerged were very similar to those found in earlier studies by Jahoda (1979) and Furth, Baur, and Smith (1976). The specific number of stages that emerged varied somewhat, but the age range in which students acquired the concepts appeared to be similar. The authors conclude that their results, based on an Asian Chinese sample, show a developmental trend similar to that found in studies of Western students. They argue that this is a meaningful finding in that the upbringing of Malaysian students is substantially different from that of students in the United States, Britain, or Australia.

One might expect that informal learning plays an important role in students' economic understanding. In spite of the conclusions by Tan and Stacy (1981), there is evidence that familiarity and direct experience are related to economic reasoning. When students have firsthand experience with the economic world, their understanding of some economic ideas can be enhanced. For example, Jahoda (1983) investigated thinking about profit with children in Zimbabwe in much the same way as he did in an earlier study (Jahoda, 1979). An important difference between the students in the Scottish sample and those in the Zimbabwe sample is that the African children had been involved in trading activities. Jahoda concluded that the Zimbabwe children were far superior in their understanding of profit to European students in Scotland, the south of England, and Holland.

STAFF DEVELOPMENT

There is evidence that offering special training for teachers can improve the economic knowledge of teachers and their students. While most studies have focused on teachers at the secondary level, key studies have used elementary teachers as the focus. For example, Walstad (1980) included 24 teachers and 563 fifth and sixth grade students in a study of the effectiveness of *Trade-Offs*, a series of fifteen 20-minute films and videotapes on economics, designed for students 9 to 13 years old. He concluded that while trained and untrained teachers using *Trade-Offs* can contribute to the increased economic understanding of students, the trained teachers appear to be significantly more effective. Chizmar and Halinski (1983) had similar results. Using the *Basic Economics Test* (BET) in 56 classrooms in 23 states, they found that teacher training in economics is a significant factor in the performance of students on this test. Other studies of the effectiveness of in-service programs show similar results. Taken together, they offer evidence of the positive influence of economic education workshops and courses on teachers and students.

WHAT INSTRUCTIONAL PRACTICES ARE EFFECTIVE?

A large body of research supports the idea that young people can learn economics. Most of this research was done during the 1960s and 1970s, shortly after the development of nationally normed tests of economic understanding published by the Joint Council on Economic Education. Lawrence Senesh, for example, was a pioneer in the development of instructional materials at the elementary level. Larkins and Shaver's study (1969) of the *Our Working World* materials, developed under Senesh's leadership, tended to confirm Senesh's optimism that economics is an intellectually appropriate subject for elementary students. Their research results supported the idea that conventional teaching approaches can be used successfully at the elementary level. Dawson (1977) summarized the results of several early studies and concluded that students at almost any age in elementary and secondary schools can learn economic concepts in a structured school setting. Students' ability to learn economics varied with many factors including age, socioeconomic status, academic ability, reading level, and motivation. However, research clearly shows that students perform better on posttests after instruction in economics than they do on pretests.

Perhaps the most widely noted instructional approach at the elementary level is that used by Marilyn Kourilsky in the Mini-Society and the Kinder-Economy. The goal of this approach is to teach economics in a way that enables students to directly experience economic concepts. In the Mini-Society, for example, students establish their own simulated economy and earn money by becoming entrepreneurs and selling goods such as wallets or services such as needlepoint lessons. They choose to become salaried workers in the simulated private sector or in the civil service sector. The Mini-Society approach affords students active participation, real economic experiences, and decision making wherein

146

they bear the consequences of their decisions. Kourilsky (1977) found that 96 children in five kindergartens learned such concepts as scarcity, supply and demand, and opportunity cost after participating in economic learning activities 30 minutes per day for a semester.

More recently, Kourilsky and Graff (1985) investigated how experience in the Mini-Society might affect students' ability to use cost-benefit analysis to recognize that decisions involve forgoing one alternative for another. Students in grades one through four were presented with concrete situations. For example, a student would recognize that $500 for a small package of candies would be a very high price. Next, students would be interviewed concerning their ability to use cost-benefit analysis. The following is an example of the response pattern:

0 = "Yes" or "no"—with no additional or incorrect information forthcoming after prompting.

1 = "Yes, it costs me a lot. Five hundred dollars is a lot of money." This response shows a beginning recognition of opportunity cost.

2 = "Yes, it costs me a lot. I could get the best bike in the world for that money, and that's worth more than a package of candy." A reason is given; the alternative forgone is explicated.

Kourilsky and Graff found that participation in the Mini-Society produced greater understanding of cost-benefit analysis. They also found that age is a powerful factor in determining economic reasoning. As students got older, their understanding of cost-benefit analysis improved, and they were able to apply it to everyday situations. The researchers concluded that students have the potential to use cost-benefit analysis and that its use can be accelerated by instruction.

Televised instruction can be an effective way of teaching economics at the elementary level. Walstad (1980) and Chizmar and Halinski (1983) investigated students' performance on tests of economic knowledge after using the *Trade-Offs* television series produced by the Agency for Instructional Technology. Walstad (1980) found that students in the groups that used the *Trade-Offs* series learned significantly more economics than did those in the control groups that did not use the series. Chizmar and Halinski (1983) also examined the influence of the

Trade-Offs series on students' learning of economics. Increased instruction with *Trade-Offs* was associated with improved student performance. The Chizmar and Halinski results seem particularly impressive. Students with instruction of 13 weeks or more improved by more than three-quarters of a standard deviation.

The work of Berti, Bombi, and their colleagues has added considerably to our knowledge of how children think about the economic world and how their thinking may be influenced through instruction. In one recent study Ajello, Bombi, and their associates (1987) investigated the effects of third grade curriculum materials on student knowledge. Teachers were trained in how to use the curriculum materials that introduced children to the ideas of profit, price, and the production process. Seventy-six children were pre- and posttested, using an interview. The results showed a significant improvement in student performance for all the ideas in the curriculum, with the best result occurring regarding the idea of profit. Fifty-three percent of the children gained an understanding of the idea of profit. The researchers found that not all children benefited equally from instruction. For example, youngsters with lower initial scores on the interview improved quite a lot, while those who scored high in the beginning did not display much improvement. One interesting result was that many children tended to give up initial incorrect ideas, but did not always replace them with better explanations. Children moved from a lower stage of thinking to an intermediate level. This suggests that children need to move through each stage of economic thinking on their way to achieving the highest level of understanding.

Berti, Bombi, and De Beni (1986) experimented with two differing teaching approaches in teaching the concept of profit to children. One was a critical training approach inspired by the work of Piaget in which children were presented with a situation and encouraged to come up with their own explanations. The second was a tutorial situation in which children were presented with a similar situation, but the answers were given to the children. The results of this study revealed that the progress of students in both groups was significant, but not dramatic. The researchers presented several suggestions in teaching the concept of profit to third graders. First, neither teaching approach—the critical training or the tutorial—differed much in improving children's understanding of the concept of profit. Second, failure to understand some basic ideas in mathematics may have interfered with students' learning the concept of profit. Finally, it may be worthwhile just to get students to talk about economic ideas. The experience in itself would be a helpful instructional tool.

Instruction in particular economic concepts is guided by many variables including the discipline of economics, the thinking of students, the existing school curriculum, and the skills of teachers. Our knowledge in each of these areas is incomplete. Nonetheless, school leaders have to make decisions about how to sequence economics into the school curriculum. The Joint Council on Economic Education recently developed recommendations for sequencing economics into the K–12 curriculum (Gilliard et al., 1988). The authors took into account the structure of economics, cognitive development theories and research, and school practices. The guide shows grade levels at which economic concepts should be introduced. The authors take a useful first step to assist school leaders in designing curriculum. They also offer researchers a framework for experimentation to test how economic content can be sequenced to ensure learning.

IMPLICATIONS FOR CURRICULUM AND INSTRUCTION

A few generalizations can be made on the basis of the studies that have been discussed. First, students' reasoning about economic ideas, including economic concepts such as ownership, profit, and price, tends to follow a developmental sequence. Students' reasoning becomes more abstract and flexible with age and includes greater recognition of others' points of view. With age, students depend less on concrete, physical appearances to explain their ideas.

Second, reasoning about nearly all the economic concepts reported in these studies shows a pattern of gradual improvement with age. Nonetheless, mature reasoning about some concepts appears more rapidly than does an understanding of other concepts. Advanced reasoning about concepts that have more concrete referents or that are in students' immediate experiences seems to emerge sooner than does mature reasoning about concepts that are more remote. This, for example, might be inferred from cross-cultural studies. Conversely, learning some economic ideas—even though they may be defined as basic or fundamental—may be difficult. Perhaps the best example is the notion of profit. While understanding profit is central to understanding how a market economy works, a clear understanding does not seem to emerge until around age 11.

Third, staff development appears to be an effective method to improve the economic understanding of students. Students in the classrooms of trained teachers perform better on nationally normed tests of economic understanding than do students in the classrooms of untrained teachers.

Finally, there is ample evidence that students can learn economic ideas from formal instruction. Moreover, there is some initial evidence that students' reasoning about basic concepts such as cost-benefit analysis and profit can be improved through their involvement in concrete learning experiences. Still, there seem to be levels of understanding through which students progress. Lack of understanding in other areas, such as mathematics, may slow some students' development of economic understanding. Age remains an important factor in students' economic thinking.

What does all this mean for classroom teachers? Overall, the research supports economic education for elementary students. As early as age five or six, children are developing an understanding of some economic ideas. Clearly, some instruction can begin even at the early grades. Yet, it is also clear that reasoning about some economic ideas develops gradually. One implication is that we need to be careful in the selection of economic concepts for instruction. The Joint Council on Economic Education has offered beginning assistance to answer this question (Gilliard et al., 1988). Some concepts—such as scarcity—should be stressed early. Other concepts—such as profit—may need to be taught later. A second implication is that economic instruction for youngsters aged 9 to 12 may be especially appropriate.

Teachers need to understand the type of "confusion" that they might expect from their students as they begin instruction in economic ideas. Students are not ignorant about economic ideas such as profit. In fact, they construct their own understandings of these economic ideas, especially when they are exposed to puzzling situations that invite their reflection. Learning activities designed by teachers need to take account of the type of thinking students use to understand economic problems if instruction is to be appropriate to the needs of these students.

Eaton, Anderson, and Smith (1984) stress that students' misconceptions of the world are sometimes quite different from scientific conceptions. They note that researchers have found that misconceptions affect the way students understand a variety of ideas. Teachers and economics teaching materials need to show recognition of the types of confusion that many students have about economic ideas and must explain directly how the scientific view differs from the misinformed views that many students possess. For example, it is easy to imagine a teacher patiently explaining how market factors like supply and demand determine price. However, many students in the class believe that size or function determines price. By failing to acknowledge the students' misunderstanding at the beginning, this naive understanding may go unchallenged even while students respond correctly to the teacher's questions about market factors.

Teachers should be encouraged to avoid pressure to teach economic ideas quickly or superficially. The importance of age in much of this research strengthens the idea that students need instruction in economics over several years. It is also likely that students do not easily transfer an economic idea from one area (shops) to another (factories) (Berti, Bombi & De Beni, 1986). What is most important is to identify key economic principles and teach them thoroughly, drawing heavily on the personal and family economic experiences of students. Moreover, teachers should not rush to include many new economic concepts. Teaching a few economic ideas at several key points in the elementary curriculum will allow students ample opportunities to assimilate basic economic ideas. To encourage real economic understanding, teachers should select key ideas such as scarcity and opportunity cost and build numerous teaching activities with rich, concrete examples.

REFERENCES

Ajello, M. A.; Bombi, A. S.; Pontecorvo, C.; and Zuccinermaglio, C. (1987). Teaching economics in primary school: The concepts of work and profit. *International Journal of Behavioral Development* 10(1):51–69.

Berti, A. E.; Bombi, A. S.; and De Beni, R. (1986). The development of economic notions: Single sequence or separate acquisitions? *Journal of Economic Psychology* 7:415–24.

Berti, A. E.; Bombi, A. S.; and Lis, A. (1982). The child's conceptions about means of production and their owners. *European Journal of Social Psychology* 12:221–39.

Burris, V. L. (1976). The child's conception of economic relations: A genetic approach to the sociology of knowledge. Ph.D. diss., Princeton University.

Chizmar, J. F., and Halinski, R. S. (1983). Performance in the Basic Economics Test (BET) and Trade-Offs. *Journal of Economic Education* 14(1):18–29.

Danziger, K. (1958). Children's earliest conceptions of economic relationships (Australia). *Journal of Social Psychology* 47:231–40.

Dawson, G. G. (1977). Research in economic education at the precollege level. In *Perspectives on economic education*, ed. D. R. Wentworth, W. L. Hansen, and S. H. Hawke, 85–104. New York: Joint Council on Economic Education.

Eaton, J. F.; Anderson, C. W.; and Smith, E. L. (1984). Students' misconceptions interfere with science learning: Case studies of fifth-grade students. *Elementary School Journal* 84(4):365–79.

Furth, H. G. (1978). Young children's understanding of society. In *Issues in Childhood Social Development*, ed. H. McGurk, 228–56. Cambridge, England: Cambridge University Press.

Furth, H. G.; Baur, M.; and Smith, J. E. (1976). Children's conception of social institutions: A Piagetian framework. *Human Development* 19:351–74.

Gilliard, J. V.; Caldwell, J.; Dalgaard, B. R.; Highsmith, R. J.; Reinke, R.; and Watts, M. (1988). *Economics: What and when—Scope and sequence guidelines, K–12*. New York: Joint Council on Economic Education.

Jahoda, G. (1983). European "lag" in the development of an economic concept: A study in Zimbabwe. *British Journal of Developmental Psychology* 1:113–20.

―――― (1981). The development of thinking about economic institutions: The bank. *Cahiers de Psychologie Cognitive* 1(1):55–73.

―――― (1979). The construction of economic reality by some Glaswegian children. *European Journal of Social Psychology* 19:115–27.

Kourilsky, M. (1977). The Kinder-Economy: A case study of kindergarten pupils' acquisition of economic concepts. *Elementary School Journal* 77(3):182–91.

Kourilsky, M., and Graff, E. (1985). Children's use of cost-benefit analysis: Developmental or non-existent. Paper presented at the annual meeting of the American Educational Research Association, Chicago.

Larkins, A. G., and Shaver, J. P. (1969). Economics learning in grade one: The USC assessment studies. *Social Education* 33:955–63.

Schug, M. (1983). The development of economic thinking in children and adolescents. *Social Education* 47(2):141–45.

Schug, M., and Birkey, C. J. (1985). The development of children's economic reasoning. *Theory and Research in Social Education* 13:31–42.

Strauss, A. L. (1952). The development and transformation of monetary meanings in the child. *American Sociological Review* 17:275–84.

Tan, H., and Stacy, B. G. (1981). The understanding of socio-economic concepts in Malaysian Chinese school children. *Child Study Journal* 2(1):33–49.

Walstad, W. B. (1980). The impact of Trade-Offs and teacher training on economic understanding and attitudes. *Journal of Economic Education* 12(1):41–48.

10. DEEP ACROSS THE STATE

by Bonnie T. Meszaros and James B. O'Neill

In many ways, the state of Delaware and the Delaware Center for Economic Education are unique. As the facilitator of the Delaware Council on Economic Education (DCEE), the center services a statewide teacher/student population that is smaller than that serviced by many individual centers for economic education in other states in the Joint Council on Economic Education's network. Delaware is small in square miles as well as population, currently under 650,000. Travel time to cover the length of the state is $2^1/2$ hours. The number of public school districts (17) is small, and communication among teachers and state agencies is simplified through a statewide courier at no cost to the users. However, the smallness does not mean the state is without diversity. The state has an economic base that includes industry, retail businesses, and agriculture; population centers ranging from urban to rural; and a diverse socioeconomic population.

SETTING THE STAGE

The Delaware Center for Economic Education was established in 1971 on the main campus of the University of Delaware. This campus is located in northern Delaware, the most densely populated region of the state. By its mere location at the university, the center from its inception was held suspect by many teachers and administrators in the state's two southern counties. Citizens in these two locations often believed that they had been neglected and slighted by the University of Delaware. They felt past promises were not kept and that any involvement with the university was due to efforts on their part and not the university's. As a result, when the center opened, a representative group of the teaching population in two-thirds of the state did not look favorably on university programs, including those from the center.

With the arrival of the first center director, James B. O'Neill, a public relations program was undertaken. A plan was initiated to create center

153

visibility and to establish good will between the center and the local administrators.

The first step was to create awareness. Individual meetings were scheduled with each district to provide administrators with some understanding of the center, its role in the education process, and the services it could provide to local school districts. The center director vividly remembers the response he received from one district superintendent in southern Delaware. The superintendent indicated he had had previous visitations from members of the university community who made promises and then ultimately faded into the night, never to be heard from again. The response was short and simple. He obviously was doubtful that the center would follow through on any commitments to his district. The center director informed the superintendent that the center was in its early formation and was not in a budgetary position to make promises; however, if a promise was made, it would not be broken.

As the center's program spread and its commitment to quality economic education programs for all Delaware students was acknowledged by Delaware teachers and administrators, the center's credibility grew. A friendship evolved between this doubting administrator and the center director. Eventually, this district became one of the first in Delaware to receive an Exemplary DEEP School Award—a national award sponsored by Kraft, Inc., and administered by the Joint Council on Economic Education to recognize schools with outstanding DEEP programs.

A second step was to determine the status of economic education in the state's schools. In 1973 a study was conducted involving 175 public school teachers and 9,500 students in grades 1 through 12. The results showed that economic literacy in the First State was on a level with that in other states around the country. Delaware's teachers and students scored average or below on Joint Council–prepared standardized tests of economic knowledge, which was well below what experts considered adequate.

The newly formed Center for Economic Education at the University of Delaware faced a dismal picture and substantial problems. In the early 1970s the school population was highly diverse, and the resources of the public schools ranged from adequate at best to severely inadequate. Half the teachers who were responsible for courses that logically could incorporate economics lacked formal training in the discipline. A large majority of those (80 percent) were apprehensive about the prospect of

154

teaching even the most fundamental concepts to students. Furthermore, the teachers felt pressured for time and did not look favorably on an addition to their already crowded curriculum.

The good news was that the teachers indicated a desire for opportunities to learn more about the subject of economics and were willing at least to explore ways to teach economics if it could be incorporated into their existing programs.

Instructional materials did not seem to be a major problem. Even in the early seventies some resources existed. But Delaware lacked a comprehensive program to make optimum use of these instructional materials.

THE DELAWARE APPROACH

Having laid the groundwork by meeting with each district superintendent and carrying out a needs assessment, the Delaware center assembled a planning group of interested educators and asked them to propose a program that was tailored to local needs, had clearly defined goals, examined immediate needs within a long-term framework, and represented the various sectors of the state economy.

This planning group offered the following guidelines, which were carefully implemented:

- Start with a core of committed professionals. A small group of experienced teachers from across the state who had taken the center's early courses and workshops provided this base.

- Take one step at a time. Begin with selected teachers in a few school districts. Add teachers within these districts and move on to additional districts once a strong economic education program is underway in current DEEP schools. Initially emphasize teaching the teachers.

- Stress quality, not quantity. Add new DEEP schools gradually. Make sure existing DEEP schools have adequate support and service from center staff before expanding to new districts.

- Offer many options. Since materials had to be infused into courses already in the curriculum, economics had to be harmonized with these subjects and adjusted to the ability of specific student groups to absorb the message.

- Put teaching objectives and related resources together in a logical sequence. The objective was to make the programs dovetail and to build on them year by year as students moved on to higher grades.

- Build a solid base of support. Program advocates explained their purposes to affected teachers and administrators and thus earned a place in the budget as well as administrative blessings.

- Define the goals. From the outset, the DEEP program was shaped to enable students to discuss, in their own language based on their own experience, nine key economic concepts: scarcity, resources, creation of wealth, inflation, jobs and unemployment, government economic policy, the public sector, and alternative economic systems. Some of these concepts were to be started early on, although at lower grade levels, progress would have to be more gradual. Later, this list of concepts seemed inappropriate for all grade levels and was lacking some fundamental concepts. It was revised and today follows a scope and sequence modeled after that of the Joint Council on Economic Education, as outlined in its *Economics: What and When* (Gilliard et al., 1988).

DEEP IMPLEMENTATION— LAYING THE GROUNDWORK

During the first few years, courses were offered for Delaware teachers, generally attempting to develop a better understanding of the principles of economics and how these basic concepts could enrich their curriculum. From these early courses, teachers with unique talents and commitment were identified. During the early stages of the program, those teachers who were willing to commit additional time served as advisors and helped shape the future direction of the center's economic education programs and ultimately the DEEP program. From the beginning, the center believed direct involvement of teachers with periodic input from administrators was crucial if change and implementation in the classroom were to occur.

Through 1975 the center continued to offer courses primarily for secondary teachers. At this point, the Board of Directors for the Delaware Council on Economic Education, through the direction of Council President Lazslo Zsoldos and Chair Richard Heckert of E. I. duPont de Nemours and Co., devised a plan based on the recommendations from the center's planning group. The council stressed two objectives: (1) to start economic education early, in the primary grades, and work toward a capstone course at the secondary level and (2) to provide services and ongoing follow-up to trained teachers.

At the request of the center director, the council laid the groundwork to hire a field consultant who could more effectively work with teachers as more teachers were trained and added to the state's DEEP network. Bonnie Meszaros, who had classroom experience along with the leadership skills necessary to work with teachers, was hired as the first field consultant, initially through a grant from the National Science Foundation, followed by funds from the Delaware council, and ultimately with support from the state of Delaware.

The follow-up component of Delaware's DEEP network serviced by a field consultant was initially unique to Delaware. The Delaware council still supports the notion of field consultants based on the belief that this concept of ongoing support was a crucial factor in the establishment of the strong statewide DEEP network that exists today. Teachers were not trained and forgotten. Their skills were continually updated and refined. They were kept abreast of new materials and strategies. And the center was always available for input, advice, and guidance. The center also continues to strengthen and nurture its network through a newsletter distributed to all public school teachers statewide and to most private and parochial schools. Through the dissemination of a catalog of educational resources, printed curriculum and resource materials are provided on free loan to teachers. Future plans call for an economic education professional association for elementary teachers and expansion of the Delaware Council for Social Studies' programs for secondary economics teachers.

With the additional staff person, the Delaware DEEP program could move beyond the awareness objectives to those focusing on training and reinforcement beginning in the elementary grades. During this transition period in the training program, fortuitously, a training program in Mini-Society was jointly sponsored by the Delaware and Maryland councils on economic education. Marilyn Kourilsky, creator of Mini-Society, trained ten teachers from each state on how to implement and maintain a Mini-Society. The following year the center director, the field director, and a future DEEP coordinator attended a training class at the University of California at Los Angeles on how to teach teachers the Mini-Society program.

The Mini-Society provided an important impetus for the Delaware program. With proper training and center support, teachers easily implemented the program, material costs were minimal, and teachers, students, and parents were excited about the program. Over the next five years the center's program blossomed. Approximately 200 teachers were trained throughout the state, and a half-time field consultant, Nina Lou Bunting, was hired in order to better serve teachers' needs in southern Delaware.

Mini-Society enabled administrators, business people, and parents to become aware of the center's economic education programs. Center visibility was enhanced through increased news articles, presentations to service groups, and periodic features on television. In addition, the Mini-Society program generated a core of teachers who eventually worked with the center to establish DEEP programs in their districts. Today, all DEEP coordinators who are also elementary teachers have participated in Mini-Society training.

As the Center for Economic Education grew, its first priority was to establish a track record with a core of qualified, talented teachers statewide, initially involving secondary teachers and then enlarging the group to include those involved in Mini-Society. These teachers returned to their schools and generated enthusiasm and excitement for economic education, encouraging their colleagues to sign up for the center's course and workshops offerings. It was not until this network of teachers was in place that the Delaware DEEP program began to emerge.

As the Delaware DEEP program expanded, the center began to rely increasingly on teacher input. The DEEP coordinators felt that the elementary program was well established and that the focus of the center's program needed to expand. They recommended that more resources be devoted to secondary programs. Although the center had a core of secondary teachers to provide advice and input into the direction for an expanded secondary program, the center wanted to generate a data base regarding what social studies teachers were currently teaching, the amount of past course work teachers had in economics, and the extent to which economics was included in each school district's secondary curriculum.

With a grant from the Department of Public Instruction, a statewide survey of all secondary schools was undertaken. A teacher from each school district in the state was assigned to gather the information and compile a composite of the economic education program in his/her district. Teachers who worked on this project were familiar with the center and were paid for their work. The project resulted in a statewide profile of the status of economic content at the secondary level and the extent of the economics background of secondary teachers throughout the state.

The results were not surprising. Secondary teachers lacked course work in economics, the economic content of courses was weak, and teachers often taught capstone courses with minimal formal economics training. With an emphasis on the elementary grades, the obvious trade-off was that the center had devoted less time and resources to the secondary-level program.

The message was clear. To promote quality DEEP schools, the center needed to design a training program for secondary teachers. The Department of Public Instruction funded a planning committee consisting of five secondary teachers. The committee organized the course—a sequence of three semester-length graduate classes—and established recruitment procedures. An additional grant from the state funded the tuition, books, and a $1,500 stipend per teacher for the courses in 1987–88. The state has continued this level of support for subsequent courses. The first class was comprised of predominantly secondary economics and social studies teachers. Later classes have included secondary mathematics, business, education, and special education teachers and guidance personnel. This has increased the participation of teachers from these disciplines in other center-sponsored programs. As a result, the center's influence has gone beyond the social studies department.

DEEP IMPLEMENTATION—FORMAL COMMITMENT

From its early days, the center's increased emphasis was on establishing a large pool of trained, talented teachers who represented most districts statewide and who were involved in past center programs. A DEEP program was not initiated until this core of teachers was active in a school system. Once trained, the teachers and the center staff met with the district administrators to explore strategies for incorporating economics into that district's curriculum.

The center's grassroots approach proved successful. Teachers appreciated the fact that they had a voice in the planning process and that it was not another program dictated from the top down—from administrators to teachers. Teachers responded positively to center course offerings and workshops and, more importantly, to the concept of economics as an important theme throughout the school's curriculum.

When administrators were presented with a DEEP plan and a rationale from the teachers working with the center, the responses were favorable. The center worked with each district to train teachers, develop curriculum, evaluate programs, and provide follow-up. However, this was not undertaken until the school district's teachers and administrators had designed a plan for implementing an economic education program specific to that district's needs. Some focused initially on elementary teachers, others on a specific grade level, and a few on the secondary grades or, more specifically, the capstone course. After receiving input from the center staff, the district chose where and how to begin.

A DEEP commitment was not the beginning of economic education in a school district. Strong DEEP commitment emerged after teachers had been involved in economics through center activities and had recognized the need for economics in the curriculum. With teachers playing a strong advocacy role, school district administrators readily conceded the importance of economics in the curriculum and had no objections to formal acknowledgment of their schools as DEEP schools.

Once the plan was finalized, the center designed training programs to meet each district's needs. As a result, each DEEP district's economic education program is different, and together they represent various stages of development. Despite the variety, the economic education programs in Delaware's DEEP schools have emerged as model programs.

In the three years that the Joint Council on Economic Education has sponsored the DEEP Exemplary School Awards Program, the state of Delaware has received seven awards, more than any other state in the Joint Council's network. For example, a downstate school district won an award for its K–12 program which focuses on the integration of economics at the high school level in English, mathematics, business, social studies, science, home economics, and science courses as well as a capstone economics course. The district philosophy is that economics is a "life skill." Two school districts were recognized for their outstanding capstone courses required for all students. Three winning entries focused on the districts' elementary programs, and one district was recognized for a model economic education program in a 3–6 school.

All these winners have outstanding programs and represent Delaware DEEP programs statewide. But, in addition to maintaining quality economics programs within their individual districts, each has had an impact on economic education beyond its own school setting. For example, teachers from each of these districts have promoted economic education by serving on state standards committees for economics, writing statewide curriculum guides on economics for both the elementary and the secondary levels, conducting workshops for teachers from across the state, and developing economic units printed and distributed by the Department of Public Instruction.

FACTORS CONTRIBUTING TO STRONG STATEWIDE DEEP

Despite the diversity in Delaware's DEEP school programs, the DEEP districts acknowledge a few common factors that have contributed to the success of their economic education programs. These factors exist not only in the seven DEEP award-winning schools, but also throughout all Delaware's DEEP schools. These elements, which have contributed to the strength of Delaware's statewide DEEP program, are

- cooperation among teachers, administrators, and the center;
- willingness of the center to work within district constraints, to listen to district concerns, and to be flexible;
- support from the center once the bulk of the teacher training is finished;
- professional respect for teachers by the center and a sincere desire for teacher input and involvement; and
- teacher and district ownership of the DEEP programs.

DEEP expansion in Delaware began slowly. The DCEE brought school districts on board only when the council felt capable of working with a new district without sacrificing support and follow-up services to the teachers in existing DEEP schools. Today, Delaware's DEEP network reaches over 75 percent of the state's students. Those districts that are not formal DEEP schools are small and located in the southern part of the state. Eventually, each will become a formal DEEP school. For the moment, the center's half-time field consultant for southern Delaware serves as an informal DEEP coordinator. However, the primary focus of the Delaware program is extension and enrichment of existing economic education in the statewide DEEP system.

161

To maintain a strong DEEP network of schools that continually evaluates upgrades, and enriches economic education programs, the center relies on committed and enthusiastic DEEP coordinators; maintains a dialogue with teachers and administrators; works cooperatively with school administrators, teachers, and the Department of Public Instruction; and provides continual follow-up and support services for teachers once they return to their classroom.

In all but one of the Delaware DEEP schools, the DEEP coordinator is a full-time classroom teacher. The larger DEEP districts have two to three coordinators who focus on secondary or elementary economic education programs.

Teachers were selected to be DEEP coordinators for several reasons. Most of Delaware's districts have small administrative staffs, and none of them has an individual specifically assigned to social studies. Therefore, the center felt economic education was better served by teachers who were committed to the center's goals and to economic education. These teachers were also in touch on a daily basis with the center's constituents—the teachers.

All DEEP coordinators prepare yearly reports on their economic education activities and are paid by the center through funding by the DCEE. The financial resources to fund these coordinators were initially provided by a 1985 grant from Pew Charitable Trusts. DEEP coordinator meetings are held regularly to obtain input from the coordinators and to keep them abreast of center activities and programs. Yearly, the coordinators and the center staff attend a weekend retreat to evaluate the previous year's program and plan for the coming year's activities.

Although the Center for Economic Education has several competing organizations within the state that offer economic education programs, the center has been accorded respect and credibility from all sectors of the community. The stature of the center's program and the DEEP network is epitomized by the following resolution, adopted by the state board of education in August 1986:

RESOLVED BY THE DELAWARE STATE BOARD OF EDUCATION,
That all school districts are urged to expand their economics related course offerings within the existing curriculum and to support the Center for Economic Education at the University of Delaware in its efforts to provide additional training in economics to teachers

throughout the state and are directed to report to the Department of Public Instruction of actions taken at the close of each school year.

The bases for the success of the Delaware center's statewide DEEP program can be summarized as follows:

- never promising a school district more than can be delivered
- never telling a district what it should do, but listening to district concerns and developing a program to meet these concerns
- involving teachers and administrators in policy decisions
- providing a follow-up reinforcement component
- receiving excellent support from the business community, school district, Department of Public Instruction, and University of Delaware
- developing continuing staff commitment, primarily through the leadership of the associate director
- allowing DEEP commitment to emerge from teacher and administrative involvement in economic education programs.

Following the guidelines, the DCEE's principle of teaching the teachers has proven to be sound, and the ongoing structure of in-service programs, workshops, and classes has provided a latticework by which teachers can increase their confidence and their competence. As a result, DCEE's achievement has won regional and national recognition and, most importantly, has gained a commitment from the business and educational communities to continue raising the economic sophistication of Delaware's students.

REFERENCE

Gilliard, J. V.; Caldwell, J.; Dalgaard, B. R.; Highsmith, R. J.; Reinke, R.; and Watts, M. (1988). *Economics What and when—Scope and sequence guidelines, K–12*. New York: Joint Council on Economic Education.

11. DEEP AND CORE COMPETENCIES IN ECONOMICS FOR MISSOURI SCHOOL DISTRICTS

by Karen Hallows and Warren Solomon

With the passage of Missouri's Excellence in Education Act of 1985 and its provisions for identifying and testing objectives called "key skills," the Missouri Council on Economic Education (MCEE) gained a unique opportunity to become actively involved with the Missouri Department of Elementary and Secondary Education in promoting the integration of economics in local curricula. As a result of the 1985 law, students in Missouri in grades 3 through 10 are tested on economic concepts and reasoning skills by state-mandated tests called the Missouri Mastery Achievement Tests (MMATs). The implementation of the testing program has had a great impact on economic instruction within the state.

THE CHARACTERISTICS OF MISSOURI DISTRICTS AND TEACHERS

Approximately 800,000 students are enrolled in Missouri's 545 school districts. The average district has 1,500 students, but districts range from over 46,000 students in the largest district to less than 100 students in each of the 50 smallest districts.

As for Missouri students, 37 percent are currently enrolled in 52 DEEP districts. Of the state's largest districts, five DEEP districts are located in the St. Louis area, with 19 non-DEEP districts also in this area. Located in the Kansas City area are nine DEEP districts and four non-DEEP districts. It has been the philosophy of the MCEE to provide quality economic education in a restricted number of DEEP districts, rather than expanding DEEP in the state without the ability to provide effective service.

Missouri has approximately 50,000 classroom teachers, of whom about 7,000 have attended MCEE workshops, courses, and seminars in the past two years. Systematic economic education programs, which include teacher courses, district curriculum advisement, and follow-up activities, have been in operation in the Kansas City area since 1987. This type of program has also been implemented in four St. Louis districts starting in 1989–90.

A statewide economic education survey, designed by the MCEE and sent to a random sample of about one-third of Missouri's teachers in the spring of 1988, revealed a relatively strong demand for the economic education services provided by Missouri's nine centers for economic education. Over 60 percent of the sample surveyed indicated a desire to receive in-service training on how to teach economics. Over 75 percent said they would like most to receive training activities based on the state's tested key skills objectives, and 92 percent responded that more information about their area's center for economic education would be desirable.

In Missouri, about 13 percent of the state's districts require students to take a separate course in economics before graduation. A separate economics course, however, is not required by the state. Instead, infusion is encouraged throughout the curriculum by testing students in economics at all levels where state social studies testing is conducted. Approximately 5 percent of the test questions on the state test relate to economics.

MMAT CONSTRUCTION AND TESTING

Section 4 of the Excellence in Education Act of 1985 requires the Missouri Department of Elementary and Secondary Education to identify objectives, called "key skills," for language arts, mathematics, science, and social studies; to test a sample of students throughout the state on those key skills; and to report state performance results to the Missouri General Assembly annually. Local school districts are required to implement their own testing programs, embedded within which are the state's key skills that are to be assessed by state-designed or state-approved criterion-referenced tests.[1] The advent of the MMATs marked a significant expansion of mandatory testing for public school students in Missouri.[2]

The Objectives

Economics objectives are found in the social studies portion of the state program. There are three categories of objectives in the Missouri core competency/key skills program. First, there are the general goals, called *core competencies*. The economics core competencies developed in 1985 are

M: Analyze economic decision situations with an awareness of opportunity costs and trade-offs.

N: Understand factors of production, their interrelationships, and how investment in them relates to productivity.

O: Understand economic relationships (flows of money, goods, and services) among households, businesses, financial institutions, labor unions and governments of this and other economic systems.

P: Understand relationships among supply, demand, price and quantity of goods and services in market economies.

Q: Understand how a nation's level of output, income, employment and distribution of income is determined.

R: Understand principles related to trade (personal, regional or international).

For each of the core competencies at the various levels from grades 2 through 10, more specific objectives are listed. For example, for Core Competency M at level three, the objectives are

1. Give examples of wants in homes or communities that may not be satisfied because of scarcity of resources.
*2. Identify opportunity costs and trade-offs in choices made by individuals, families or communities in economic decision situations.

Objective M-2, preceded by an asterisk, is called a key skill because it is included in the state's testing program. All other objectives, like M-1, may be taught and assessed locally by whatever means districts choose.

The objectives at each level are to provide a foundation for subsequent learning and to serve as a basis for planning instruction and monitoring student progress.[3] It is hoped that local districts will not concentrate exclusively on state-tested key skills. Many of the objectives were not included in the state testing program because they do not lend themselves to multiple choice testing, not because they are of less importance.

166

Testing

New in the Excellence in Education Act are the requirements for districts to include criterion-referenced testing for all students at periodic grade levels in specific subjects, to monitor student progress on key skills, and to identify areas for instructional improvement.

Because of these requirements and the requirement that a sample of students be tested on state key skills, the Missouri Department of Education developed tests that it and local districts could use to assess students on the key skills. Reports on student performance on the tests are sent directly from the test publisher to the local districts from which those students come, together with summary reports on the district and the buildings in the district. Statewide reports are made annually on the state sample for grades 3, 6, 8, and 10.

DEVELOPMENT OF KEY SKILLS AND TEST ITEMS FOR ECONOMICS

The process of developing the core competencies, key skills, and test items for economics was carried out with considerable involvement of teachers, the MCEE, and staff from the centers for economic education.

Developing the Objectives

Warren Solomon, the Department of Education's social studies consultant, led the task of developing objectives. A committee of 25 educators, which included teachers of social studies from the primary grades through high school, district social studies coordinators, elementary principals, professors of curriculum and instruction in social studies, and the director from the Southeast Missouri State University Center for Economic Education, was selected to assist in the process.

A first draft of the objectives was made using a set of objectives found in Chapter 5 of *A Guide to Social Studies Curriculum Development for Missouri Educators* (Missouri Department of Elementary and Secondary Education, 1980). Subcommittees for primary, intermediate, junior high, and senior high levels examined the objectives and selected appropriate objectives. Using the reports of the subcommittees, Solomon formulated a new draft set of objectives. Subcommittees made suggestions for revisions, and new drafts were made, examined, and

167

subsequently revised. In the process of making drafts, Solomon incorporated ideas from such sources as *A Framework for Teaching the Basic Concepts* (Saunders et al., 1984) and *A Guide to Trade-Offs* (Agency for Instructional Television, 1978). Objectives finally included in the state program were arrived at by consensus of the subcommittees.

This process was used in 1985–86 for levels 3, 6, 8, and 10, which were seen as milestone years; level 3 representing learning gained during the primary years, level 6 during the intermediate years, level 8 during the middle school/junior high years, and level 10 during the first two years of high school. Subsequently, objectives were developed for levels 2, 4, 5, 7, and 9 in 1987.

Once objectives were specified, the task of developing test items rested with the Center for Educational Assessment (CEA), an organization affiliated with the School of Education at the University of Missouri. The CEA invited a group of teachers to review and arrive at test content specifications for each key skill.

The next phase of drafting the test items was carried out by the CEA with the assistance of the Missouri Department of Education and educators. The CEA then arranged for piloting the items, following which small committees of teachers examined the data and decided which items to keep in the item pool. Throughout the process a major concern was to make certain that key skills, test content specifications, and items were in direct alignment. Another concern was that the content of items be acceptable to scholars in the field. To help in that regard, Solomon was in frequent contact with the staff at the centers for economic education and the MCEE.

Implementation Efforts

The Missouri Department of Education faced the major challenge of helping teachers in the state understand the program and how it might be meshed with their local curricula. To this end, *Core Competencies and Key Skills for Missouri Schools: For Grades 2 Through 10* (Missouri Department of Elementary and Secondary Education, 1988a) was developed by the department, and workshops were conducted throughout the state to inform teachers about the program. In addition, the department developed a resource called *Key Skills Sets* (Missouri Department of Elementary and Secondary Education, 1988b), which, for five key skills at every level, explains the main idea of each key skill, provides suggestions for evaluation, includes sample test items, and offers suggestions for teaching each key skill.

In addition, the MCEE developed guides for teaching the economics key skills at the primary, intermediate, junior high, and senior high levels and conducted workshops on the key skills. The *Guides for Teaching the Missouri Core Competencies in Economics, Grades K–3, 4–6, 7–8, and 9–10* (Missouri Council on Economic Education, 1987) present and explain the core competencies in economics, explain the economic concepts contained in the competencies, and offer teaching activities to assist classroom teachers. Core competencies and learner outcomes for each grade level covered in the particular *Guide* and for all other grade levels are included, allowing teachers to place their grade-level concepts within the total economics curriculum requirements.

The MCEE distributes the *Guides* through its nine centers for economic education, and the centers conduct workshops on the *Guides*. Over 1,000 *Guides* have been distributed in the past two years. Indirectly, the testing program has increased the amount of teacher training in economic education in the state.

Test Results for 1987 and 1988

Test results for the economics key skills for 1987 and 1988 are listed in Table 11.1. The general trend for the sample between 1987 and 1988 was one of improvement in most cases. Performance was quite low on some of the key skills, with less than half of the students demonstrating mastery (three out of four items correct for the key skill) in three cases: N-1 and O-2 in level 3 and O-1 in level 10. Performance is unspectacular on a number of other objectives.[4]

For objectives on which performance is low, several alternative steps might be—and have been—taken. For example, the *Key Skills Sets* (Missouri Department of Elementary and Secondary Education, 1988b) were developed in particular for those key skills on which student performance was low. In addition, the state has been revising the key skills. In the case of Key Skill O-2, which deals with sources of household income, it was decided that having students distinguish among wages, interest, profit, and rent as sources of income could be saved for assessment at grade levels above grade 3. In the case of Key Skill O-1, which deals with the distinction between market and command economic systems, it was decided to incorporate the objective in the

TABLE 11.1
Student Performance on the MMATs for Levels
3, 6, 8, and 10, 1987–88

KEY SKILL	PERCENTAGE OF SAMPLE STUDENTS DEMONSTRATING MASTERY		
	1987	1988	Change
Level 3			
M-2 Economic Choices	79	79	0
N-1 Types of Economic Resources	21	24	+3
O-2 Sources of Household Income	25	35	+10
Level 6			
M-1 Trade-Offs in Decisions	85	87	+2
N-1 Production Terms	44	50	+6
O-2 Government and Economy	69	66	–3
P-2 Price and Supply/Demand	77	78	+1
R-1 Regional Specialization	46	54	+8
Level 8			
M-2 Economic Decision Making	74	78	+4
N-1 Results of Economic Changes	70	77	+7
P-1 Changes in Supply/Demand	68	75	+7
Q-1 Economic Growth/Decline	64	72	+8
Level 10			
M-3 Economic Decision Making	62	77	+15
O-1 Market and Command Economics	36	37	+1
O-5 Government and Economy	52	58	+6
P-4 Price and Supply/Demand	69	68	–1
Q-1 GNP and Living Conditions	44	51	+7
Q-2 Influences on GNP	48	62	+15

program at earlier levels so that students would have more opportunities to be exposed to the concepts before being tested on them.

Of greater importance, local districts are asked to look at key skills on which performance is low and to plan strategies for improvement. Specific strategies might vary from district to district because in Missouri local districts have responsibility for determining their own scopes and sequences of units and courses. The fact that the MMAT is a test that is criterion referenced to explicit, public key skills should make it quite possible for districts to make major improvements in their performance on any key skills for which performance is deemed unacceptable by the local district. Both the Missouri Department of Education and the MCEE stand ready to assist any district with its efforts.

Revision of the Core Competencies and Key Skills

Since the inception of the core competencies and key skills program, the state department of education has planned to make modest revisions in the program every five years. The first effort to revise the program began in the fall of the 1988–89 school year with a request for local districts to submit statements of their concerns and related recommendations. At the same time, state curriculum consultants in language arts, mathematics, science, and social studies identified committee members from local school districts and universities in the state. The committees first examined the criticisms of the present program from the surveys sent to the department. On the basis of committee input, Solomon made draft revisions of the core competencies and key skills which were examined by the writing and review committees to help make certain that the final product reflects the vision of outcomes that a quality social studies program should produce. Solomon has also sought out suggestions from economics educators and made use of *Economics: What and When—Scope and Sequence Guidelines, K–12* (Gilliard et al., 1988) in preparing the drafts. The challenge facing the revision committees will be to make improvements in the objectives, yet keep continuity with the program as it was developed earlier.

DEEP IMPLEMENTATION AND MMATs IN A DISTRICT

For the past several years, many Missouri school districts have been floundering in response to the state-mandated assessment program. In others, there have been success stories. In March 1988 the St. Joseph School District Elementary Economics Program was named one of ten exemplary economic education programs in the country by the Joint Council on Economic Education. A major input into this success was the integration of the core competencies into the existing curriculum.

From the outset, the St. Joseph School District had supported the Excellence in Education legislation, but at the same time had been apprehensive about the state-imposed program because the existing social studies curriculum had been developed years before the MMAT was devised. By 1988, however, the district had successfully integrated the economics core competencies and key skills into its existing curriculum. Teachers were given the option of adopting a prepared economics curriculum based on the key skills and core competencies in economics or developing materials of their own.[5] Even though teachers were expected to teach the Missouri key skills and core competencies in economics, no teacher was coerced into using one of the packaged programs.

The St. Joseph program was a joint effort by the school district teachers and the Missouri Western State College Center for Economic Education and was enhanced by individual teacher training in economic education through DEEP. The revision of the curriculum was a deliberate district effort to achieve curriculum alignment. Although the MMAT cannot be said to have caused the curriculum alignment, it did provide a vehicle to revise the curriculum in a systematic fashion, which is a major goal of DEEP. The MMAT served as a tool for examining a local curriculum, and DEEP provided the vehicle to implement the process.

The St. Joseph School District's program exemplifies all four elements of the DEEP model: It is (1) developmental, (2) integrative, (3) institutionalized, and (4) buttressed by an outside support system. The St. Joseph program is developmental because it embraces all elementary grades, and plans have been made to continue the process into the secondary grades. The program is integrative because appropriate economic concepts were defined for all grade levels and integrated into the existing curriculum. The program is institutionalized because the school board and the administration have made a commitment to raising the economic literacy of students within the district. Finally, the program is buttressed by an outside support system, with the Missouri Western State College Center for Economic Education providing teacher training, curriculum advisement, and economic education materials.

DISTRICT AND COMMUNITY ATTITUDES TOWARD THE MMATs

To determine how the MMATs are being used; what attitudes district administrators, teachers, and parents have toward the program; and the impact the MMATs have had on economic education in Missouri, a survey was sent by the authors to a random sample of superintendents and/or directors of curriculum in the spring of 1989. Questions on the survey pertained to the MMATs in general and the core competencies in economics specifically. Another purpose of the survey was to determine if responses were significantly different between the DEEP and non-DEEP districts. The survey was sent to 82 non-DEEP districts and 49 DEEP districts in the state.[6]

Overwhelmingly, 63 percent of the responses from district administrators/curriculum directors indicated that they believe students will leave their school districts better educated as a result of the MMATs. Reasons given were the quality of the tests themselves, the additional teacher training addressing the MMATs, and the pretesting of students on the MMATs. Seventy-three percent of the DEEP districts and 68 percent of the non-DEEP districts indicated that their school district provided special workshops or courses for teachers addressing the core competencies and key skills in general on the MMATs. Many of the surveys indicated that more workshops were offered at the elementary level than at the secondary level. Of the DEEP districts surveyed, 54 percent indicated that they encourage their teachers to pretest their students on the MMATs. In non-DEEP districts, 45 percent of the respondents encouraged teachers to pretest.

Respondents were asked the question, "What impact has the MMAT had on the teaching of economics?" Sixty-eight percent of the DEEP responses indicated that more economics is taught as a result of the implementation of the MMATs, compared to a 52 percent response from non-DEEP districts. None of the DEEP district respondents believed that less economics is taught as a result of the MMATs, but 2 percent of the non-DEEP districts indicated that this is the case. Generally, district administrators view the core competencies and key skills program as a valuable educational device.

Two of the fears voiced by educators and others at the onset of the testing program were that the state-mandated test might inadvertently dictate a state-defined curriculum and that teachers and students might experience a test-overload effect. In the survey the administrators and curriculum directors were asked to what degree there was ill feeling among their teachers about the MMATs. In general, 57 percent of all district administrators believed there is some ill feeling among teachers about the testing program. In non-DEEP districts, 13 percent of the responses indicated that there is a great amount of ill feeling among their teachers about the MMATs, compared to 8 percent of the DEEP district responses. As far as how the community views the MMAT program, the results showed that 32 percent of the district administrators believed their community likes the program because it provides a yardstick by which to judge the district, 60 percent indicated their community knows little about the program, and 3 percent said they believed the community residents use the program to vent their frustrations with the district. In general, it appears that the testing program is accepted by local communities.

When the administrators were asked in which of the social studies/civics core competencies they felt students are in most need of improvement, an overwhelming 55 percent indicated economics, compared to 35 percent in geography, 19 percent in government, and 11 percent in history. Perhaps the lack of economics in textbooks at all grade levels is responsible for this result. These responses may also indicate a need for further teacher training in economics.

As for the types of economic education training or materials they believed teachers in their district would most like to receive, responses indicate that the most desired training by districts is in-service workshops on how to teach economics and that there is a perceived need for more economic education curriculum materials.

CONCLUSION

The identification of core competencies and key skills in economics is consistent with DEEP, which is a program designed to facilitate curriculum change in the local schools, especially when identification of those objectives involves inputs from economics educators and the materials they produced. In addition, the core competencies and key skills approach can encourage systematic curriculum change and alignment. This has been illustrated by the St. Joseph School District.

The state testing program is based on the philosophy that if student learning outcomes are clearly stated, if activities are focused on those outcomes, and if those same learning outcomes are assessed to determine student learning, schools will be more effective. The testing program is a resource to help "align" objectives, teaching activities, and testing.

The DEEP approach is to view the curriculum as the totality of teachers, students, and administration so that the process of curriculum change can be examined and modified to achieve results based on local needs. The key skills in economics approach can serve as a complement to the DEEP process.

Successes and Needed Improvements

When the Excellence in Education Act was passed, the student testing provisions were among the most controversial sections of the law, and the MMATs are not without their critics. Some educators contend that the new tests are forcing local school districts to adopt a state-defined curriculum. They say that the key skills, which form the basis of the MMATs, and the state testing program have forced districts to revise their curricula to fit the tests.

According to Commissioner of Education Robert Bartman, "It is not our intent to dictate curriculum through testing. The MMATs cover key skills which teachers and citizens in Missouri have agreed are essential for all students to learn at each level. These skills provide only a skeleton for any school's curriculum. They do not determine how schools should teach" (Missouri Department of Elementary and Secondary Education, 1989c, p. 6). In fact, the key skills may be addressed in the context of a variety of social studies courses of study.

The story of the Missouri program of core competencies and key skills is far from complete, it being in its third year. From what has been observed, however, some conclusions may be drawn—some positive, some negative.

On the positive side, the program has made economics a matter of concern to elementary teachers and secondary social studies teachers who have had the freedom to ignore the subject entirely. This concern is reflected in the increased demand for economic education courses and materials from the MCEE network. In addition, the objectives themselves, by their being related to concepts and thinking skills identified as important by the Joint Council on Economic Education, offer the possibility of broadening the vision of teachers on what students should learn as a result of their economic education. Finally, the program, by being focused on outcomes, should encourage local educators—as indeed it has in some cases—to plan for instruction starting from objectives, with alignment of those objectives, teaching strategies, and assessment strategies as an end in mind. In the long run, these factors should result in improved economic understanding and skill development among Missouri students.

Unfortunately, there have been problems in implementation, which

175

pose a hazard for economic education. It is important to remember that Missouri's list of core competencies and key skills is quite broad, with 21 objectives listed, for example, in level 10. Yet from that set of objectives, only six are tested on the MMAT because of the practical needs of keeping the test manageable in length and having a machine-scorable test. A problem may occur when local districts or teachers narrow their vision of outcomes to only those that are state-tested. In such cases many important economic educational outcomes will be missed.

It is critical, if problems are to be avoided, that there be sound leadership at the local level in integrating the objectives into the school district's curriculum. This can be accomplished best if there are good lines of communication among local districts, the state department of education, and the MCEE network.

Implications for Teaching Economics

The following implications for teaching economics in the schools are a result of the implementation of the core competencies and key skills in economics:

- More economics is being integrated into the curriculum as a result of the identification and testing of core competencies and key skills in economics. More economic education means greater consistency in instruction statewide as well.
- The implementation of the testing program, including economics, has made the MCEE, the centers for economic education, and the Department of Education more visible throughout the state because the demand for economic education services has increased to a great extent. Many school districts have sought out these sources of information because of a pressing need to incorporate economics into their curricula.
- More teachers are integrating economics into the curriculum at all grade levels, rather than just at the high school level. A state mandate that a student must have an economics course before graduating from high school, although important, does not integrate economic instruction throughout the curriculum at various grade levels. A greater understanding of economics can occur when instruction begins in the earlier grades and proceeds through the upper grades.
- More economics curriculum materials for Missouri teachers and students have resulted from the passage of the state-mandated

176

testing program. In addition, more economic education workshops, seminars, and courses are being attended by Missouri teachers. As a result, students in Missouri are being provided with more economic instruction. As teachers are required to teach economics, they learn it themselves, and they, in effect, become more effective consumers, producers, and citizens.

- Teachers seem to have a greater focus on what economics is—rather than what they think it is—and how it can fit into their existing curriculum. Dispelling the notion that economics is simply learning how to write a check or how to count money is important if good economic education is to be provided in the schools.
- Teachers have been made aware that economics instruction can be integrated into the other disciplines and that this is a desirable thing to do. The economics portion of the MMATs can easily be integrated into history, government, and geography courses and units, as well as into other subject areas.

The identification of core competencies and key skills has provided the state of Missouri with a framework to align curricula statewide at all grade levels.

NOTES

1. The Missouri Mastery and Achievement Tests (MMATs) are a battery of criterion-referenced achievement tests based on selected learning outcomes, or "key skills." The key skills are published in the book *Core Competencies and Key Skills for Missouri Schools: For Grades 2 Through 10* (Missouri Department of Elementary and Secondary Education, 1988a). The major distinction between the MMATs and other standardized achievement tests is that the MMATs are criterion referenced rather than norm referenced. This means that unlike some other standardized achievement tests, which may be designed to comparatively rank students, the MMATs measure students' mastery of just the particular set of Missouri key skills on which each MMAT is based. Individual student MMAT scores are reported in terms of the student's performance on each key skill. The MMATs are designed so that student performance is amenable to instruction. As a result, no passing scores for subjects have been established for the MMATs.

2. The only other state-mandated test in Missouri was the Basic Essential Skills Test (BEST), required since 1979 under state board of education policy.

Because the MMATs are more comprehensive than the BEST in both content and grades covered, the state board voted in July 1988 to drop the BEST.

3. The tests are unique to Missouri, and their results cannot be directly compared with national averages on well-known, commercial achievement tests. Because of this factor, students included in the statewide MMAT sample also take portions of the Iowa Tests of Basic Skills (ITBS) in grades 3, 6, and 8 and the Tests of Achievement and Proficiency (TAP) in grade 10. With these data, scores on the MMATs can be equated directly with scores on the two widely used national tests.

4. Of particular interest to the MCEE is the question of whether DEEP district involvement has an impact on student economics achievement on the MMATs statewide. To this end, a statistical study was conducted in the fall of 1988 by Karen Hallows, using a randomly selected sample from grades 3, 6, 8, and 10 in 242 districts, to examine the impact of school district resources and varying levels of formal DEEP involvement (initiating, implementing, and sustaining) on the core competency performance of students in economics.

In general, the study indicates that if a district is enrolled in DEEP in the implementing stage, there is a positive relationship between the average district economics score on the MMATs and district DEEP involvement. However, the results in general do not add up to a major DEEP victory, and it appears that the promise of DEEP has not yet been realized in many districts. This study indicates that there is a need to expand DEEP.

5. Zooconomy and Exchange City are the prepared packages. Zooconomy is a program developed by the University of Missouri–St. Louis Center for Economic Education, and Exchange City was developed by the Learning Exchange in Kansas City.

6. Fifty-six of the eighty-two non-DEEP districts and 37 of the 49 DEEP districts responded to the survey.

REFERENCES

Agency for Instructional Television (1978). *A guide to Trade-Offs*. Bloomington, Ind.: the Agency.

Gilliard, J. V.; Caldwell, J.; Dalgaard, B. R.; Highsmith, R. J.; Reinke, R.; and Watts, M. (1988). *Economics: What and when—Scope and sequence guidelines, K–12*. New York: Joint Council on Economic Education.

Missouri Council on Economic Education (1987). *Guides for teaching the Missouri core competencies in economics, Grades K–3, 4–6, 7–8, and 9–10*. Columbia, Mo.: the Council.

Missouri Department of Elementary and Secondary Education (1989a). *Missouri school directory, 1988–89*. Jefferson City, Mo.: the Department.

_____ (1989b). MMAT scores still climbing. *Missouri Schools* 56(1):6.

_____ (1989c). *1988–89 report of the public schools of Missouri.* Jefferson City, Mo.: the Department.

_____ (1988a). *Core competencies and key skills for Missouri schools: For grades 2 through 10.* Jefferson City, Mo.: the Department.

_____ (1988b). *Key skills sets.* Jefferson City, Mo.: the Department.

_____ (1980). *A guide to social studies curriculum development for Missouri educators.* Jefferson City, Mo.: the Department.

Saunders, P.; Bach, G. L.; Calderwood, J. D.; Hansen, W. L.; and Stein, H. (1984). *A framework for teaching the basic concepts.* 2d ed. New York: Joint Council on Economic Education.

12. STATE MANDATES ON ECONOMICS IN THE CURRICULUM: THE IMPACT ON DEEP

by Sanford D. Gordon and Kenneth Wade

In 1974 the Joint Council on Economic Education established a policy against state mandates on economics in the curriculum. On 3 October 1986 this policy position was revised, urging "state departments of education, state governments and teacher education institutions to develop and implement requirements that will foster the goal of improved economic education for students in the K–12 grades." Why did the Joint Council oppose mandates, and why did it to change its policy?

REASONS FOR OPPOSING A MANDATE

In 1974 few social studies teachers had adequate academic training in economics. The network of affiliated councils on economic education and their regional centers was small and not capable of providing the needed training for a large cadre of teachers already in the field. The increased demand that a mandate would be likely to create could put a strain on most state councils. Worse yet, to require economics to be taught by those who knew little or nothing about the subject could prove worse than not teaching it at all. In addition, it made little sense for those who professed the virtues of the free market to support state mandates when local boards of education resisted mandates in general. In addition, mandates in economics most frequently meant requiring a separate twelfth grade course in the subject, an action totally inconsistent with the Joint Council's avowed position calling for an infusion of economic concepts throughout the entire curriculum. Then, also, if the twelfth grade mandate became a reality, the incentive to teach economics in all the other grades would be less. With the growing number of school dropouts, we could wind up with many young adults who have no knowledge of the economy. With these compelling reasons for opposing a mandate, something had to happen to force a change in policy.

REASONS FOR CHANGING THE POLICY

The revised 1986 statement calling for a mandate identifies how the environment had changed during the preceding 12 years and includes the findings of recent research. Many other disciplines, including the sciences, mathematics, history, and geography, lobbied successfully to increase their share of the curriculum. This meant that other subjects were prone to being crowded out of school programs. Such prestigious organizations as the National Science Foundation seem to be most impressed with disciplines that all students are required to take.

With the National Assessment of Educational Progress soon to measure student achievement in economics, chambers of commerce, legislators, and state commissioners of education are likely to become more sensitive to mandated economics offerings. In addition, some recent research indicated that the most effective way to teach economics is not by infusing basic concepts into the general curriculum, but by having a one-semester course devoted completely to economics. However, the best programs include both approaches. Finally, it has become apparent that those states where there is a mandate have the strongest councils on economic education. Which is the cause and which the effect is hard to say, but it is likely that they go hand in hand.

THE NEW YORK EXPERIENCE

The first state syllabus, published in 1880, called for six courses in the social studies area—namely, American, English, Greek, and Roman histories; civics; and economics. Eleven years later this 4-page outline for social studies was expanded to 182 pages, providing a course of instruction to prepare pupils for the state's regents examinations. While this would appear to have given economics an important place in the curriculum, it was not required at any specific grade level until 1934 when world geography and economic citizenship were included in the grade 9 program.

In 1940 the state launched a major reformation of the curriculum, combining the separate courses in the disciplines into an overall social studies program. Nevertheless, history and geography represented the major part of the curriculum. Later, in the 1960s, world geography and economic citizenship were dropped as a ninth grade requirement, and the study of Asian and African cultures was substituted. In reality, this action did not reduce the amount of economics taught in grades 7 through 11 because economic concepts were infused into most of the program, but particularly into the eleventh grade American studies course, which includes a major unit on American economic life. Requirements in the state called for three years of social studies, but most schools had well-developed senior year electives. While economics was offered in many schools, sociology and psychology were much more popular choices with the students who chose senior electives in social studies.

New York City was an exception to the statewide requirements. In the 1930s economics became part of the mandated social studies curriculum. It was usually taken in the twelfth year, although some students took it concurrently with their eleventh grade American history course. What was the course like? It depended on the teachers' background and the students' ability. Mostly the course emphasized economic institutions and current economic problems. Where teachers had good training (some had graduated as economics majors), economic theory was taught. However, students who were not in the upper tracks academically received a heavy dose of consumer education along with some instruction in economic institutions and current economic problems.

Moving Toward a Real Mandate

In the 1970s the Board of Regents, the governing body of New York's education system, established as one of the major goals for elementary and secondary education that students should be provided with the knowledge and skills that would enable them to function as effective and informed citizens in the economy of the United States and the world. The board recognized that basic economic concepts were needed by producers and workers and by consumers and citizens for intelligent decision making. The function of the state syllabus in social studies was to translate that goal into a program that would provide teachers and students with the knowledge and skills necessary to enable them to achieve that goal.

In 1984 the Board of Regents approved an Action Plan that had a far-reaching effect on the entire curriculum through all grade levels. However, revisions for the social studies curriculum for grades K–6 had already begun in the late 1970s and for grades 7–12 in 1980.

For grades K–6 ten overarching concepts are highlighted regardless of the specific content in each grade level. Three of these—scarcity,

182

interdependence, and technology—are primarily considered economics, but the other major concepts such as change, the environment, and culture have strong economic elements. Within each grade level the K–6 program is divided into five strands or categories of content: social, political, economic, geographic, and historical. For example, a content understanding for the grade 3 syllabus is that "People must make economic choices due to unlimited wants and needs and limited resources." For grade 5 the syllabus calls for this understanding:

Production, distribution, exchange and consumption of goods and services are economic decisions with which nations must deal. These issues centered around:

- what and how much to produce
- how to combine and use resources in production
- how goods and services will be distributed.

The syllabus makes these abstract understandings meaningful by suggesting activities that teachers may select according to the needs and backgrounds of their students. Suggested resources are listed. The part that the New York State Council on Economic Education (NYSCEE) had in the development of the syllabus and curriculum resources and the preparation of teachers for implementing this new program will be described later.

In 1980 a survey taken of New York State secondary social studies teachers showed strong support for this statement: "The curriculum should promote the development of economic literacy and should include instruction in basic economic concepts and in economic decision making." The following year this sentiment was translated into a discussion paper prepared by representatives of the social studies professional organizations and the Bureau of Social Studies, recommending that a fourth unit of social studies should be required and that "at least one semester should be devoted to the study of economics in order to meet the need for economic literacy."

In 1982 the Board of Regents began the formal process of developing what eventually became the Regents Action Plan, a series of major changes in the curriculum. Ten regional conferences were held around the state in which all interested parties were asked to provide their recommendations for improving elementary and secondary education in the state. The NYSCEE had representatives at each of these regional hearings and in each presentation made a strong case for a state curriculum that would promote economic literacy. These hearings plus the sentiments expressed by the teachers' professional organizations provided the necessary support for the Bureau of Social Studies Framework Committee to proceed with its work of infusing economic concepts throughout the 7–12 curriculum and to prepare a syllabus for a required twelfth grade capstone course.

The revised curriculum for grades 7–8, the history of the United States and New York State, while primarily social and political, paid special attention to the economic development of the nation and state, providing an understanding of economic life and how people met their economic needs in each of the periods covered.

For grades 9–10, global studies, the overall goals of the course included the following:

That the student will be able to demonstrate knowledge of

- the major . . . economic forces and events that have shaped the global community and individual nations
- the . . . economic interdependence of major nations and cultures
- the means used by various nations and cultures to deal with human needs
- the economic significance of various nations and cultures.

This global studies course is divided into the seven areas of the world, including nations with different economic systems and in different stages of economic development. The international context not only broadens the pupils' understanding of economic differences, but also points out the universality of economic concepts.

The new course for grade 11 is a return to U.S. history, chronologically organized with the greatest emphasis on the periods when our nation became industrialized and a power in the world. It provides the historical setting for the one-semester economics course.

The capstone course in economics concentrates on the 22 basic concepts identified in the Joint Council on Economic Education's publication *A Framework for Teaching the Basic Concepts* (Saunders et al., 1984). It builds on the foundation of understandings developed in the K–11 program and attempts to provide students with the ability to apply economic principles, to analyze information, and to make decisions based on this analysis. Consumer education is given little attention. The major goal is to make it possible for students to deal with economic issues for many years to come, whatever those issues might be.

But what about the student who is not academically talented or highly motivated? The state syllabus deals with this problem by suggesting model activities that can be used to make abstract concepts meaningful to all levels of students. Teachers are provided with sources of relevant materials geared to many levels of student abilities including simulations, role playing, and actual case studies from the past. All students, as consumers, producers, and citizens, are affected by the realities of prices, unemployment, productivity, the balance of payments, taxes, wages and profits, interest rates, and government involvement in the economy. They will have to make decisions on these and other economic issues. It is the expectation that the knowledge and skills they acquire in economics in the total K–12 social studies program will prepare them to make decisions more rationally.

The Department and the Council Working Together

The State Education Department (SED), working through the Bureau of Social Studies Education, and the NYSCEE have worked cooperatively to improve economic education in the state since the founding of the council in 1965. Most of the early efforts were directed toward disseminating information about curricular materials and cosponsoring workshops for teachers. In the late 1970s Dr. John Youngers, executive director of the NYSCEE, was a major contributor to the evolving K–6 curriculum. The bureau chief of social studies during the latter part of the seventies became a member of the council's board of directors. Nevertheless, it was not until 1980 that the bureau and the council worked hand in hand in developing a total economic program for the state. Kenneth Wade of the Bureau of Social Studies Education and Dr. Sanford D. Gordon, executive director of the council, worked together in a mutual effort to expand and strengthen the program.

The council recognized that the best approach to creating a demand for economic education was to push for a state mandate. The most appropriate vehicle to achieve the mandate was the curriculum changes being considered by both the bureau and the regents. Through the efforts of the council's board members, center directors, sympathetic superintendents of schools, social studies department heads, and the New York

State Council for the Social Studies, and as a result of the many awareness sessions held throughout the state, the pressure built to mandate a separate twelfth grade capstone course in economics. As mentioned above, the regents approved the mandate in 1984, creating a sudden demand for assistance to teachers preparing to implement the course in September 1988. Both the bureau and the NYSCEE began receiving telephone calls from frantic teachers, department heads, and superintendents. They wanted to know what was being done to help teachers prepare to meet the mandate. The demand for expanding and improving economic education was in place. Since the education department provided no specific allocation for economic education, the major task fell to the NYSCEE.

The resources of the council began to expand at a slow, but consistent rate as the corporate community became aware of the level of economic illiteracy in the schools and how that might impact on their own well-being. Nevertheless, in 1980 there were only seven centers for economic education widely scattered throughout the state, and of these, only three were actively training teachers. Four small school districts were signed up for the council's DEEP program, but none of these was active. Workshops were few in number, and most of these were held for only a portion of a day. Two centers were developing some curricular materials, but their distribution was limited. The annual creative teaching awards contest attracted only a handful of entries. Indeed, few people had heard of the council, and those who had were not sure what services it performed. By 1984, the date the regents passed the mandate, the number of centers had grown to 13, all active; 84 school systems were affiliated with DEEP, including 4 of the 6 largest in the state; the Joint Council's curriculum materials were being widely disseminated; and over 800 teachers had participated in 40 workshops during the year. Many of these workshops now offered credit and ran for one, two, or three weeks. The NYSCEE participated actively in all economic education sessions sponsored by the New York State Council for the Social Studies and by its local councils. Even though resources for the NYSCEE nearly doubled, it still could not keep up with the expanded demand. Either new resources would have to be found, or the needs of the teachers of the state could not be met. The next step in the progression toward establishing an effective program was to get state funding, an essential component if all teachers were to be prepared to meet the new curriculum requirements.

State Funding

An attempt to secure financial support from the state began in 1980, using several state council board members' experience and influence to open doors to influential legislators. At the same time, meetings were held with members of the SED to submit a request for funds specifically designated for economic education. Interested legislators disagreed as to whether funding should be initiated in the SED's budget or should originate with the legislature. The decision was made easy when several sympathetic, well-placed, and influential legislators agreed to sponsor a bill. Key staff people on the Ways and Means Committee drew up the legislation in 1983, appropriating $50,000 to the SED "for the purpose of contracting to a non-profit organization services for improving the economic education of teachers of social studies, business education, home economics and distributive education (marketing)." Everything seemed to be in place for passage. Unfortunately, the Education Committee was not contacted in time to send the bill to appropriations.

In the 1984–85 session nothing was taken for granted. Lobbying was done by superintendents of schools affiliated with DEEP, by the SED, by the teachers union, by major banks and corporations that supported the council, by the Farm Bureau, and even by the Business Council which almost always opposed any increase in state expenditures. Because 1984 was a tight budget year in New York and the Bureau of the Budget recommended vetoing the appropriation, letters and phone calls were directed to the governor, urging him to sign the bill. Upon passage of the bill, 1984–85 marked the first state funding specifically designated for economic education.

Subsequent legislation raised the amount of funding to $200,000 and included entrepreneurial education. In 1987–88 and 1988–89, funding was placed by the legislature directly into the budget under aid to local governments. This protected it from a budget freeze, a not uncommon occurrence in New York. The weakness in the funding process is that it requires a separate renewal each year. To overcome this kind of uncertainty, legislation was introduced in 1989 that would require the SED to place funds in its budget for economic, entrepreneurial, and labor education for the next three years. Unfortunately, 1989 was a budget crisis year for the state, and no public funds were appropriated specifically for economic education. Money was available for staff development through the Boards of Cooperative Educational Services, but under this arrangement, economic education has to compete with all other disciplines. How well this approach will work is not known at this time.

Response to the Mandate and State Funding

From 1984–85 to 1988–89 the growth of the economic education movement in New York State was impressive indeed. Sixteen centers for economic education located on college and university campuses throughout the state served nearly 300 school districts, including the four largest in the state. Workshops were attended by more than 25,000 teachers, curricular materials were distributed to nearly 400 school districts, and cooperative programs were given by the NYSCEE with Boards of Cooperative Educational Services as well as with Teacher Centers. Center directors worked with school districts to develop curricula at all grade levels, and these materials were made available to other systems. The NYSCEE developed an annual publication, *The Evaluation of Frequently Used Textbooks for the Twelfth Grade Economics Course*, and distributed it to all DEEP systems. It also published a supplementary textbook, *The Economy of New York State*, 59 essays designed to link economic concepts to a world that students would find relevant. In addition, an inventory of human resources was developed. It included bankers, labor leaders, business people, and government officials who would be available in most regions in the state, allowing classroom teachers to show the relevance of the curriculum to their students and to make economics more exciting.

The state mandate that includes both an infusion of concepts and a separate twelfth grade course and that is supported by a combination of state and private funding has set the stage for a major improvement in the economic literacy of teachers and students in New York. Dr. Raymond Calucciello, director of curriculum and instruction in Schenectady, expressed what was happening in many parts of the state when he said:

When the Regents signaled economics as a high priority for social studies, K–12, and for business education, home economics and distributive education our faculty was not prepared to implement the changes. NYSCEE and its Center for Economic Education provided our teachers with workshops, curricular materials and guidance in writing our own curriculum so that our teachers now feel prepared, some even confident as they approach a discipline that just a short time ago frightened most of them. Thanks!

THE FLORIDA EXPERIENCE

A group of prominent business people, aware of what they perceived as a void in the curriculum, urged the Florida legislature to require free enterprise and consumer education. In 1975 the Free Enterprise and Consumer Education Act was passed, calling for changes that would infuse economic concepts into the curriculum. In addition, the act created the Florida Council on Economic Education and provided $100,000 to implement its program. The passage of this act represented the first formal action taken by Florida to do something about economic illiteracy in the schools. The effort was well received by the educational community. By 1980 the council had set up six centers on university campuses throughout the state to work with teachers in each region.

In 1983 the legislature went a step farther when it passed the RAISE Act which revamped the secondary school curriculum. Designed to improve academic standards in general, one of the specific focuses was economic education. Starting in 1986–87 the act required every student seeking graduation to take a one-semester course in Introduction to Economics, Economics, or Advanced Economics. The differing titles actually reflect differing tracks of difficulty. Again, the legislature recognized the importance of training teachers to implement this mandate, stating "the Florida Council on Economic Education shall provide technical assistance to the [Florida Department of Education] and local school boards in developing curriculum materials for the study of economics." To implement the teacher preparation program, the legislature increased its appropriation to the council to $348,700 from the previous year's $250,000. Additional public funds were provided through local districts. The Florida council has now increased its centers to eight in order to better serve its school districts.

THE CALIFORNIA EXPERIENCE

Two pieces of legislation set the tone for the mandate in economics in California. Both were largely the result of the leadership of State Senator Gray Hart. Senate Bill 813 (the Hughs-Hart Educational Reform Act of 1983) placed strong emphasis on economics in the curriculum. To make sure the objectives of the act were carried out, tests to measure performance (the California Achievement Program), were instituted for grades 4, 8, and 12. Many of the questions were on economic concepts.

189

More directly oriented toward economics was Senate Bill 1213. It mandated a one-semester course in economics for all graduating high school students by 1989. To support teacher education for the mandate, the regular state funding given to California state universities and colleges was augmented by $150,000. This legislation was passed overwhelmingly by both houses and then signed by the governor. Following this 1985 legislation, Section 51210 of the California Education Code was put into place: "instruction shall provide a foundation for understanding . . . the development of the American economic system, including the role of the entrepreneur and labor." Infusion of economic concepts occurs at all grade levels. Regular public funding comes from the chancellor's office to all 19 California state university and college campuses.

STATE MANDATES TODAY

The Joint Council on Economic Education recently made a survey of where states stood with regard to mandating economic instruction:

- 28 states mandate that students receive some form of instruction in economics.
- 16 states require at least a one-semester course in economics for graduation.
- 25 states have an economics/free enterprise mandate.
- 4 states require that an economics elective be made available.
- 9 of the 28 states that mandate economic instruction provide funding support for teacher training.
- 10 states mandate that economic concepts be infused into their K–12 curriculum. (Highsmith, 1989)

The population of the 28 states mandating economic instruction represents two-thirds of the population of the United States.

CONCLUSIONS

If state mandates are used as the criterion to measure how deeply entrenched economics is in the curriculum, it is obviously well established. Probably more important is the fact that the largest and most important trend-setting states of California, Florida, and New York all require a one-semester course in economics for graduation and are supporting teacher-training programs so that these mandates may result in quality offerings. To require the teaching of economics without a cadre of teachers who are adequately prepared would be worse than ignoring the subject. It is in the preparation of teachers to carry out the mandate that the state councils on economic education have their most important mission.

REFERENCES

Highsmith, R. J. (1989). *A survey of state mandates for economics instruction, 1989.* New York and Washington, D.C.: Joint Council on Economic Education and NFIB Foundation.

Saunders, P.; Bach, G. L.; Calderwood, J. D.; Hansen, W. L.; and Stein, H. (1984). *A framework for teaching the basic concepts.* 2d ed. New York: Joint Council on Economic Education.

13. A PARTNERSHIP WITH A HISTORY: FUNDING THE DEEP EXPERIENCE

by Michael A. MacDowell and Peter V. Harrington

The DEEP program began in 1964 as a partnership between the private sector and the schools. As such, it is one of the oldest public/private educational partnerships in existence. It also remains unique because it requires, and in most instances delivers, the commitment of a school district to curriculum change. In school districts that accept and engage in the systematic teacher-training program and the increased instruction in economics that go with a commitment to DEEP, students score significantly higher on national tests of economic understanding (Walstad & Soper, 1988). In school districts that are not part of DEEP, students understand less about our economic system and are less favorably disposed to it.

DEEP is as much a financial innovation as it is an innovation in curriculum change. Financially, the DEEP hypothesis is simple. Since the private sector has much to gain by a public that is more economically literate, the private sector would be willing to finance the development of the special materials and teacher training necessary to increase that economic literacy. There are precedents for this. Many other disciplines use public, private, and school district funds to bring about curriculum change. The massive curriculum programs of the late 1950s and early 1960s in the sciences, mathematics, and social studies are cases in point. But the DEEP program goes farther. DEEP requires a commitment on the part of a local school district not only to accept economic education in the schools, but also to support the program by providing release time for teachers and for a DEEP administrator and by providing some funds to purchase materials for the teachers and students. Another unique feature of the DEEP process today is that curriculum change is driven by school system needs, rather than by a set of prescribed materials produced at the national level.

Does the process work? As measured in terms of total private dollars raised, DEEP has been an unqualified success. The Joint Council on Economic Education has seen its budget income increase threefold in the past ten years, and much of that was a result of a special effort to emphasize DEEP. The DEEP capital campaign was begun in 1984 and had raised $4.6 million by early 1989. The Joint Council operates through 50 independent state councils on economic education, and their budgets—which according to Suglia (1989) averaged $35,000 in 1975—now average $185,000 with some state council budgets exceeding $500,000 a year. Total funds raised by state councils exceed $8.5 million, and many of these dollars support DEEP.

DEEP growth in the field has also been substantial. Some 1,700 school districts with close to 40 percent of the nation's K–12 students are now enrolled in DEEP. State departments of education are also engaged in this effort. Thirteen state departments now allocate funds specifically to economic education, often directly in support of DEEP.

As DEEP operations in schools have evolved over the years, so have the financial aspects. Today many more causes compete for corporate and foundation support than was the case in the past. Consequently, school districts must start to pick up more of the "DEEP burden." Moreover, when DEEP began in 1964, instruction in economics was a rarity in schools. Nowadays, 28 states require some sort of economic education. One of the major purposes of the DEEP program was to institutionalize economic instruction, and now much of that goal has been reached. Because economics is becoming a mainstream subject in the K–12 curriculum, school systems have less claim on outside monies to handle the necessary and often required teacher education and materials purchases for instruction in economics; the necessary financing must be at least partially shifted to the schools.

DEEP: THE BEGINNINGS

The DEEP concept was developed by M. L. Frankel, president of the Joint Council on Economic Education from 1952 to 1976, and by S. Stowell Symmes, executive director of school services at the Joint Council. The curriculum philosophy of DEEP, discussed elsewhere in this book, initially emphasized the development of an experimental curriculum for grades K–12 that could be written in one district and adopted by another. DEEP started with an initial grant of $100,000 from the Ford Foundation in 1964.

The purpose of the Ford grant was to begin DEEP in 30 pilot school districts and to underwrite the development of special materials and the services of a resident economist in three special districts: the Minneapolis, Pittsburgh, and Contra Costa school systems. The funds from the Ford Foundation were matched by contributions from major corporations. This marked the first time the Joint Council engaged in the solicitation of funds directly from business.

The original 1964 financial model behind the pilot DEEP program was to develop a set of curriculum materials that could be "purchased" from the Joint Council and that would serve as a model for the creation of similar materials in new DEEP school districts. In reality, however, the diversity among school systems, as well as the difficulty of writing an economics curriculum at the local level, necessitated amendment of the initial funding schema. Since most school districts were not capable of producing their own materials in economics, a new, more systematic method for materials development and adoption had to be determined and funded.

By 1973 the Business Roundtable released a study on economic education that strongly endorsed the Joint Council and extolled its approach because the council affected not only students, but also teachers—"the gatekeepers of the classroom." Buoyed by this pronouncement, the Joint Council initiated its first general corporate fund-raising drive, and by 1974 corporations supplanted major national foundations as the Joint Council's prime funding source.

A systematic approach to curriculum development was conceived in 1973. Grants from several corporations and foundations allowed work to begin in 1975 that resulted in the Joint Council's *Master Curriculum Guide*. The *Guide* consists of a set of teaching strategies for various subjects and grades at the precollege level. The purpose of the strategies is to provide a foundation for all national economic education materials developed by the Joint Council. By doing so, it also provides a uniform base for DEEP instruction and materials. Equally important to the Joint Council was the fact that the *Guide* would make all its economic education materials more homogeneous, thereby lessening the time it would take to "develop" local material in any school district, and thus extending the time and resources available for teacher training. The 1977 *Framework for Teaching Economics* (Hansen et al., 1977) (concise statements of the basic concepts used to teach economics) and a few of the now ten strategies sections began to appear. Subsequent publications and film series, such as *Trade-Offs* (1977) and *Give & Take* (1981), funded by private and public dollars, provided further substantive support for DEEP. Grants from the Amoco Foundation, for example, financed regional DEEP coordinator training.

DEEP EXPANSION

In the 20 years from 1964 to 1984, 725 school districts joined the DEEP program—an average of 55 districts per year. In 1984 the then new chairman of the Joint Council on Economic Education, Louis V. Gerstner, Jr., who was president of American Express and is now chairman of RJR/Nabisco, asked the Joint Council staff and Executive Committee a rather simple question: "If DEEP works so well, why are only 22 percent of the nation's students fortunate enough to be part of it?" He proposed an extensive expansion program that would attempt to enroll a majority of the nation's school districts in DEEP by 1990. So large a goal for growth was unprecedented for the Joint Council and represented a significant challenge to the national staff and, most particularly, to the network. Even if so ambitious a project could be funded, how could the network service close to 30 million students and 1.6 million teachers?

Through a series of discussions with various members of the National Association of Economic Educators and a study conducted by the firm of Payne, Wester, Forrester & Olsson, a plan was developed.[1] The plan called for attempting to enroll 70 percent of the nation's students in DEEP by 1990. A prospectus for DEEP expansion was written that put forward a national budget of approximately $7 million. Additionally, it was assumed that the Joint Council would help its state affiliates raise an additional $4 million for the initial servicing of DEEP school districts.

Consultants were then hired to review the DEEP fund-raising plan. Their comments were telling and spelled out why DEEP, as a fund-raising rubric, had some liabilities. DEEP's flexibility and adaptability to meet local needs were attractive to schools, but less so to prospective funders. Prospective funders, particularly corporate entities, desired and were drawn to a more structured, centralized program. DEEP seemed fuzzy to funders, who wanted greater specificity. Also, DEEP relied solely on educators. Funders wanted to participate. Moreover, the DEEP process was difficult to explain and created questions on the part of funders about what was supposed to be achieved.

The DEEP funding effort was begun despite the reservations voiced by the consultants and to date has raised close to $5 million of the original $7 million goal. While the prognosis for reaching the $7 million sought is good, many of the donated funds have come with the proviso that they be tied to specific projects or regions not contemplated in the original DEEP prospectus. Funder designation of DEEP funds to particular geographic areas or projects has led to spotty DEEP growth. For example, some areas of the country far surpass others in the number of new school districts enrolled in DEEP.

Nevertheless, as already noted, significant funds have been raised for DEEP on both the national and the local levels. Many of these funds would never have been available for economic education had it not been for the DEEP expansion effort. DEEP partnerships have also helped clarify the responsibilities of the national office and of its state affiliates and have sharpened the Joint Council's focus on the delivery of economic education programs.

FUNDING THE DEEP OF TOMORROW

Some people who are interested in economic education find it difficult to comprehend that the corporate sector does not "flock to fund" DEEP. After all, who benefits more from support for a vibrant, strong economic system than business does? And corporate executives themselves declare economic illiteracy a major issue. A 1985 study by the Opinion Research Corporation (Joint Council on Economic Education, 1986) found that four out of five executives of major U.S. corporations are concerned about the lack of efforts to educate the public about how our economic system works. In rating those who have the greatest effect on the next generation's understanding of economics, corporate executives say social studies teachers have the best potential for eradicating the problem of economic illiteracy. Yet, according to Opinion Research Corporation, only 5 percent of these same corporate executives say that teachers are well enough informed about our economic system to carry out that task. Apparently the corporate sector is ripe to support programs that would alleviate these situations, but it does not seem anxious to do so. Why?

A possible explanation may be that business is geared to seeing faster results than the educational process can achieve. In addition, business people have a natural "take charge" mindset. Thus, they seem to tend to prefer specific projects that promise an immediate return or in which they or their subordinates can directly participate. Such factors seem to

196

have been at work during the past five years for in that period there has been a significant shift away from economic education based on business and school system partnerships to programs fairly directly tied to business' specialized interests. Among business' highest priorities have been programs to generate new engineers and scientists, as well as the complete reform of local schools. Many organizations have been developed to meet such goals. Hence, while corporate funding for elementary and secondary school programs has increased in recent years, the Joint Council and its state councils, which are not geared to meeting such immediate curriculum goals or concerns, have not shared equitably in this recent increased funding.

Moreover, the competition for corporate dollars has increased significantly since DEEP was initiated. Beginning with a call from the Reagan administration for increased corporate philanthropy to substitute for a decline in federal dollars, many existing and new nonprofit endeavors entered the corporate fund-raising arena. At first, between 1981 and 1986, corporate contributions increased substantially, which allowed funding of the newcomers and helped ameliorate the developing squeeze on DEEP. Since 1986, however, the growth in corporate funding has begun to taper off, according to a 1987 survey by The Conference Board (1988). It grew at only 2 percent in 1987–88. DEEP, as a result, has begun to feel the pinch.

Funding from foundations also experienced a surge of growth in the early 1980s, but this surge, too, began to level off in the latter part of the decade. Contributions by individuals were the only type of funding that continued to grow substantially during the entire decade. But few individuals feel comfortable about giving to DEEP because it provides little name recognition for them and hence is less attractive than a variety of other options.

Adding to the concern of many who raise funds from corporations has been the surge of mergers, acquisitions, and corporate restructurings in recent years. These activities severely cut into the sheer number of companies that support various nonprofit causes, as well as the amount that those that remain can give.[2]

THE SCHOOL DISTRICTS

The direct funding of their "wants and needs" has become big business for many major school districts. These districts directly solicit funds for programs and projects. According to the *Chronicle of Philanthropy* (6 December 1988), Los Angeles' education partnership raises about $2 million a year while the Boston Compact has raised close to $10 million for general educational improvements in the schools.

Fund raising by school districts offers a unique opportunity for economic education. The lack of interest in general economic education that businesses have expressed in regard to national or statewide DEEP campaigns can be overcome when a DEEP fund-raising drive concentrates on specific schools or even districts. Businesses seem to have become much more attuned to giving to local programs for economic education than to national or statewide programs. It is a fact that a local program of quality that boasts demonstrable results can attract funds.

Can a fund-raising system that was based on national and statewide drives adapt to the new corporate—and foundation—preference to give locally? The answer must be yes if DEEP is to survive as the basis for economic education in this country. But funds for DEEP can be raised in conjunction with local schools only if the school districts themselves make economic education a funding as well as a curriculum priority. Financial partnerships between school districts and local centers for economic education must be established and maintained. And the districts themselves must be intimately involved in asking for DEEP money.

State councils and university centers, as well as school districts, can benefit from cooperative fund-raising efforts for several important reasons. First, economic education through DEEP produces results. A relatively small portion of jointly raised DEEP funds can produce significant consequences, and thus build credibility between schools and businesses. This credibility, in turn, serves to leverage additional funding for other projects. Meanwhile, many of the large general educational partnership programs such as the Boston Compact have produced mixed, if not dubious, outcomes (Rothman, 1988). Businesses are beginning to ask questions about the efficacy of these programs that do not produce quantifiable effects.

Second, while, as mentioned, businesses are often not interested in economic education on a national level, they are interested in local endeavors. The ability to obtain future employees who understand why businesses do what they do is important to business people, and they are willing to pay to get such employees. In particular, business prizes employees whose actions and values it finds compatible. In addition, since economics provides a foundation for rational decision making, business feels that an economic education assists in its constant goal to improve employee productivity substantially.

Third, the new projects under DEEP, such as *Choices & Changes* and *Economics & Entrepreneurship Education*, are directed at audiences of particular interest to business—students who are economically disadvantaged and/or at risk of dropping out of school. These programs help such students learn that they can become part of the economic system. This possibility is particularly appealing to many local business people who increasingly share a commitment to assist the economically disadvantaged students in the nation's public schools.

Finally, there is the issue of U.S. international economic competitiveness. The Joint Council on Economic Education was created by the Committee for Economic Development in 1949, not to produce more economists, but to help give the country a labor force that understood how and why balanced economic growth is important both domestically and internationally. That is still a primary goal of the Joint Council. It is also the rationale for many of the recent studies about America's education system. Indeed, *A Nation at Risk* (National Commission on Excellence in Education, 1983) and the many studies that follow based several of their recommendations for change in American schools on the need for the United States to be competitive. It seems logical that the citizens of tomorrow must understand what competition is and why it is important for this country to remain competitive in the world at large. These are key purposes of economic education.

SPECIFICS OF PRIVATE SECTOR FUNDING AT THE STATE AND LOCAL LEVELS

Previous fund-raising experience for DEEP suggests some general guidelines for future successful fund raising at both the state and the local levels. Here are some capsulized suggestions on the emphasis state councils and university center networks should place on various fund-raising initiatives.

- *Securing local leadership.* Key community leaders or their subordinates should be invited to serve on university center advisory boards. If there is no local university center, a community advisory board representing all sectors of the local economy should be

199

established. Members of the advisory board should have firsthand knowledge about and contribute advice to present DEEP program activities, as well as to future DEEP activities in their community. Their direct involvement and "sense of ownership" in school program initiatives will make them more cooperative partners in fund raising at the local level.

- *Capitalizing on restricted giving.* As noted earlier in this chapter, corporate and foundation funders are now placing greater emphasis than before on funding specific projects that meet their needs, have a limited time span, demonstrate results, involve them in program activities, and bring recognition to them and their employees. Proposals that address these matters and that are crisp and well written have the best chance of being funded.

- *Leveraging with other nonprofit organizations.* With the growth of privately funded Public School/Community/Economic Development/Partners-in-Education Foundations, there is significant potential for raising additional funds and in-kind support because these groups have a common interest in promoting excellence in education, particularly as it relates to economic education. In addition to the cover letter that highlights the rationale for the project, the proposal should include the project's purpose, needs, strengths, uniqueness of organization, desirable results, and long-term benefits, and a budget that includes indirect costs.

- *Developing joint proposals.* Foundations or corporations with strong regional or national connections are also potential sources of funding for the major DEEP projects of state councils and, in many instances, those of the Joint Council. Advance planning and communication among all the entities that may be involved will help ensure that the needs of all the organizations at work on the project are met. A proposal should be thoroughly reviewed and agreed on with respect to goals, feasibility, potential usefulness, employment of resources, time lines, and allocation of funds.

- *Encouraging interstate cooperation on unrestricted giving.* State councils can assist one another by sharing their individual knowledge about the major corporations and trade associations that have plants or offices in various states. Councils should also develop strategies (phone calls, letters, meetings, etc.) through which

200

contributing firms contact their counterparts in other states in order to broaden support.

- *Expanding unrestricted giving.* Since restricted giving is becoming more commonplace as a funding strategy than ever before, councils that must also rely on funds to support their general operating expenses may be finding it more difficult than before to obtain the necessary monies. The following guidelines should enhance unrestricted giving at all levels and, in the long run, strengthen public/private partnerships for DEEP:

— *Leadership.* Council directors and corporate leadership are crucial from planning to implementation. In some instances corporate leadership can serve in an honorary capacity to provide visibility and credibility to the campaign.

— *A well-conceived plan.* The plan should include the overall goal of the particular DEEP program, regional goals, types of giving (challenge grants, endowments, restricted giving, unrestricted giving, etc.), amounts to be sought from each prospective donor, and a time line.

— *A strong case for giving.* Stress should be on the vision and mission of the local DEEP program; the nature of the economic education problem; the program's financial needs—current and future; public acknowledgment (such as listing) of contributors; DEEP's results in terms of school, teacher, and student outcomes; and endorsements.

— *Well-developed fund-raising strategies.* Emphasis should be on personal contact. Report luncheons, letter writing, telephone calls, etc., should play secondary roles. Develop a list of large and/or steady contributors to get the strongest possible response.

— *A cadre of dedicated and trained volunteers.* Select individuals from different sectors of the economy who can best approach their counterparts in manufacturing, agriculture, agribusiness, labor, utilities, accounting, high tech, insurance, banking, etc., in order to raise funds from their own sectors of the local economy.

— *Timing.* Fall (October and November) and spring (March and April) are the most opportune times to raise funds for DEEP.

— *Quality public relations/fund-raising materials.* Such materials should be geared to each fund-raising strategy used and each type of contributor sought.

201

— *Strong university support.* Such support will provide a clear signal to potential givers that the university is willing to serve the community. University support also frees DEEP resources to increase or enrich DEEP educational efforts.

— *Active centers.* The stronger a local university center's programs are and the more active its center advisory board becomes, the more visibility, credibility, and commitments accrue to DEEP fund-raising campaigns.

—*Communication, follow-up, and recognition.* Continual communication with fund-raising volunteers, follow-up on non-responders to funding campaigns, and wide and full public recognition of givers/volunteers ensure continuing success for raising unrestricted funds.

Fund-raising efforts that use the foregoing hints and guidelines should broaden the base of support and strengthen the relationships among the Joint Council, its state affiliates, university centers, the private sector, and local DEEP programs.

THE ROLE OF PUBLIC SECTOR FUNDING

The success that the Joint Council and its state affiliates have enjoyed in raising funds for DEEP has a minus side. Because the Joint Council's funding endeavors have been successful, many school districts are happy with the status quo and feel that their own fund-raising efforts would be better spent to assist areas of the curriculum other than economic education.

Unfortunately, many state departments of education have the same inclination. Only 12 states provide any funding for teacher training by state councils. Many states that require economics do not support the necessary teacher training. They justify this omission on the ground that since the private sector benefits from economic education, that sector should fund it. For example, former Governor Jerry Brown of California several times "lined out" a special allocation in the state's budget for teacher education in economics. His reason was that business would pay for an economics program and that therefore public funds should be spent on educational programs that are less immediately attractive to the private sector. The rebuttal to this argument, of course, is that economic knowledge is, in many respects, a public good. When citizens—as consumers or as wage earners—exercise rational economic thinking, they benefit not only their employers, but also themselves, their families, their communities, their states, and their country. All these entities should help pay for economic education.

In 1985 the Joint Council revised its longstanding policy of opposing state-mandated economic education. The Joint Council now endorses such mandates, but vigorously recommends that if states feel strongly enough to require the subject, they should also help pay for the necessary teacher training and, if possible, the proper materials for economic education. These efforts should be matched by school districts. They should pay for teacher release time and other incidental costs associated with putting a quality economic education program into practice.

The case for state and local financial support for DEEP transcends the inherent worth of the subject matter. The fact is that the DEEP process also addresses most of the concerns of those school districts and teachers profoundly interested in the process of educational reform. DEEP treats teachers as professionals; it does not hand them a box of materials and expect them to replicate whole cloth a specific set of classroom exercises. DEEP allows—indeed it requires—teachers to learn while doing; it also gives teachers the necessary training and the necessary basic materials. DEEP individualizes teaching and learning. Consequently, the materials used in inner city New York and in Shawnee Mission, Kansas, cover the same conceptual base, but are not presented in the same way. The decentralized decision-making process used in DEEP also emphasizes continuing collaborative arrangements between universities and school districts. All the aforementioned features are considered essential by today's educational reformers, and all have been part of DEEP since the mid-1960s. DEEP's consistency with reform and the fact that economic literacy is extremely important are the major reasons why school districts and state departments of education should support DEEP.

SUMMARY

DEEP has a long and distinguished history as a partnership process. The program has maintained its intellectual integrity while, at the same time, meeting the explicit needs of teachers and school districts. Over the years it has also raised more private money for a specific discipline-based curriculum than have most other educational programs. At the same time, the process that makes DEEP so appealing to the schools—its attention to local needs and its general adaptability and flexibility—have seriously inhibited the raising of funds nationally. Similarly, the unique federalist structure of the Joint Council and its independent state and local affiliates already in place makes the additional division of labor between state and national offices required by DEEP difficult to maintain and enforce. These conditions have sometimes led to less than optimal funding for DEEP from the private sector.

DEEP has a solid future as a curriculum design and as a financial model. It offers a unique partnership that can be leveraged into significant funding dollars. But the days when all DEEP funding was generated by the private sector at the national or statewide level seem to be over. DEEP is too big, too complex, and, in the current competitive environment for private monies, not sufficiently appetizing to maintain the former pace of fund raising. Instead, the future of DEEP lies in a greatly increased number of local partnerships funded by local companies or branches of national companies, local foundations, state departments of education, and school districts themselves.

NOTES

The authors would like to express their appreciation to Michael Watts of Purdue University for his review of the first draft of this chapter.

1. The study was conducted for the Joint Council between February and May of 1985 and outlined potential strengths and weaknesses associated with a DEEP capital campaign.

2. Robert Mertz's (1989) article in the *Houston Chronicle* was one among many that investigated the impact of mergers on nonprofits. Others have appeared in the *Chicago Tribune*, *New York Times*, and *Boston Globe*.

REFERENCES

Business Roundtable (1973). *Report of the sub-committee on economic education.* New York: the Roundtable.

The Conference Board and the Council for Aid to Education (1988). *Annual survey of corporate contributions, 1987.* New York: The Conference Board.

Hansen, W. L.; Bach, G. L.; Calderwood, J. D.; and Saunders. P. (1977). *A framework for teaching economics: Basic concepts.* New York: Joint Council on Economic Education.

Joint Council on Economic Education (1986). Corporate executives say teachers can best provide education. Press release.

Mertz, R. (1989). Takeovers may impair corporate giving. *Houston Chronicle*, 1 February, 1.

National Commission on Excellence in Education (1983). *A nation at risk: The imperative for educational reform.* Washington, D.C.: U.S. Government Printing Office.

Rothman, R. (1988). Businesses refuse to sign Boston Compact II. *Education Week*, 9 November, 5.

Suglia, A. F. (1989). Terms, conditions, and salary data, state councils on economic education. New York: Joint Council on Economic Education. Typescript.

Walstad, W. B., and Soper, J. C. (1988). A report card on the economic literacy of U.S. high school students. *American Economic Review*, 78(2):251–56.

14. DEEP IN THE INNER-CITY SCHOOLS

by Judith Staley Brenneke

DEEP implementation is not simply the collection of a group of interested or trained teachers; it is the *systematic* inclusion of economics throughout the school curriculum, being taught by trained teachers. This systematic implementation of DEEP can be described by three basic models:

1. Implementation in a single discipline (such as social studies or business education) or at a specific grade level (such as twelfth grade)

2. Development of a model school using an exemplary economics curriculum which serves as a model for the rest of the district

3. Districtwide implementation, with the economics curriculum articulated across grade levels throughout the district

Two school districts, Cleveland Public Schools and East Cleveland City Schools, will be used to illustrate these processes, based on descriptions of the people and programs as of the spring of 1989. The basic characteristics of the school districts are reported in Table 14.1.

CLEVELAND PUBLIC SCHOOLS

While both of the districts are urban with a large minority population, one district, Cleveland Public Schools (CPS), is representative of the dominant large inner-city district. This district has had racial imbalance (which predicated federal district court control); teacher discontent, unionization, and strikes; a large bureaucracy; a limited general funding base with generous availability of special funds; politicization of the school board; and a high turnover of superintendents.

Working with any bureaucracy is difficult. The superintendent of the Cleveland Public Schools is vice-chair of the board of trustees of the Cleveland Center for Economic Education (CCEE) at John Carroll

206

TABLE 14.1
Characteristics of the School Districts

	CLEVELAND[1]	EAST CLEVELAND[2]
Year of DEEP enrollment	1974	1978
1988 student enrollment	72,116	8,170
Enrollment trend	declining	declining
Faculty size	4,689 certified 2,557 noncertified	500 certified —
Number of schools	128	10
Location	inner city	inner city
Estimated family income	low (60% daily free lunch)	low (75% daily free lunch)
Approximate racial composition	69.9% Black 23.5% Caucasian 5.2% Hispanic 1.4% other	99.5% Black 0.2% Caucasian — 0.3% other

1. This district has been under federal district court control since 1979 due to racial segregation. It was also placed in receivership by the Ohio State Department of Education from 1979 through 1987. The student retention rate for high school graduation in 1988 was approximately 43 percent. Reading scores in 1988 were drastically below grade. Between 1982 and 1987 the district had three superintendents, and continuing animosity between the superintendents and the school board was evident.

2. In 1988 the average classroom teacher had 158 semester hours of training and 11.25 years of experience. By the third year of "intensive DEEP implementation," six of the nine district personnel involved in the process had left the district (including the DEEP coordinator). Another two members of the district committee had advanced to administrative positions. The mobility rate of the student population in 1988 was approximately 27 percent.

University. The superintendent or a surrogate usually attends two-thirds of the center's board meetings during the year. In addition, the president of the Cleveland Teacher's Union serves on the center's board. The current DEEP coordinator is in a districtwide position with a portion of her district assignment being to coordinate economic education programs (she also coordinates law-related education and assists the social studies coordinator). The original DEEP coordinator (who served from 1974 through 1986) was the districtwide coordinator of consumer education and economic education.

207

However, districtwide supervisors/coordinators have limited power to effect change. They report to individuals several layers below the assistant superintendent for curriculum. To work directly with classroom teachers they must first work with seven cluster superintendents (the court subdivided the district into seven clusters with busing occurring between schools in each cluster) and then be *invited* into the individual school by the principal. Interaction among district supervisors themselves (economics, career education, social studies, mathematics, etc.) is negotiated due to the individual power base of each of these supervisors. Some of these relationships are cooperative; some are wary. All progress slowly because of the reporting structure and concerns about decisions of higher bureaucracy.

Seldom can decisions be made quickly—and almost never can decisions be made individually. Everyone in the system (classroom teachers, principals, cluster superintendents, etc.) must have decisions approved by someone else in the structure. Even the superintendent must clear decisions with the district court, the Ohio Department of Education, and an extremely strong school board. The success of district supervisors or coordinators depends on their ability to maneuver within the political structure and to identify and amass resources to carry out their desires.

The movement of classroom teachers and building administrators between buildings in the district is constant and is determined by district personnel and union contracts (not necessarily by building principals). Personnel changes often occur *during* the school year with little warning. This process is complicated by a lack of information and a delay in the formal distribution of information that is available. The informal chain of command and information is extremely active.

Because of this, DEEP curriculum development is approached tentatively and sporadically. Many times outside funding must provide the stimulus for curriculum revision. Although the identification of curricular areas to be addressed may appear to be haphazard, it is usually based on an analysis by content-area coordinators who are ready, willing, and/or able to cooperate in a revision. Because the CCEE staff members are seen as "outsiders" to the system, the administration tends to be somewhat wary of suggestions. However, because our active board of trustees is composed of local business, labor, and community leaders, we are also seen as a conduit to outside community involvement (an interest mandated by the district court). Likewise, since we are "outsiders," we can sometimes avoid the chain of command within the system. We can work directly with classroom teachers and many times use them to encourage building administrator support for our activities. However, every attempt is made to, at a minimum, make the DEEP coordinator aware of our activities throughout the system.

Last, but definitely not least, conducting an evaluation or any type of testing program is next to impossible. The district is "gun-shy" of any evaluation because of the past use of results from other disciplines or programs. The media are ruthless in headlining the most recent negative results from testing. Building principals are wary of evaluation, and classroom teachers are extremely defensive. The Office of Research and Evaluation, while knowledgeable about evaluation and research procedures, is so heavily involved in developing population statistics and mandated testing for the district court and the state that additional evaluation of classroom activities is not a high priority. If approvals from all levels are finally obtained for a testing program, if the building administration does grant approval for this testing, and if the classroom teachers *do* actually administer the exam, the chances are 50 percent that an "outsider" will ever actually see any resulting data.

Implementation in a Single Discipline or at a Single Grade Level

This approach to implementation has tended to be the most successful in the Cleveland Public Schools. The infusion of economics into the American history, consumer education, and career education curricula showed varying outcomes due to several factors. Primarily, the results of the implementation depended on the coordinator, the amount of staff involvement, and the economics background of all parties involved.

American History

The 1984 development of a new American history curriculum was coordinated by the district social studies supervisor (an individual highly respected by the social studies teaching staff). The project involved a teacher from each school and each grade level in a nine-month process. The development committee met weekly with center staff for a one-semester-hour course on teaching economics in American history. The participants were required to develop a classroom project for each unit introduced in the course as well as to fulfill university requirements for a graduate course. At the conclusion of the course, selected classroom teachers were invited to work during the summer to review, revise, and compile the classroom activities into an integrated elementary, middle, and high school teacher's guide. The production of this guide was under the direction of the social studies supervisor with the assistance of the center.

By the following fall, draft copies of the teacher's guide were available to every American history teacher in the district for their review and pilot use. After a one-year pilot, the district supervisor and several teachers reviewed comments and produced the final American history curriculum which continues to be used throughout the district.

Consumer Education

The 1985 consumer education curriculum revision was not as successful. The process was coordinated by the DEEP coordinator who personally had an appropriate background in economics. However, classroom teachers used in this project were not exposed to any significant amount of economics training either prior to or during the development of the curriculum. In addition, the actual curriculum was developed primarily by the district coordinator (with assistance from the CCEE) rather than directly by classroom teachers.

Thus, with minimal economics background, extensive prior experience with consumer concepts, and little teacher input into the development of the new curriculum, consumer education teachers throughout the district displayed minimal interest in the adoption of the new curriculum. In addition, four years after development of the curriculum, the Ohio Department of Education eliminated funding for consumer education and further lessened district interest in this subject. There was little indication that the economics included in the new curriculum was ever taught in the classroom.

Career Education

Ohio has had extensive funding for career education, with economic understandings being one of the seven basic teaching modules. However, seldom have career education coordinators had any background in economics. The CPS DEEP coordinator convinced the career education office that a career economics curriculum should be developed in 1986. The process was then directed by a career coordinator, with assistance from the DEEP coordinator and the center.

210

The process began with a one-day in-service for a select committee of classroom teachers (teachers with extensive contact with the career education office, but with minimal economics background). The CCEE attempted to present "all you ever needed to know about the economics of career decisions" during this day. After the one-day in-service, the committee of teachers, under the direction of the career coordinator (and with limited assistance from the DEEP coordinator and the center), then proceeded to produce a curriculum guide and a set of suggested teaching activities. A final copy of this curriculum and the activities has never been received by the center.

Summer UpBeat

This 1988 five-week summer program, developed for eighth grade nonpromotes, utilized CPS teachers and students, a curriculum developed solely by the CCEE, monies from the Job Training Partnership Act (JTPA), and the computer and organizing resources of a for-profit company with expertise in working with summer JTPA funds. Participants in this program were 275 students who had failed eighth grade and whose family incomes fell within JTPA requirements. These students were paid to work and to attend class during the five-week period. Their studies revolved around economics of the working world. Mathematics, science, and English skills were integrated into the classroom and were reinforced through computer-assisted instruction. Economics exams were developed by the CCEE for each week of the program. However, we received only 10 percent of the student test sheets from these exams. Apparently the teachers did not give the exams even though these exams had been approved by the district administration.

This was a massive, big-budget program, with 66 percent of the students being promoted to ninth grade on the basis of an evaluation of their mathematics and English course work. Although this project was apparently successful, with evaluation results that were positive, there is no indication that it will be continued during future summers.

Implementation Through a High School Economics Course

Economics is required to be taught in all the comprehensive high schools in the district. During the spring of 1984 the CCEE carried out a pre/postevaluation of student performance in the economics courses at six of the Cleveland high schools, using the *Test of Economic Literacy*

211

(TEL) and the *Survey on Economic Attitudes* (SEA). This evaluation was directed by, and at the request of, the same social studies coordinator who had conducted the American history project.

The cognitive TEL results show that the mean pretest scores were all substantially below the national norms for "students with no economics instruction." In addition, the results show that none of the six classes achieved the posttest norms on the test. In fact, the mean scores for two of the six classes actually *declined* relative to their pretest means.

On the "Attitude Toward Economics" portion of the SEA, two of the six classes showed *worsened* attitudes toward economics as a result of the course. On the "Economic Attitude Sophistication" portion of the SEA, three classes showed *worsened* economic attitude sophistication as a result of the course.

Shortly after completion of the evaluation, the social studies supervisor retired and was not replaced for a year and a half. The CCEE submitted a report to the district with the recommendations that a new high school economics curriculum be developed, that new texts be identified and purchased, and that a training program be required for all teachers of this course, and the center followed up with the new supervisor once he was in place. Finally, in the spring of 1986, a social studies department chairpersons' meeting was held where the results were released.

It was decided that a major proposal to accomplish these recommendations should be submitted by the center and the school district to local foundations. After one and a half years of negotiating with the district and pursuing the internal district approval process, the proposal was finally sent to the foundations which then promptly called the superintendent asking where this project fit in his priority schema. In part because of the low district priority, this proposal was never funded, and *none* of these steps was ever taken to improve the course.

Implementation Through a Model School

In 1980 the district (with the encouragement of the center) designated a single elementary school as a magnet school for economics and the basic skills. The Fundamental Education Center (FEC) program involved approximately 30 handpicked teachers, a building principal, an assistant principal, the district DEEP coordinator, and the CCEE. During the 1981–82 school year the CCEE conducted weekly training sessions on economics for the teachers in this school, a K–6 curriculum was

212

developed, and a culminating business-in-the-classroom simulation was set up throughout the school.

By the following fall, three-fourths of the original trained teachers remained in the school building. The CCEE conducted pre- and posttest evaluations in all classes; however, results from this evaluation were never released to the center. By the fall of 1983 less than half of the original teachers remained, and the principal and assistant principal had been replaced. An attempt was made by the CCEE to train teachers new to the building; however, these sessions were voluntary, and when only one or two teachers showed up, the sessions were discontinued. During the 1983–84 school year (with continued losses of the original teachers during the school year) the FEC decided to eliminate the economics orientation and concentrate on the basic skills. In 1987 the new principal of the FEC (the third since 1983) decided that the economics emphasis should be reinserted. However, a formal plan for training teachers was never completed (this was the first year for a new DEEP coordinator), and the economics emphasis resulted in the delivery of several classroom activities (the Stock Market Game and the CCEE's puppet show).

Due to the movement of teachers from one building to another at any time during a school year, it was determined that the model school approach is not feasible. New teachers did not have the background or the interest in pursuing economics in their classrooms.

Districtwide Course Work for Classroom Teachers

The Cleveland Public Schools have been in turmoil for at least the last ten years. The conclusion of three-year contracts many times has led to strikes. The union negotiated away teacher released time for training or personal development, while mandating extra teacher pay from the district for any in-house training programs (at a ridiculously low rate). Meanwhile, local and national foundations were extremely interested in helping this district. This meant a wide variety of funded programs were introduced into the district that offered graduate credit at no cost and with minimal requirements. The first time the CCEE attempted to offer a graduate-credit course in the district with the usual requirements (15 hours of course work for each semester hour, a project to be completed, and a final examination) we were laughed out of the building. Apparently in the prior year a funded program enabled the teachers to obtain a master's degree in one year with minimal (if any) class meetings and with credit based on their classroom teaching.

213

Although this kind of degradation of graduate credit has been reduced and the hiring of teachers without master's degrees has resumed, graduate credit continues to provide very little incentive for these teachers.

EAST CLEVELAND CITY SCHOOLS

The second district, East Cleveland City Schools, has had a more stable administrative structure and teaching staff. Although its minority population is 99.8 percent, test scores tend to be higher than in most inner-city schools, and, in fact, one of the elementary schools was designated as an Exemplary School by the U.S. Department of Education in 1987.

Although the district had been a DEEP district since 1978, minimal activities had taken place until the fall of 1982. The DEEP coordinator requested the development of an "intensive DEEP curriculum" tied to the district revision of the K–8 social studies curriculum.

K–8 Curriculum: Phase I

During the 1983–84 academic year, a curriculum committee for economics was established as a subcommittee of the district social studies committee. The chair of the social studies committee also served on the economic education subcommittee. This subcommittee, composed of ten people from the district (teachers, assistant principals, and districtwide curriculum representatives) and the codirectors of the CCEE, met for two to three hours every two weeks for eight months.

During this phase, a set of 11 generalizations (or Broad Understandings) that students leaving eighth grade should understand were developed. Competencies or objectives were then identified for each of these eleven generalizations. These competencies were written with the existing grade-level objectives in mind and were designed to be "testable" utilizing varied taxonomic levels of understanding.

Finally, the economic concepts to be used in the analysis of each objective were identified, and grade-level assignments were made for the introduction and basic mastery of each objective.

K–8 Curriculum: Phase II

During the spring of 1984 the teacher-training process began. Using the draft curriculum developed by the district subcommittee, teachers from the district were trained in the basic economic concepts to be utilized in the new curriculum through three-semester-hour graduate-credit courses conducted by the CCEE. From the spring of 1984 through the summer of 1985, about 90 teachers were trained through this process.

K–8 Curriculum: Phase III

Evaluation of students' preinstruction economic knowledge began in the spring of 1985 with the administration of nationally normed economics tests: grade 3, the *Primary Test of Economic Understanding*; grade 6, the *Basic Economics Test*; and grade 8, the *Junior High Test of Economics* and the *Survey on Economic Attitudes.*

In addition, information was obtained on general ability (through the use of standardized reading scores), socioeconomic status (using the "free lunch" variable), and student gender. A follow-up postimplementation evaluation of student progress was scheduled for 1988, but was never conducted.

1986 Qualitative Evaluation of the K–8 Curriculum

During the spring of 1987 a graduate student in the John Carroll University Department of Education, under the direction of the center, conducted an in-depth study of the K–8 curriculum implementation. The research procedures were based on the comparison of goals, objectives, and expectations for this curriculum, both written and expressed, with actual practices in the classroom. This research was accomplished through administration of a 22-item questionnaire, personal interviews with administrative personnel and classroom teachers, site visits to all eight schools, school and classroom observations, and an analysis of pertinent written materials.

Of the 171 teachers surveyed by the questionnaire, 66 percent responded. Nineteen personal interviews with classroom teachers were conducted (five with members of the original subcommittee). Also interviewed were five elementary principals, one middle school assistant principal, two curriculum specialists, two career economics facilitators, the district DEEP coordinator, and the district director of curriculum and instruction.

As stated by the administration and the teachers, the educational emphasis of the district was that of providing academic knowledge, essential life skills, and psychological support, with priority given to quality in reading, writing, mathematics, and critical thinking skills. However, among the teachers and principals, a complexity of differing

215

priorities emerged—each competing for time, program development, and highest priority. Approximately 80 percent agreed that economics could contain life skills and basic knowledge and thus would be of benefit to their students. About 75 percent of the teachers found their students to be "enthusiastic" or "interested" in economics.

Of those responding in the elementary schools, 29 percent used the DEEP economics curriculum in their classroom regularly, and 3.4 percent used it sometimes. Teachers felt that economics was not taught because of time pressures. Interviews with teachers revealed that the majority of teachers followed the textbook and that "the textbook manual was the curriculum." At the middle school level one-third of the teachers responded that they were "enthusiastic" about economics, with almost 90 percent of the teachers claiming they had taught some economics in their classes.

More important, both teachers and principals concurred that social studies and economics were not priorities of the school administration even though they *were* stated as such. In the scarce curricular space of the elementary school, the basic skills of reading, language arts, and mathematics held higher priorities. Standardized achievement tests were administered in all subjects at the end of every school year, but economics was not included in the social studies test. The teachers expressed their need to teach what would be tested; therefore, their teaching emphasized the topics and skills that would be included in the standardized tests.

1988 Revision of the Social Studies/Economics Curriculum

By the fall of 1986 the DEEP coordinator had retired, and a new coordinator had been selected. She had *not* worked on the 1984 K–8 development subcommittee. During the 1987–88 school year the district was scheduled to revise the K–8 social studies/economics curriculum. A committee was selected, and the curriculum was revised. The DEEP coordinator was unhappy with this revision so she asked a classroom teacher with a master's degree in economic education to assist with further revisions. Although the CCEE continues to work closely with the new DEEP coordinator on a variety of projects, we were not asked to help with this revision process. The center has not yet seen the newly revised curriculum; however, since no one on the original subcommittee served on the 1988 revision team, the suspicion is that little of the original economics curriculum remains.

216

SUMMARY AND CONCLUSIONS

Inner-city schools have problems common to other districts. They also tend to have additional problems caused by sheer size, the socioeconomic backgrounds of the students, media exposure, the politicization of the educational process, and expansive bureaucracies.

- As with most DEEP implementation projects, the success or failure of the process is dependent on the district personnel to be involved. The center for economic education can offer expertise, materials, ideas, and possible funding to assist the process. However, the center is an "outsider" and must be invited into the district to be successful.

- Dropping an existing program into the district (such as the Cleveland Summer UpBeat) may be successful in the short run. But in the long run it will disappear unless nurtured from within the system.

- Formal curriculum development can be accomplished—but formal curriculum does not necessarily dictate district priorities or what will be taught in the classroom.

- Teacher training in economics is essential to classroom implementation. However, with the aging master's-degree-plus teacher population, there is little incentive for teachers to undertake additional training in anything, let alone economics. Additional incentives, beyond graduate credit, must be identified for teachers to learn and teach economics.

- The only way to ensure that economics is taught is through district or statewide testing and evaluation. As long as teachers are held accountable for their students' test results, these teachers will teach what is to be tested. Likewise as long as economics is not included on the tests, it will remain a low teaching priority.

A successful DEEP curriculum implementation project may be accomplished. However, schools tend to be cyclical in their interests and approaches—therefore, this successful curriculum may be forgotten in a short period of time.

To continuously have an impact on education, we must increase our efforts in pre-service training, materials and audiovisual development, competency testing in economics, and, most important, textbook revision. Reaching teachers while they are still impressionable, providing new and innovative materials to catch the classroom teacher's attention, ensuring that economics has a high classroom priority through testing, and making certain that economics plays a major role in textbooks used in the classroom are all essential. We, unfortunately, will never be successful enough to "work ourselves out of a job." We must be in the schools every year encouraging the teaching of economics and providing assistance to do so. The teaching of economics, unfortunately, can be described as "out of sight, out of mind." Meanwhile we must demand quality and accountability in all our efforts—from ourselves and from others with whom we are working. Our resources are too scarce to require anything less.

15. THE URBAN DEEP EXPERIENCE: SAN ANTONIO, TEXAS

by Howard R. Yeargan

San Antonio, located in the southwest part of Texas, is on the cultural boundary between the Hispanic culture along the U.S.-Mexican border and the Anglo culture of northern Texas. With a population of 786,023, San Antonio is the third largest city in Texas and the eleventh largest city in the United States, according to the 1980 census. Metropolitan San Antonio, including its 30 suburbs, encompassed an estimated 1.31 million people in 1987.

THE ENVIRONMENT AND ECONOMIC EDUCATION

While the state of Texas has a population that is 21 percent Hispanic, the population in the city of San Antonio is 53.7 percent Hispanic. The metropolitan area's Hispanic population is diluted to 51.5 percent. Either way, Hispanics are the dominant "minority" in San Antonio.

San Antonio, with five Air Force bases and one Army post, has long been known as a military town. More recently there has been some diversification, and it is also a major trade center for most of south Texas and northern Mexico. Still, San Antonio has a low per capita income, ranking 23rd out of 30 standard metropolitan statistical areas in Texas.

Public education throughout Texas is produced by political subdivisions of the state called independent school districts. They each levy and collect ad valorem taxes on real property located within their boundaries. The state, through an elected state board of education, provides additional funding to these local districts based on a legislated formula. In 1984–85 there were 1,059 such districts in Texas.

Economics is mandated in the state curriculum. In 1981 the Texas legislature passed a statewide curriculum law that mandated a one-semester economics course for high school graduation and the inclusion of economic topics at all grade levels. The specifics of the new curriculum were left to the state board of education. After a series of statewide meetings which included economic educators, the "essential elements" of the new curriculum were adopted. The new curriculum specified what the content of the high school course would be. In addition to the concepts recommended in the *Master Curriculum Guide* of the Joint Council on Economic Education, the state curriculum also specified a number of consumer and personal finance topics.

The state mandate started many, many school districts "teaching" economic concepts for the first time. The law made no provision for implementing the new curriculum. Specifically, no teacher-training programs were even suggested. Since economics historically had not been in university pre-service teacher-training programs, many totally untrained teachers were faced with the prospect of teaching economic concepts that they had never studied and often did not understand themselves.

Several universities are located in San Antonio. The University of Texas has a branch in San Antonio. There are also three four-year, private, church-affiliated schools and a large multicampus community college. All of the universities have economics programs at the graduate and undergraduate levels, but none of them has specifically developed economic education programs for teachers. One exception was a foundation affiliate of Trinity University which developed some curriculum materials under a three-year grant from the Greater San Antonio Chamber of Commerce.

Southwest Texas State University (SWTSU) is located in San Marcos, Texas, 49 miles from San Antonio. This is about midway between Austin, the state capital, and San Antonio. SWTSU is considered a comprehensive regional university. It has an enrollment of just over 20,000 students.

Southwest Texas State University has a long history as a teacher-training institution. It was founded in 1903 as a state normal college and since that time has often produced more teachers each year than any other institution in the state. Prior to the establishment of a Joint Council–affiliated center for economic education in 1981, the center director had worked in the economic education field since 1970. Weekend programs offered for high school students evolved, because of the multiplier effect, into weekend programs for teachers. When the need for a longer-term relationship became apparent, summer workshops for teachers were begun. Six such programs were conducted prior to the establishment of a center. Therefore, the DEEP process in San Antonio

220

did not begin from a zero base. Many programs and relationships had been developed and maintained prior to the first DEEP affiliation.

Another factor in the economic education environment in San Antonio is the large number of Junior Achievement (JA) programs in San Antonio schools. During the 1987–88 school year there were 161 Applied Economics classes (5,039 students), 120 Project Business classes (3,611 students), and 169 Business Basics classes (4,623 students) in metropolitan San Antonio. The center programs were in place prior to the introduction of the JA classes. The JA area executive contacted the center, and the two have maintained a cooperative arrangement from the beginning. The center has done several teacher-training programs for JA teachers.

THE DEEP PROCESS

Five of the seventeen independent school districts in metropolitan San Antonio have become affiliated with the Joint Council network as DEEP districts through the SWT Center for Economic Education. This section will describe the process of their affiliation.

The Initial DEEP District

The initial DEEP recruitment approach was to select one of the smaller districts in metropolitan San Antonio to be the pilot affiliate. This would permit the center to learn about DEEP implementation without risking overcommitment of resources. Several conversations with persons in the local educational establishment led to the selection of Judson as the pilot district.

With a student population of 12,591, Judson is the sixth largest district in metropolitan San Antonio. Its ethnic mix is 64 percent Anglo, 21 percent Hispanic, and 11 percent Black, which is closer to the state average than the San Antonio metropolitan average, which shows a 49.3 percent Hispanic school population. While Judson is a suburban district, its boundaries do include some significant industrial/commercial areas. It also serves a wide variety of income groups and neighborhoods. It has 1 high school, 2 junior high schools, and 11 elementary schools. There were 800 faculty in the district.

One of the most significant characteristics of the district is that the central administration explicitly attempts to be a leader in curriculum areas. Largely because of this, DEEP recruitment was relatively easy. Prior to, and in anticipation of, the results of a needs assessment, the district decided to begin the DEEP process by encouraging a number of elementary teachers to participate in the next three-week summer program the SWT center conducted. One of the encouragements was that the district paid a travel stipend to cover the cost of the daily 100-mile commute.

With district encouragement, 12 Judson elementary teachers participated in the 1982 Summer Economic Institute. This was the initial economic education experience for most of these teachers. Five of the eleven elementary schools in the district were represented. The result of this experience was positive and is still being felt within the district and beyond. A group of four teachers from one school developed a comprehensive schoolwide economics program which is still in place. Other individual teachers developed units that were successful and have been emulated by others. One kindergarten teacher not only developed a highly successful unit for kindergarten children, but also has done a large number of in-service programs for peers inside and outside the district. More recently, she has become a regional educational leader as president of the university's Teacher Council.

After the district became a DEEP affiliate, a needs assessment was conducted during the fall 1982 semester. The instrument used was based on the listing of economic concepts shown in Part I of the Joint Council's *Master Curriculum Guide*. It asked every teacher in the district which of these concepts they were teaching presently and which ones they might teach with additional training.

Based on the results of the needs assessment, five half-day and two full-day in-service workshops have been conducted for Judson teachers. Four of the half-day workshops were for elementary teachers; the two full-day workshops were for high school teachers. One of the high school workshops presented the *Give & Take* video series when it was new. The other high school program was A Day at the Fed, held in cooperation with the San Antonio Branch of the Dallas Federal Reserve Bank. Additionally, Judson teachers have participated in a number of other center-conducted workshops which also included teachers from other school districts.

Judson teachers have participated in six full-semester classes for graduate credit conducted through the SWT Center for Economic Education. Twelve of these were the elementary teachers who attended the previously noted 1982 Summer Economics Institute. The other 14 were secondary teachers who enrolled in night classes such as consumer economics forums and economics, energy, and environment courses. Ten district teachers have had classes participate in the Securities Industry Association–sponsored Stock Market Game.

In addition to teacher-training activities, the SWT center director made 18 separate consulting visits to central administrative and school personnel. These visits ranged from brief planning sessions for various programs to a full-day, joint grant-proposal-writing session. Beyond this, the center called on the area chamber of commerce several times to secure community support for economic education in general and to obtain financial support for two elementary programs conducted in district schools. Two service club presentations were also made to enlist community support for DEEP affiliation.

The results of these efforts have been measured only anecdotally. The first noticeable change has been in the interest in economics on the part of faculty members. The programs done with elementary teachers in the district have decreased the "economic hostility" so often found in uninitiated teachers. Several of them have begun encouraging their colleagues to undertake economic topics in their classes. One teacher in particular has done several in-service presentations.

Of the original 12 elementary teachers enrolled in the three-week summer program, half were still teaching in the district after seven years. Each of these has taught the unit(s) he or she developed as a result of the summer program. Two have submitted these units to the Texas awards program that is preliminary to the national Joint Council program, and one of these projects has received honorable mention in the state contest. In conjunction with that award, the teacher and some of the children in the project made a presentation to the local school board. This created a very favorable impression on the part of board members and central administrators. Additionally, a local chamber of commerce executive, who had been involved with securing some financial assistance for this project, was so pleased with its outcome that he wrote and sent out a news release about it. The news release was picked up on a news wire and was printed in several newspapers far away from San Antonio. In fact, the story was mentioned by Paul Harvey on his nationally syndicated radio program.

Several junior high school teachers have written economics curricula for their grade levels and are successfully incorporating economics into their history classes. The state curriculum does not provide for separate economics classes at the junior high school level. It does specify economic essential elements that are to be taught in these grades.

In the high school the social science faculty has gone from an overt avoidance of teaching economics to a situation where one teacher has volunteered to teach an advanced placement class. Others within the department are now teaching economics and incorporating economic concepts into their world history and American history classes.

Significant strides have been made in this district to increase and enhance the teaching of economics. DEEP put a focus on this objective and has helped to achieve it.

The Second DEEP District

The second school district to affiliate as a DEEP district was Northside. With 46,822 students, Northside is the second largest district in metropolitan San Antonio. Northside has not only four times the student enrollment and faculty of the Judson district, but also double the proportion of Hispanic students, 43 percent. Its 7 high schools, 9 middle schools, and 39 elementary schools serve a very large geographic region that is the fastest-growing area in metropolitan San Antonio.

The DEEP recruitment here began with several teachers from the district who had participated in center-conducted classes. They communicated their interest in becoming a DEEP district to their administration. Contact with the secondary social studies supervisor was established, and after investigating the initial district's affiliation, he became highly supportive of affiliation. Given the size of the district and the limited resources of the SWT center to service its needs, the original DEEP plan was to focus on secondary education.

Immediately after affiliation, a DEEP committee was formed with representatives from each of the district high schools. After looking at several alternatives, this group decided that the needs assessment for their district should involve districtwide testing at the high school level to determine which economic concepts were being taught and which needed strengthening. They developed a test for this purpose which combined materials from the Joint Council's *Test of Economic Literacy* with test items developed by the committee.

The test results revealed a desire to strengthen the money and banking section of the high school course. Based on this finding, the program called A Day at the Fed was arranged for teachers in the district at the San

224

Antonio Branch of the Dallas Federal Reserve Bank. In-service programs dealing with *Give & Take* and *Tax Whys* were also conducted through the center. The thrust is now turning to the elementary grades where, until now, very little has been done in an organized fashion.

As with the first district, the results of DEEP have been measured only by anecdotal means. For instance, the enthusiastic incorporation of *Understanding Taxes* in one teacher's class led to her appearance on a television program dealing with the use of these materials. Another district teacher has become very well known for the development of curriculum materials for the high school course. Still another has begun to use the new advanced placement materials and is scheduled to make a presentation on these to a state economic education meeting in the near future. These and other similar stories seem to indicate that DEEP has had a positive influence on the quantity and the quality of economic instruction in the district. Given the programs in other disciplines such as history, geography, and government that compete for teachers' time and attention, economic instruction might well have suffered without the attention that DEEP affiliation has focused on the subject.

The Third DEEP District

The third DEEP affiliation in the San Antonio metropolitan area was the suburban Seguin district, with a student population of 6,722 in one high school, two middle schools, and nine elementary schools. Like the Judson district, Seguin has a very progressive administration, eager to maximize the students' academic opportunities. After an inquiry from the district curriculum director in January, the district moved quickly to affiliate as a DEEP district in April.

A full-day in-service program was conducted for elementary and high school social studies teachers at the beginning of the next school year. Several elementary teachers began economics units immediately. Further workshops and consulting visits were made to two of the nine elementary schools. One of these schools has undertaken a schoolwide economics program which culminates in using their annual Halloween carnival as an economic market for the "goods and services" produced by each class's "corporation." When two teachers from another elementary school completed their units, they felt that they were so successful that they submitted them to the state awards program. They won second-place honors and made outstanding presentations about these units to the annual meeting of the Texas Council on Economic

225

Education (TCEE). Another teacher participated in the center's 1988 Summer Economics Institute and has become a positive force for economic education in her elementary school.

Two teachers are involved with the required high school economics course at the single district high school. One of these teachers has been a most enthusiastic participant in the Security Industries Association Stock Market Game since its beginning. The other has completed a center-conducted graduate class in anticipation of teaching an advanced placement economics class. Additional teachers at the elementary and high school levels have participated in center classes, as has the director of vocational education for the district.

It is clear that smaller districts can achieve momentum faster than can the larger ones. Results are also more easily recognized and communicated to the community at large.

The Fourth DEEP District

The third largest district in San Antonio was the next district to affiliate with the DEEP program. The North East district, with 38,688 students, formally affiliated at the 1989 annual meeting of the state council. North East, with 27 percent Hispanic students, has a Hispanic proportion lower than Northside, but somewhat higher than Judson. The district includes 6 high schools, 8 middle schools, and 26 elementary schools.

The recruitment of this district came from within. Over the years a large number of North East teachers have participated in center programs and have learned about the DEEP designation from these. They, in turn, have recommended to central administrators that they investigate DEEP affiliation. When a new school superintendent familiar with DEEP was employed, the district decided to become a DEEP affiliate.

A districtwide DEEP committee will be formed and the planning process begun as it was in the Northside case. The plans developed by this group will guide the DEEP process in the future.

The Fifth DEEP District

Finally, the largest district, San Antonio, has also become a DEEP district. Affiliation occurred in August 1989, and the planning process is beginning. The district is the third largest school district in Texas, and its affiliation will push the number of students in DEEP schools in Texas over the one million mark.

Recruitment of San Antonio came largely from within the district. After many teachers and the social studies coordinator had participated in SWT center programs, they became advocates for DEEP affiliation. However, it took over four years for the district administration to decide to affiliate. During that period of time Joint Council and TCEE staff met with various administrators to explain the benefits and responsibilities of being a DEEP district. A meeting of the TCEE and center directors and the school superintendent was the final step prior to the decision to affiliate.

The San Antonio district serves 61,501 students, 80 percent of whom are Hispanic. It has 9 high schools, 17 junior high schools, and 70 elementary schools. The size of this district poses a significant challenge to the center to service its economic education needs.

SUMMARY AND CONCLUSIONS

DEEP recruitment thus far has been intentionally tentative. The major limitation has been the capability of the SWT Center for Economic Education to deliver programs and services. It is widely felt by center directors in Texas that their credibility is at stake when DEEP schools affiliate with their centers. Therefore, many have moved rather slowly so as not to promise more than they could deliver.

In metropolitan San Antonio, recruitment has been largely determined by school district inquiries or previously developed linkages from programs conducted over a 15-year period. The DEEP districts thus far do not include the richest or poorest districts. Neither do they represent the highest or lowest Hispanic concentrations. They represent districts where the center already had a high degree of credibility from previous programs.

The experience thus far seems to indicate that the size of the district is much more important than its Hispanic composition is. Hispanic teachers, students, parents, and business people seem to be no different from their Anglo counterparts with regard to economic education. There are those who enthusiastically support economic education. There are those who strongly favor no changes in the curriculum. It is likely that it is not "economic education" that fosters this attitude. Rather, it is some general resistance to any change. Some of this resistance may stem from the political polarization of elected school boards. In other cases it simply reflects an institutional rigidity toward change. Clearly, the attitudes and outlooks of the people involved are the most critical element in DEEP affiliation.

Progressive teachers, administrators, and parents can see the importance of economic literacy for Hispanic children in much the same way Anglo teachers, administrators, and parents do. Ethnic background has little apparent impact on their attitudes. While one might make an argument for bilingual teachers and materials at very early grades in some schools, economic education is no different in this regard from any other subject area. Except for language, there appears to be no difference in capabilities related to ethnicity.

16. DEEP IN THE LARGE CITY DISTRICT

by James Dick

The Omaha Public Schools (OPS) were among the original Developmental Economic Education Program schools when DEEP was created in the mid-1960s. Under the leadership of Dr. Norman Sorensen, the OPS social studies supervisor, the district sought to improve the teaching of economics. Teacher-training workshops were offered to district teachers at the Center for Economic Education at the University of Nebraska at Omaha (UNO) with support by the Nebraska Council on Economic Education (NCEE). An economics course was offered as an elective for seniors in the district's high schools; economic concepts were also incorporated in business education courses. The district's interest in and commitment to economic education remained at this level throughout the 1970s.

A renewed concern for economic education emerged in the early 1980s under the leadership of Gary Caldwell, Sorenson's successor as social studies supervisor for the district. Caldwell, while serving on an education subcommittee of the Greater Omaha Chamber of Commerce, convinced the chamber representatives of the need to go beyond the existing community support for economics in the schools. He encouraged the committee to provide teacher training in addition to continuing to provide guest speakers and field trip sites and to sponsor business/education days. The committee, with financial support from the InterNorth Foundation, agreed to Caldwell's proposal. This community support provided the basis for greater infusion of economics throughout the scope and sequence of the OPS curriculum, the training of many teachers, and the development/adoption of new curriculum materials and teaching strategies. As a result of these efforts, based on strong support from the school administration and the community, OPS was selected as an outstanding DEEP district by the Joint Council on Economic Education in 1988. At the National School Boards Association's annual meeting in New Orleans, OPS was recognized as a true DEEP school district with a long-term commitment to comprehensive economic education.

The Center for Economic Education at UNO was a strong partner in

229

the efforts to improve and expand economic education in OPS. The center, which languished during the 1970s, was revitalized as the Omaha schools developed a renewed commitment to economics. In cooperation with the Chamber of Commerce education subcommittee, the Center developed the first teacher-training program, a three-week summer workshop for secondary teachers in 1981. Follow-up activities for teachers were conducted during the 1981–82 school year; a second summer workshop was conducted for elementary teachers in 1982. The center's work with the Omaha schools has continued to the present day.

THE NATURE OF THE SCHOOL SYSTEM

The Omaha Public School District is the largest in the Omaha metropolitan area; the population of the metropolitan area including Council Bluffs, Iowa, is over 600,000. The economic base of the community is very diversified with over 15,000 businesses. Omaha is the corporate home of Union Pacific Railroad, Mutual and United of Omaha, and ConAgra; 44 of the Fortune 500 companies have manufacturing operations in the metropolitan area. The employment pattern is as follows: service 26.8 percent; trade 25.6 percent; government 15.0 percent; manufacturing 11.3 percent; finance, insurance, and real estate 9.6 percent; transportation, communication, and utilities 7.6 percent; and construction and mining 4.1 percent (Greater Omaha Chamber of Commerce, 1988).

The district enrolled 41,251 K–12 students in 1989. Of those students, 24,678 were in grades K–6, and 16,573 were in grades 7–12; 67.7 percent of the students were white, 26.7 percent Black, 3.1 percent Hispanic, 1.3 percent American Indian or Alaskan Native, and 1.1 percent Asian or Pacific Islander.

On the California Achievement Tests, OPS students in grades 2–6, 8, and 10 exceed the national norms. Students' scores on the American College Testing (ACT) profile are at the national norms; 56 percent of the seniors take the ACT. Student performance on the Scholastic Aptitude Test (SAT) exceeds the national norms; however, only 13.6 percent of the seniors take the SAT. The 1987 graduates of the district pursued the following activities: 49.3 percent attended colleges or universities, 3.7 percent attended business or trade schools, 22.1 percent were employed full time, 9.7 percent were employed part time, 4.8

percent were unemployed, 6.0 percent entered the armed forces, and the status of 4.4 percent was unknown.

There are over 2,800 teachers and administrators in the district. The pupil/teacher ratio is 18.6:1 in the senior high schools, 17.1:1 in the junior high schools, and 22.2:1 in the elementary schools. Approximately 50 percent of the teachers have completed the master's degree or a higher degree; about one-third of the teachers have taught 17 or more years in the district (School District of Omaha, 1988).

In the district there are 7 senior high schools, 10 junior high schools, and 57 elementary schools, plus alternative high schools and a career center. District enrollment reached a peak of 63,000 in 1970; after a period of sharp decline, enrollment has leveled off at approximately 42,000. OPS is a member of the Organization of Great City Schools and is accredited by the North Central Association and the Nebraska Department of Education.

In 1976 the U.S. Court of Appeals for the Eighth Circuit ordered the district to prepare a desegregation plan to address racial balance in the district. The court withdrew its mandatory busing order in 1980; however, the district has continued its desegregation efforts including creating magnet elementary schools in minority neighborhoods and busing students to achieve racial balance.

THE DEEP IMPLEMENTATION

During the last eight years OPS has revised its curriculum to include economics at all grade levels from K through 8 and to incorporate more economics into social studies courses in grades 9 through 12. The high school economics course for both regular and honors students was redesigned for tenth graders. Also, at the high school level, the business education department has completed curriculum revisions that incorporated more economics and new materials into the business education courses. The purpose of these efforts is based on the following curriculum goals of the school district:

- To help students become citizens who understand and apply the principles of economics; and

- To prepare students for effective economic decision making, thus developing responsible citizenship.

231

With a grant from the NCEE and with assistance from the UNO Center for Economic Education in 1984, OPS curriculum supervisors, under the leadership of Gary Caldwell, the social studies supervisor and DEEP coordinator, reviewed the existing curriculum and developed plans for infusing more economics into the K–8 curriculum. Curriculum planners including supervisors and teachers developed new curriculum guides based on *A Framework for Teaching the Basic Concepts* (Saunders et al., 1984) and other materials from the Joint Council. These efforts complemented earlier curriculum revisions in the district.

At the same time the district began to implement Outcome Based Education. This program, which incorporated mastery learning, provided specific objectives at all grade levels and in all courses. Tests were designed to determine if students had achieved the objectives, and remediation strategies were developed for those students who initially did not achieve the objectives. Specific economic objectives were incorporated into Outcome Based Education: All K–8 teachers are required to include economics in the social studies or CORE curriculum, and all 9–12 social studies teachers must include economics in their course objectives. There are also economics objectives in appropriate business education courses.

The school district conducted a series of staff development programs to make teachers aware of the K–8 curriculum guide and the 9–10 social studies curriculum guides that outlined the economics objectives incorporated into Outcome Based Education. Special sessions on using the computer to teach economics were conducted for the teachers of the senior high school economics course. Many other teacher-training activities have been conducted within the district and in cooperation with the UNO Center for Economic Education. Over 150 OPS teachers have completed the UNO economic education course for teachers, a three-week graduate-credit course that is offered each summer. Over 300 teachers per year attend after-school workshops conducted by the UNO center. These workshops have focused on using Zooconomy to teach economics, the infrastructure, international trade, using local museums to teach economics, and using the newspaper to teach economics. At the beginning of the 1987–88 school year, the UNO center conducted a workshop for the district's business education teachers at the Federal Reserve Branch Bank. Field trips to the Kansas City Federal Reserve Bank have also been provided for teachers.

The district has implemented DEEP through additional strategies:

232

- The OPS DEEP coordinator attends planning meetings conducted by the UNO center.
- Project Business is a part of the eighth grade CORE program; Junior Achievement is available for senior high school students.
- The high school economics course based on the Joint Council's *Framework* and *Master Curriculum Guide* was revised, and an honors course was created. Teachers of this course have evaluated the Joint Council's *Master Curriculum Guide* prior to publication.
- The Joint Council's *Framework* was used as part of the criteria for evaluating high school textbooks.
- Microcomputer materials for the high school course were developed by David Ross, a high school economics teacher. Ross was a coauthor of the microcomputer guide published by the Joint Council.
- An economics section was incorporated in the *River City Roundup Guide.* This guide for upper elementary students is used during the annual festival that celebrates the city's western heritage.
- After attending workshops and courses conducted by the UNO center, many teachers have contacted the center to use a variety of curriculum materials including *Give & Take*, *Trade-Offs*, and *Income/Outcomes.*
- The business education department participates in the Academy of Finance Program.
- There are honors sections in the high school economics course and applied social studies courses for basic students.

RESULTS OF THE DEEP IMPLEMENTATION

Economics is included in the social studies and CORE curricula for grades K–8; as a result, over 29,000 students receive instruction in economics. In grades 9–12, economics is infused into social studies courses, and there is an elective one-semester course for sophomores. All students must take geography in the ninth grade and American history in the eleventh grade. These course requirements and social studies electives increase the number of students affected by the OPS economics program. Additional students receive economic instruction in business education courses. Counting the number of students at the high school

233

level without double counting is difficult, but one can conclude that a high percentage of secondary students in the Omaha Public Schools receive instruction in economics each year.

Benchmark tests were created as part of the Outcome Based Education program; these tests are given in each course, or at each grade level, at the end of the semester, and the results are added to the district's student achievement records. Where appropriate, questions for various tests prepared by the Joint Council were incorporated into these exams. Some economics teachers in OPS also participated in the development of the revised version of the *Test of Economic Literacy* (TEL) published by the Joint Council. Test results using the TEL with tenth graders indicated that students made significant gains in their understanding of economics.

Information collected from teachers who attended summer courses conducted by the UNO Center for Economic Education indicated that these teachers increased their understanding of economics, developed more positive attitudes toward economics, and understood how economics could be incorporated into their classrooms. Teachers also gave high ratings to the after-school workshops conducted by the UNO center.

As a result of the variety of curriculum development efforts, the district and the teachers at all grade levels have won Cooper Awards, Nebraska's awards for outstanding economic curriculum development. Omaha teachers have made presentations at local, state, regional, and national professional meetings, describing their successful curriculum development projects. Teachers and supervisors have written individualized instructional materials, microcomputer materials, curriculum guides, and articles for the state social studies journal.

The Omaha School District has indicated its support for economic education. The board has endorsed a statement of educational goals that includes goals for economic education and also has endorsed K–12 curriculum guides that contain specific economic objectives.

Dr. Norbert Schuerman, the superintendent, is an active member of the board of trustees of the NCEE. He has assisted in fund raising for the Nebraska council and has spoken at DEEP recruiting luncheons sponsored by the UNO center. He is currently a member of the state legislature's Committee of Education and Economic Growth.

Superintendent Schuerman, in remarks prepared for a luncheon honoring the district when it was selected as an exemplary DEEP school district in 1988, stated:

234

...DEEP has provided our classroom teachers with extremely valuable teacher/student materials. These materials range from nationally normed tests to student activities and lessons which definitely can be utilized in the classroom.

DEEP has been very helpful and instrumental in providing teacher economic education for hundreds of our teachers in the form of staff development, college credit and other in-service activities. (Schuerman, 1988)

The district has identified a DEEP coordinator. Released time and travel funds are provided so the coordinator can attend both local and national economic education meetings. The district has also provided released time for teachers attending workshops conducted by the UNO center. Professional growth credit and salary increases are provided for these teachers who participate in the center's teacher-training programs. Funds have been made available to purchase curriculum materials at all grade levels.

The NCEE and the UNO center have provided and continue to provide support for economic education in the Omaha Public Schools. Each semester the NCEE conducts the Stock Market Game for students. The NCEE also provides a tuition subsidy to OPS teachers who complete the UNO summer course and subsidizes the costs of the after-school workshops. The UNO center's program coordinator plans workshops and other activities for OPS teachers, provides materials, duplicates tapes, and consults with teachers. Requests for guest speakers are also handled by the coordinator's office. The UNO center has supported a variety of student programs including the junior high school computer fair; Handelmass, a simulated trade fair for foreign language students; History Day; and awards to the outstanding economics student in each of the district's high schools.

The Omaha community has provided extensive support for enhancing economic education in the Omaha Public Schools. As described earlier, the InterNorth Foundation and the Omaha Chamber of Commerce provided funds to revitalize the UNO center. Omaha businesses, agencies, and institutions including Mutual of Omaha, the Joslyn Art Museum, U.S. West, and the Federal Reserve Bank of Kansas City–Omaha Branch have provided financial and human resources to support improved economics programs in the schools.

The *Omaha World-Herald* and Kirkpatrick Pettis Smith Polian Inc. cosponsored the Stock Market Game each semester. The newspaper also funded the development of a curriculum guide on *Using the Newspaper to Teach Economics* and cosponsored a series of related teacher workshops. Many local business representatives have served as guest speakers in classrooms; several businesses that are adopt-a-school partners have provided resources for economic education. The Cooper Foundation in Lincoln provides awards each year to foster curriculum development projects in economics. There is widespread coverage of school economics programs in the newspaper and on the local television stations.

FACTORS CONTRIBUTING TO DEEP SUCCESS

Probably the most important reason for the success of DEEP in the Omaha School District was the critical role played by the secondary social studies supervisor. Gary Caldwell had both a personal and a professional interest in economic education; he majored in economics and taught high school economics courses before he became a curriculum supervisor. Caldwell, a link between the district and the community, and between the district and the UNO center, identified key teachers who were opinion leaders in their buildings to participate in the early stages of the program. He recruited other supervisory colleagues as participants in center workshops and courses. He was responsible for making certain that economic goals and objectives were included in the district's curriculum scope and sequence. He even taught an economics class for high school honors students while carrying out his supervisory duties.

The support of School Superintendent Schuerman helped to ensure the success of DEEP in the Omaha schools. He participated in several activities to publicize the role of economics in the curriculum, including making public service announcements that were shown on television stations across the state.

The initial involvement of key teachers in the district also helped to make DEEP successful. Such involvement increased the credibility of DEEP projects and materials throughout the district. The UNO center staff continues to work with these teachers to create awareness of new materials and strategies. These teachers have participated in local curriculum development projects and in NCEE and Joint Council curriculum development projects including the revisions of the *Test of Economic Literacy* and the *Test of Economic Knowledge*. These key teachers are invited to be presenters at workshops and courses sponsored by the UNO center.

236

The success of DEEP can also be attributed to the incentives made available to the district and to individual teachers. The original funds from the InterNorth Foundation and the follow-up support from the Omaha Chamber of Commerce and other businesses made possible the first two summer courses for teachers. Tuition was subsidized; businesses provided guest speakers, lunches, and sites for field trips. As a result, the teachers felt good about their experiences, were excited about teaching economics, and encouraged colleagues to enroll in future courses. The NCEE, with funds provided by the Joint Council, supported the development of the K–8 curriculum guide in 1984–85. Supervisors and teachers also received awards from the Cooper Foundation, the sponsor of the statewide curriculum development competition. Some teachers, as mentioned earlier, have participated in Joint Council projects, and other teachers have made presentations at regional and national economic education meetings. The school district or the NCEE covered their travel expenses.

Another reason for the success of DEEP in Omaha was highlighted by Superintendent Schuerman. DEEP is a process, not a prescription; local autonomy, exceptionally important in Nebraska schools, was assured. The center, with the support of the NCEE and the Joint Council, made an extensive variety of curriculum resources available to the district. However, the final curriculum decisions were made by teachers, supervisors, and administrators in the district. This approach, which differs from those of other groups promoting economic education, was compatible with the approach to curriculum development that existed in the district (Schuerman, 1988).

The opportunity provided by the district's commitment to Outcome Based Education was another reason for the success of DEEP. This commitment provided an opportunity for curriculum revision that could incorporate a comprehensive economic education program across the curriculum.

RECOMMENDATIONS FOR DEEP ENHANCEMENT

In the second and third sections of this chapter, the nature of DEEP in the Omaha schools and its effects have been presented. However, the most innovative feature of OPS is that it truly is a DEEP school district. The program is comprehensive; economics is integrated throughout the curriculum. The program was developed by the school district in cooperation with the UNO Center for Economic Education and the NCEE. In addition to the comprehensive K–12 program, there are areas where economics has been highlighted. The school board and the superintendent have a strong interest in and support for economic education; there is strong community support also.

The results of these efforts to improve economic education should become more evident as the district completes the implementation of its economic education program and Outcome Based Education and as it continues its commitment to DEEP. Being selected as an exemplary school district in 1988 is evidence DEEP in OPS has been a success.

While the success of DEEP in the Omaha schools has been acknowledged nationally, there is a need

- to provide additional in-service work to help teachers fully implement the economic objectives for grades K–6.
- to develop closer relationships among the K–6 curriculum supervisors, the CORE supervisor, and UNO center staff. While there are extensive working relationships with the secondary social studies supervisor and the business education supervisor, the supervisors at the primary, elementary, and junior high school levels are not as aware of DEEP and the resources available at the UNO center.
- to develop closer ties between OPS staff development specialists and the UNO center so that economic education in-service programs can be developed specifically to meet district needs.
- for the district to document the impact of its economic education program by examining student scores on the various districtwide tests. It would be advantageous to use tests developed by the Joint Council on Economic Education to determine how the district compares with the national norms.
- to attract more teachers to workshops and courses offered by the UNO Center for Economic Education. The codirector of the center is well aware that the center's programs tend to attract the same group of teachers over and over. There are many more teachers who are unaware of, or lack interest in, the center's economic education courses and its workshops.
- for the center and the NCEE to continue to provide incentives to encourage teacher participation in economic education programs.

- for the center to make new curriculum materials and other resources available to teachers. This is particularly important in grades K–8 where teachers need to know how to infuse economics into the existing curriculum.
- to find overall strategies for continuing the district's commitment to K–12 economic education after being recognized for its efforts by the Joint Council. This is important so that the district will not be content with its current program. Continuing curriculum improvement in economics may be difficult since other areas in the social studies, especially history and geography, have been identified by several national organizations as areas needing curriculum reform. Global educators are also calling for curriculum reform. In the midst of these concerns, the district must not lose sight of the importance of economics.

REFERENCES

Greater Omaha Chamber of Commerce (1988). *Trends in the Omaha economy.* Research Report no. 206. Omaha: the Chamber of Commerce.

Saunders, P.; Bach, G. L.; Calderwood, J. D.; Hansen, W. L.; and Stein, H. (1984). *A framework for teaching the basic concepts.* 2d ed. New York: Joint Council on Economic Education.

School District of Omaha (1988). *Statistical and financial facts 1988–89.* Omaha: the School District.

Schuerman, N. J. (1988). Remarks at economics luncheon, Omaha.

17. ECONOMIC EDUCATION IN SUBURBAN SCHOOL DISTRICTS: THE CLOVIS DEEP EXPERIENCE

by Don R. Leet and Peter G. Mehas

This is a case study of DEEP in the Clovis Unified School District, a relatively large suburban school district in central California. By outlining the process we went through in this case, we hope to offer some guidance to educators who face similar conditions today. Our story is not one of great success in the face of adversity, but rather one of seizing the opportunities presented to us and then building on the natural strengths of the district and the community.

A PORTRAIT OF THE SCHOOL SYSTEM

The Clovis Unified School District has a student population of approximately 20,000 students. It is located in the Central San Joaquin Valley adjacent to the city of Fresno. For much of its history the district was classified as largely rural in nature. However, for the last 20 years it has been directly in the path of urban development. As the city of Fresno grew northward, developers built acres of housing tracts where grapevines and orchards of fruit trees once stood. The rural nature of the district was largely replaced by a suburban environment, although pockets of agriculture exist to this day.

District Size

The Clovis Unified School District had almost 14,000 students when it entered DEEP, compared with more than 20,000 today. It is a rapidly growing district with 15 elementary schools, 2 intermediate schools, 2 high schools, a continuation school, and an adult school. Within the next five years the district expects to build six elementary schools, one intermediate school, and one high school.

Ethnic Composition

The composition of the students in the district is fairly typical of a suburban, middle-income community in California. Almost three-quarters of the students are classified as white. Hispanics, the second largest ethnic group, comprise about one-sixth of the students. Asians are the third largest group with a 9 percent share, while Blacks and American Indians make up equally small shares of the student population.

Special Circumstances

The Clovis district was led by a very talented superintendent, Dr. Floyd Buchanan. He emphasized the importance of excellence in the basics long before such programs were fashionable. As a result, the pupils in this district could be expected to be on grade level in reading, writing, and mathematics. He also initiated a competition model of testing whereby the results of districtwide classroom tests were reported by school. This added a component of accountability for teachers and school-level administrators that proved very helpful with DEEP. Lastly, the district had a history of being willing to cooperate with the university and the private sector.

INITIATION PHASE: PRE–DEEP

Clovis DEEP began with a meeting between the coauthors of this article and Gary Fisher, chairman and chief executive officer of Fisher Industries, one of the largest employers in Fresno at that time. Fisher was convinced of the need to improve the level of economic literacy among the population, but he was skeptical of the long-term impact of programs like Junior Achievement. After he was apprised of the Developmental Economic Education Program, he was willing to fund the planning phase with the understanding that he would support a larger project if it proved meritorious. Thus, with an initial grant from Fisher Industries, the Fresno Center for Economic Education and the Clovis Unified School District began the task of evaluating the state of economic education in the Clovis district in March 1981. A task force of teachers and administrators was formed with three goals: first, to survey the school district for current economic education content; second, to evaluate the level of economic knowledge among Clovis high school students; and third, to complete the evaluation process and present recommendations by June 1981.

Task 1: Economic Education in the Clovis Curriculum

The task force reviewed economic education in the school district's K–12 curriculum. At that time there were no designated curriculum guides that even mentioned economic education at the elementary or intermediate level. At the high school level some economic concepts were taught in elective courses in the home economics and business departments, but the only required courses that had a significant economics component were geography, American history, and American government. Even these courses had no systematic treatment of economic concepts. The only students who received a solid background in economics were those who elected to take an optional one-semester course in economics that was offered by the social science department. Given the nature of economics and its placement at the high school, the task force recommended that the social science strand be designated as the major area through which economics should be integrated into the curriculum.

Task 2: Evaluating Economic Knowledge Among Clovis Students

The task force decided at an early stage that the best way to evaluate the level of economic literacy among Clovis students was to identify the basic concepts that *all* Clovis students should understand and then devise a test that would establish how close students were to this level of competency. The members of the task force unanimously agreed that such a test should not go beyond a "minimum skills" level. They also agreed that the test should be administered to the students in the ninth and twelfth grades as well as to the students in the economics elective course. It was believed that the ninth grade students would be representative of students who had completed their elementary economic education, but who had only limited experience at the high school level, whereas the scores of the twelfth grade students should indicate the extent of economic education after four years of secondary education. The juniors and seniors who took the optional high school economics course were included as a benchmark for what could be expected from high school students in this district who devoted an entire semester to the economics course.

242

Identifying the Elements of Economic Literacy

There was considerable discussion about what constitutes a minimum level of economic literacy, and the task force agreed to accept the list of economic concepts as they appeared in the first edition of *A Framework for Teaching Economics: Basic Concepts*, one component of the Joint Council on Economic Education's *Master Curriculum Guide*. In addition to these basic economic concepts, the task force wanted some test of how prepared these students were to function in their roles of consumer, investor, producer, and citizen. To this end they decided to include questions on budgeting, credit, insurance, consumer protection, fringe benefits, social security, and the advantages of incorporation.

Creating the Evaluation Instrument

There are many ways to evaluate the knowledge of a student population, but in the interest of ease of scoring and national comparability, the task force chose to use 30 multiple choice questions. Given the emphasis on minimum skills, they decided to discard many of the more theoretical questions and concentrate on the application-oriented questions. On the other hand, preference was given to test questions in the Joint Council's *Test of Economic Literacy* because it had been administered nationally and thus offered a benchmark for judging the performance of Clovis students.

Administering the Test

In order to avoid the problem of test fatigue—when a student is simply too tired or unmotivated to answer a lengthy series of questions on an unfamiliar subject like economics—the task force chose to divide the test into three equal parts. Thus, most students were given only a ten-question test that was easy to administer. The exceptions to this testing rule were the students in the optional economics class who took the entire test during a regular class period. All students who were tested fell into one of three groups: freshmen, seniors, or economics students.

Evaluating the Results

The results of the tests gave us confidence in the validity of our evaluation process. The ninth grade students were least informed about economics and answered only 46 percent of the questions correctly, while the twelfth grade students averaged 59 percent correct, and the economics students achieved a 68 percent average. Thus, we concluded that Clovis high school seniors were more economically literate than their freshman counterparts were, but that neither group was as knowledgeable as students who took a separate course in economics. It is interesting to note that these findings are consistent with more recent research (see Chapter 7 in this volume). Since most of the questions used on the task force test were taken from nationally normed tests published by the Joint Council, the responses of Clovis students could be compared with those of a national sample of students. The results indicated that ninth grade Clovis students were about as proficient in economics as ninth graders in the national sample were. Clovis freshmen scored higher than their national counterparts did on 9 of the 18 questions where comparative test data were available for ninth grade students. With respect to those questions taken from the *Test of Economic Literacy*, the ninth graders scored higher than the national sample did on only two questions, but we should remember that the TEL comparison group was composed of eleventh and twelfth grade students. Clovis seniors scored above the nationally normed sample groups on 20 of the 30 questions. These results indicated that economic education was stronger at the secondary than at the elementary level.

Diagnosing Strengths and Weaknesses

While the economic education test indicated that Clovis students were at least as able as their national peers were, the evaluation also pointed out areas of weaknesses. Even on some of the very basic questions, less than one-third of the ninth and twelfth grade students chose the correct answer. When the task force members presented their recommendations to the school board, they were able to illustrate the unevenness in the average Clovis student's economic understanding.

Task 3: Recommendations

The task force concluded its report with a series of recommendations for upgrading and improving the level of economic instruction within the Clovis School District over a three-year period. These recommendations included in-service teacher training, new curriculum guides, and the development of economic education materials for elementary, intermediate, and secondary levels. In order to achieve these goals, the task force recommended that the district utilize the DEEP model:

There are many ways that we could achieve our goal, but none offer the range, scope and promise of a nationally tested process known as the Developmental Economic Education Program (DEEP). DEEP is an acronym for a cooperative venture that was first designed by the Joint Council on Economic Education to assist school districts in building more economics into their curricula from kindergarten through grade 12.

The Clovis School Board accepted the recommendations of the economic education task force and applied for official designation as a DEEP district. Fisher Industries agreed to fund the implementation portion of the program with the understanding that the district would assume the costs of maintaining the program in future years.

IMPLEMENTATION PHASE

The implementation phase is the most important part of DEEP. The structure of the organization, the plans, and the impressions that teachers and administrators have about DEEP are all formed early in this phase. We took extreme care to select key people and programs that we felt would maximize the impact of DEEP without threatening other programs or unsettling teachers. We also had the advantage of a grant from Fisher Industries that gave us a nondistrict-bound budget as well as local community involvement. The grant required us to report on our progress to the grantor as well as to the school board, and it held the promise of three years of outside funding before the school district was required to assume full costs of maintenance.

The Steering Committee

At the district level the responsibility for the success of DEEP rests largely with the Steering Committee, which is the chief organizing body for the implementation phase of the project. Selection of the members of this committee is crucial to the overall program. The committee was chaired by a district-level administrator who was responsible for the program and was designated DEEP coordinator. Our Clovis DEEP coordinator proved to be a self-starter who was adept at resolving conflict and was respected equally by administrators and teachers. The director of the Center for Economic Education at California State University (CSU), Fresno, served in an ex officio capacity on this committee in

245

order to provide advice and economics expertise to the committee, but not to direct the committee. The associate director of the center also provided valuable input to the committee from the standpoint of a professor of education. Nevertheless, it is important to note that DEEP is a cooperative venture, not one where an outside agency attempts to impose a curriculum on a school district. In the Clovis case the composition of the remainder of the committee ensured that all areas of the district would be represented. We had teachers from each major grade cluster: K–3, 4–6, 7–8, and 9–12, as well as an elementary and a secondary principal. The senior high school teachers had formed the nucleus of the economic education task force group, and two were chairs of the social studies department in their respective high schools. The elementary teachers selected were excellent teachers who were highly respected at their school sites. Ultimately, it was the quality of these people that ensured the success of the program. The steering committee reviewed the work of the earlier economics task force and agreed to a three-year time line for implementation. The first year would be devoted to establishing a K–12 scope and sequence for the district as a whole, with subsequent years to be devoted to writing and then implementing economics units at each major grade cluster: K–3, 4–6, 7–8, and 9–12.

The model adopted in the Clovis district had five major components: (1) in-service training for key teachers at a selected grade level, (2) curriculum units written by these teachers, (3) pilot testing of these specific units, (4) revision of these units, and (5) districtwide in-service training on and implementation of the units.

Teacher Training

Teacher in-service training is a key to any economic education program, but it is especially crucial in a K–12 program because the teachers trained by the center will use their newly acquired expertise to write and evaluate curriculum materials and to offer training sessions to other teachers. Thus, it was especially important to see that we had teachers who were good candidates to be trainers of teachers and curriculum developers as well as being gifted classroom teachers.

Identifying Key Teachers

We used the expertise of members of the Steering Committee to identify key teachers who might be interested in working on an

246

economics curriculum project. These teachers were contacted and then asked to meet with the Steering Committee to ascertain their interest and abilities with regard to the project. We were subsequently able to identify some of the most qualified teachers in the district. Given our outside funding source, we were also able to offer tuition scholarships for economics classes and to pay those teachers who developed and evaluated economic education materials. By offering these teachers additional compensation for working on DEEP, we made it clear from the outset that we valued their professional opinion. Furthermore, we demonstrated that we understood that there was an opportunity cost to the time they spent on DEEP.

University Courses

In the fall semester of the first year of implementation we offered DEEP scholarships to secondary social science teachers who participated in our three-unit course on teaching economics in American history. These teachers used this experience to write and then pilot economics units in the American history courses offered at the high school level. In the summer of the first year we offered scholarships to eight elementary-level teachers who attended our three-unit summer course on teaching economics. This course proved extremely valuable in many ways. First, it stimulated the elementary teachers into thinking about economics as more than "the dismal science." Second, the teachers' enthusiasm generated a variety of avenues for infusing economics into already established elementary subject areas such as language arts, mathematics, music, and literature. Third, it provided these key teachers with an economic knowledge base that served as a touchstone for future learning and instruction. To this day, the most enthusiastic support for DEEP in the Clovis School District comes from the elementary teachers.

In the second year of implementation we offered scholarships to our fall and spring weekend courses on economics, and six teachers were given full scholarships to attend our three-unit summer course. The teachers from the two intermediate schools (grades 7–8) were engaged in writing curriculum units that summer for pilot testing in the fall. In the third year of implementation our university courses offered economic instruction that correlated with the units that had been written for the elementary and intermediate levels. These classes were generally held on weekends or during in-service days when the teachers were released from the classroom and paid by the district to receive economics training.

Curriculum Materials Development

Some school districts are intimidated by the thought of having to create new economics education materials. They fear that their resources are already too scarce to afford themselves the luxury of tailoring materials to suit themselves. Nevertheless, a basic statement about what topics and concepts are appropriate at each grade level—in other words, a scope and sequence—would seem to be the least that each district should produce. Beyond this minimal level, districts can adapt and adopt previously developed materials and teaching strategies. In the Clovis case, the district probably developed more original materials than most DEEP districts would.

Scope and Sequence

During the first year of implementation the Clovis program created a scope and sequence document that integrated the basic economic concepts found in the Joint Council's *Master Curriculum Guide* with the *California Social Science Framework*. The Clovis scope and sequence included generalizations and specific examples of each concept that was considered appropriate for each grade level. It served as the base for the curriculum work that followed. By creating it, the curriculum committee learned a great deal about the logic and structure of our discipline. Now, of course, there is the Joint Council's publication *Economics: What and When* that can serve as a guideline for K–12 economic instruction. Nevertheless, it would still be beneficial for individual districts to carefully compare their current offerings with the suggested guideline as part of their initial process. If our experience is any indication, the learning gain will be significant.

Elementary-Level Materials

The K–6 level experienced the greatest activity in the Clovis DEEP. In particular, the teachers at the primary (K–3) level took some of the most fundamental economic concepts and demonstrated that even very young students could comprehend and apply them. Clovis DEEP published its own handbooks of suggested teaching strategies for both the primary and the upper elementary grades. The primary material was largely developed by three very gifted teachers: Carol Bloesser, Julie Hollenbeck, and Jan Stafford. The upper elementary grade handbook depended more heavily on outside material like the *Trade-Offs* film series.

248

Secondary-Level Materials

The secondary teachers made significant use of the *Give & Take* film series. During the second year of DEEP implementation a separate economics course was taught at the seventh grade level, using the *Our Economy* textbook. High school faculty members never developed a complete set of materials, although they did make extensive use of the Joint Council's strategy guides on U.S. history and world studies.

Materials Dissemination

The materials developed for the elementary level were disseminated via workshops for teachers at those grade levels. In the third and final year of implementation, economics resource teachers were identified at each elementary school site and designated to provide additional training for new teachers unfamiliar with DEEP. In retrospect, some of the elementary materials may have simply overwhelmed the classroom teachers, especially those at the upper elementary level. The size and weight of some of these volumes proved too imposing. In some schools the principals proved to be less cooperative and placed less emphasis on DEEP-related activities. In these cases economics became more of a voluntary activity that was highlighted in some teachers' classrooms, but not in others.

RESULTS OF DEEP IMPLEMENTATION

Looking back on a process that began almost a decade ago gives one a chance to develop a more long-term perspective. Some of the changes that seemed dramatic at the time have faded a bit. Other forces that were only barely perceived have risen in importance and have been shown to play a key role in a successful DEEP. In this section we outline a few of these factors.

Changes in School Curriculum

The most dramatic changes in the school curriculum occurred at the primary grades where social science instruction had been conspicuous by its absence. The primary grade levels were to incorporate a significant amount of economics into the curriculum by infusing it into language, art, music, literature, and mathematics. At the upper elementary level the

Trade-Offs series and the activities that were developed to accompany that series formed the backbone of the economic education experience. At the intermediate level the *Give & Take* series was heavily piloted, but never found a home in the social science curriculum. At the senior high school level the U.S. history and American government courses both had their economic content greatly improved as a result of DEEP. Ultimately, the connection between Clovis and the CSU Center for Economic Education helped the district to adjust to the state-mandated high school economics course that is currently in place.

DEEP proved the harbinger of other long-run changes in the Clovis district. For example, after DEEP implementation it was easier for other social science disciplines to gain recognition in the elementary curriculum. History, geography, government, and even sociology became part of the social science strand. Ultimately, the district developed grade level objectives (GLOs) in each social science discipline. The scope and sequence guidelines for economics were transformed into economics objectives for each grade. The district then developed tests to evaluate the success of each high school in teaching these objectives.

Student Test Scores

The Clovis student body has generally tested at or above the norm in all subject areas, just as the economic education task force discovered in its assessment of economics at the high school level. At the end of the three-year implementation process, the DEEP Steering Committee recommended that minimal competency tests be administered at grades 3, 6, 8, and 12. As they wrote in their *Progress Report*, "The DEEP Program cannot continue to show sustained progress without some regular evaluation of its impact on Clovis students."

The recommendations of the Steering Committee spurred the district to administer a social science examination for grades K–6, 8, and 11. Scores on the economics component are reported separately for grades 3 and above. In addition to this in-house testing program, a separate measure of the quality of economic instruction can be found in the California Assessment Program (CAP) test for grade 8. This test is administered at every public school in California and has a separate reporting category for economics concepts. The Clovis social science CAP scores are consistently above the state averages (e.g., 292 versus 253 in 1987–88). Moreover, economics has consistently been listed by these tests as an area of relative strength within the district.

Awards

The credibility of a program cannot be established simply by bestowing an award on it. Nevertheless, awards can be indicative of the underlying merit of the program and its participants. Clovis DEEP has garnered its share of national honors. Some of the original teaching strategies developed by primary-level teachers in the district won awards in the California Council on Economic Education Awards Program (first place) and the International Paper Awards Program (second place and honorable mention). Several of these strategies have been published in *The Elementary Economist.* In addition, the Leavey Award for Excellence in Private Enterprise Education was awarded for this project.

Maintenance

The ultimate test of the success or failure of a program is its ability to withstand the tests of time. Educational history is littered with the bones of projects that were abandoned shortly after outside funding disappeared. In the case of Clovis DEEP, however, this problem was addressed very early in the process. The economic education task force report that first recommended a formal DEEP for Clovis also contained a section on maintaining the program after outside funding ended. That report was adopted by the school board and supported by the superintendent. At the end of the third year of implementation the DEEP Steering Committee recommended that the district provide the DEEP coordinator with an annual $10,000 budget. As a result, DEEP remains as a separate budget item within the district. These earmarked resources allow district economics teachers to offer workshops, evaluate and purchase economics materials, and generally maintain the economics program developed during the implementation phase.

RECOMMENDATIONS

Although the Clovis School District cannot stand as an archetype for all districts, its DEEP experience has resulted in some important suggestions for school districts in other circumstances.

- *Partnership of school district, university, and private sector.* The partnership of the school district, the university, and the private sector was one of the strengths of the program. The strengths of each group were combined to the benefit of all. The outside funding and the planning and implementation phases enhanced the accountability of the academic partners, just as the additional resources made the task more manageable. Thus, we would recommend that whenever possible DEEP should involve some level of community-based private sector funding. This not only enhances the resource base, but also provides an added level of accountability.

- *Monitor the progress.* The Clovis program made annual progress reports from the initial planning stage throughout the implementation stage. Members of the school board as well as Fisher Industries were kept informed of the progress. A base line of students' economic literacy was established early in the process, and both teachers and administrators were aware of the evaluation component. It would be difficult to create and maintain DEEP if there were no way to monitor student achievement.

- *Use of the infusion model.* When DEEP began in Clovis there were no district guidelines for social science at the elementary level. DEEP blazed the social science trail by illustrating how an important subject could be embedded while teaching mathematics, reading, and language arts. Later this proved very helpful to other social science areas, and economics was considered a fundamental segment in this area. In the district today it is not uncommon to find economic concepts infused in science units on ecology or in art units on museums. The infusion process offers the best opportunity for teaching economics at a variety of grade levels.

- *Human resources.* The key resource for any DEEP is high-quality human capital. Clovis was fortunate to have a group of highly dedicated teachers who were skilled at learning economics and then developing strategies for the classroom. To ensure a quality program, the in-service workshops must be carefully designed with input from the classroom teachers. But the economics curriculum itself is not a matter of negotiation—DEEP empowers classroom teachers with methodology and content in economics. We found that the most successful workshops are the ones that combine teaching methods with economic instruction.

- *District commitment.* In the long run, DEEP can succeed only if the school district itself sees that the benefits of the program outweigh the costs. But if there is community support, if the local center for economic education maintains contact, and if the teachers themselves see economic education as part of their mission, then it is very likely that the school district will continue to do its part to supply resources to DEEP. In the Clovis case these long-term resources have made an important impact on the maintenance phase. By allocating specific funds to the DEEP coordinator, the district is demonstrating its commitment to economic education. We strongly recommend that DEEP receive a separate allocation within the district budget to maintain its profile within the district.

SUMMARY

The Clovis DEEP succeeded in a district that had many advantages. Nevertheless, we believe that districts with fewer endowments could benefit from our experience. The community-university-school partnership that DEEP represents is not unique to Clovis. The potential is available to all school districts. We believe this is one of the great unlocked treasures of the DEEP program. If local community involvement such as we had with the sponsorship of Fisher Industries could be achieved in a given school district, then the potential of DEEP could be translated into action. Of course, resources and local interest are not enough. You also need to provide opportunities for your local teachers and administrators to improve their own economic understanding through formal and informal meetings and workshops. Finally, and just as importantly, you must monitor and report on the progress of the schools in implementing the economics curriculum. These three key ingredients—partnership, human capital, and evaluation—are the mainstay of a successful DEEP program.

18. DEEP IN A RURAL SCHOOL DISTRICT: THE MARION COUNTY, TENNESSEE, EXPERIENCE

by Lucien Ellington with Willie Mae Beattie

In spring 1984, the Marion County (Tennessee) School District and the University of Tennessee at Chattanooga (UTC) Center for Economic Education began an effort to implement DEEP in the social studies curriculum in grades 1–12 in all schools in the district. Five years later, although we still have not fully achieved this goal, our program is quite viable and has received national recognition.

This chapter is an account of our experiences from 1984 until the present. The process by which DEEP was begun and expanded, classroom economic education activities, and evaluation procedures are described. Because Marion County is typical in many respects of the "average" rural district, particular attention is given to both positive and negative aspects of our experience which might be useful to other rural school districts. Before dealing specifically with economic education in Marion County schools, it is worthwhile to consider what general characteristics of the rural school environment tend to help or impede curriculum development.

The small size of many schools and communities is perhaps the biggest educational advantage of a rural setting. Goodlad (1984) is only one of a number of educational researchers who in recent years have found parents, students, and educators to have higher satisfaction levels in small rural schools than in larger urban ones. It is almost impossible to overstate the educational advantages that can accrue because rural schools and the communities they serve are usually small enough that people know each other personally. Large school central office bureaucracies, which often stifle new curricular innovations, are generally not a problem in rural areas. Also, rural educators can often easily draw community resources because of the regular personal contacts that often occur among a variety of people in rural environments.

Lack of adequate economic resources is a major problem that confronts most rural school districts. Because true rural (as opposed to suburban) districts are usually poor, educators often teach outside of their content fields. Also, rural teachers perform a variety of other tasks that are ordinarily the responsibility of central office personnel, guidance counselors, assistant principals, or teacher aides in larger districts. Because teachers are expected to do so much in rural schools, opportunities for professional development such as attending conferences and engaging in reflective reading are rarer for rural educators than for their urban counterparts. Lack of funds also means a chronic short supply of instructional materials and technology.

This general description of the inherent opportunities and problems of rural education is quite accurate when applied to Marion County schools. The Marion County School District consists of ten schools which serve about 5,000 students. Marion County (approximate population 24,500) is located in the mountainous, southeastern portion of Tennessee, 30 miles from the city of Chattanooga. There is little industry in the county, and most residents are small farmers, work in wholesaling or retailing, work in coal mining, or commute to manufacturing or service jobs in Chattanooga. The unemployment rate for Marion County averages 4 percent higher that the state rate, and approximately one-fifth of the students in the district come from homes below the federal poverty line.

Because Marion County schools lack adequate resources compared to what is present in more affluent districts, teachers must cope with the same workloads and materials shortages faced by most rural teachers elsewhere.

INITIATION AND IMPLEMENTATION OF DEEP

In spring 1984 Marion County administrators were invited to plan and implement a DEEP project by UTC's Center for Economic Education. The major reason for the invitation was that the district, only one of a number in the center's service area, had a demonstrated prior interest in economic education. The interest had been fostered over several years, primarily through teacher participation in summer economic education workshops held at the university. A cadre of about 15 teachers existed in the district who had received training and were utilizing center services such as audiovisuals and print curriculum materials.

Because development, implementation, and evaluation of a comprehensive economics curriculum are quite complex, it is highly recommended that a district first develop a group of trained teachers through cooperative efforts with a university center for economic education. In our case these teachers, through both their expertise and their positive attitudes, helped to create positive receptivity to economic education among their colleagues.

Although the associate director of the cooperating university center, along with a central office administrator, developed an initial DEEP proposal, teachers were involved early in the planning process. In fact, teachers were given the opportunity, which was not exercised, to reject the very notion of a DEEP project if they so desired.

The original proposal called for the initiation of DEEP in three schools: Jasper Elementary School, Jasper Middle School, and Marion County High School. These were selected because a number of faculty at each school already had training in basic economics, and the schools and the district central office were in the same community which facilitated communication and coordination among various school personnel. In the late spring of 1984 teacher representatives from the three schools met with the associate director of the UTC center and central office staff to listen to the proposal.

The proposal called for the formulation and implementation of an economics component in all social studies classes in the three schools during the 1984–85 academic year. The Marion County elementary social studies program closely follows the Tennessee framework which is based on the expanding horizons curriculum. The secondary curriculum consists of required state history, civics and world history electives, and required American history and capstone economics.

The UTC center agreed to provide a $10,000 grant the first year for teacher training, curriculum materials, and ongoing assistance at school sites. In return, the school district agreed to evaluate economic education programs and to provide release time when possible for teachers to work on the DEEP project. It was understood that if the first-year program was satisfactory to all concerned, the UTC center would appropriate approximately $3,000 annually for the project and that DEEP would be expanded until eventually all district schools would be included.

Faculty representatives conveyed the essentials of the proposal to their colleagues and took an informal poll of all primary school teachers and of middle and secondary social studies teachers to determine if they wanted DEEP. Teachers at the three schools were generally enthusiastic about the proposal and voted to accept it.

Staff development was a crucial initial task. Several teachers from each of the three schools received tuition scholarships and modest stipends to take the summer economic education workshops offered through the university. The UTC center in 1984 also brought nationally recognized economic educator Marilyn Kourilsky, who developed the middle school simulation Mini-Society (Kourilsky, 1983), to the university for a summer workshop and arranged for several Marion County elementary teachers to attend.

Also, the associate director of the center conducted several half-day in-services for teachers at each of the three schools shortly before the beginning of the school year. A major purpose of these in-services was to enable teachers to work with colleagues to develop in each school a rudimentary economics scope and sequence for use during the upcoming school year. A second purpose was to introduce teachers who had no previous training in economic education to such economics materials as the Joint Council on Economic Education's *Master Curriculum Guide* series, *Trade-Offs*, *Give & Take*, and Mini-Society.

The actual scope and sequence that resulted from these in-services took the form of economic concept lists developed by the associate center director and participating teachers. These concept lists, which were developed for each social studies subject, represented the minimal economic content students would be taught in the coming year. Concepts that were placed on the lists were drawn from the Joint Council's curriculum guides, and a deliberate attempt was made by the UTC center and central office personnel to keep the amount of economics that teachers were required to cover modest, particularly in the early grades. For example, second grade teachers were expected to cover only four concepts: scarcity, opportunity cost, division of labor, and production and consumption.

This strategy was based on a recognition of several school realities. In grades 1–3 in Tennessee, teachers spend, on average, slightly less than 30 minutes a day on social studies due to pressure to prepare students for state-mandated basic skills tests in reading and mathematics. If primary school teachers had been required to spend large amounts of time on economics, teacher stress levels would have greatly increased, and probably faculty hostility toward DEEP would have been created. However, from the beginning, elementary teachers who were most enthusiastic about DEEP spent much more time on economics than the four to five hours a year needed to teach the concept lists.

257

In middle and high school, because of greater class time for social studies, the complexity and amount of economic concepts that were considered to be a "floor" for Marion County to be a viable DEEP district increased moderately. For example, world history teachers were expected to cover seven economic concepts including economic systems, economic development, and productivity.

The relatively conservative number of concepts required of teachers reflects another reality about the process of curriculum development. Despite high levels of general enthusiasm about economic education in Marion County schools, some teachers, for various reasons including ignorance of the subject, interest in other social sciences, and resistance to change, were not particularly enamored with economics. The small numbers of required concepts have proved to be nonthreatening to such teachers, and over the years several have, of their own volition, increased the amount of classroom time spent on economics. Because attitudes of teachers about any new educational innovation are usually mixed, and because rural teachers often tend to be quite conservative about changing curriculum, it is highly recommended that rural educators who are initiating DEEP programs consider the merits of a limited set of content requirements for all teachers.

The levels of enthusiasm and attention given any curriculum project, not only by teachers but also by central office staff and university personnel, are critical to eventual success or failure. Administrative support for teachers is usually a problem in rural districts because of the numerous tasks assigned to the typically few central office administrators.

In Marion County there is only one instructional supervisor for the entire district. While this staff person was instrumental in getting DEEP into the district, her workload made it impossible for her to provide the regular assistance in the schools that teachers needed. Marion County was fortunate during the first year of DEEP in that the associate director of the UTC center had substantial release time from university teaching to work in the district.

During the 1984–85 school year the UTC center's associate director spent approximately two full days a month in the schools working with teachers and conducting demonstration lessons in classrooms. After the first year the center continued to provide teacher support by hiring a retired high school economics teacher as a part-time consultant. The consultant, who is a county resident, works with teachers and students and is responsible for several administrative tasks including planning and evaluation. Given the situations most rural central office staffers face, if rural educators desire to implement a comprehensive economic education program, it is highly recommended that the option of using a retired teacher as a consultant be examined. The Marion County DEEP program would probably have failed without the leadership and support the part-time consultant has provided for teachers.

EXPANSION OF DEEP

Since 1984 the number of DEEP schools has expanded to include three more elementary schools and another high school. Currently, approximately 3,600 or 75 percent of the district's students are receiving economic instruction through social studies classes. It is hoped by 1990 that all ten schools in the district will be included in DEEP. Expansion decisions are based on collective decision making by the UTC center, the Marion County central office, and individual schools. The degree of enthusiasm for and the background in economic education on the part of a school's faculty have been major reasons for the selection of particular schools for DEEP.

Although gradual expansion has obvious disadvantages, a strong case can be made that rural educators interested in DEEP should give careful consideration to this strategy. A program in which teachers are trained, a scope and sequence is articulated, and evaluation occurs is much more complex if large numbers of people are involved in the beginning. A major objective of the Marion County program is participation in DEEP schools by all faculty members responsible for teaching social studies. The high levels of contact among UTC center personnel, the DEEP consultant, and the small numbers of teachers in the one or two schools that have entered the program each year have ensured maximum faculty involvement in DEEP.

Also, often as much because of geography as limited financial resources, the logistics of teacher training are much more difficult in rural than in urban districts. This is certainly true of Marion County where teachers in some schools must drive 20 miles to reach the central office. By concentrating on one or two schools each year, it is possible to conduct all in-services in the school building. This is a highly effective use of faculty and consultant time.

In general, the same process utilized in the three original schools has been used in the four schools that have entered the program since 1984.

Teachers in targeted schools participate in economics in-services or workshops, develop a school scope and sequence, and implement and evaluate economics lessons. Although concept lists developed by teachers in the original DEEP schools have been used as models, changes, particularly of a sequential nature, have been made by teachers in the newer schools to best meet the needs of their students.

The result is that there is no districtwide economics scope and sequence. It is felt this is a strength of the Marion County program since the decentralization of curriculum development allows teachers in individual schools a maximum amount of freedom in program design.

OUTSTANDING PROGRAMS

Although curriculum development is important and deserves careful reflection, the two most critical factors in any educational program are the quality of teaching and the content students are learning. What follows are brief descriptions of four classroom economics activities we consider outstanding. These descriptions are a sample of the innovative and in-depth economics teaching and learning in the district.

1. *Mini-Society Programs in Elementary and Middle Schools.* Mini-Society is a six- to eight-week economics- and law-related simulation in which youngsters develop a classroom economy with a government, currency, and businesses such as banks, small manufacturing concerns, and law firms. Currently, 12–15 teachers in grades 3, 4, 5, and 6 in three elementary schools and one middle school use the program.

2. *Japan Unit in Sixth and Seventh Grades.* In three schools, geography students participate in a three-week unit on Japan which includes a large component on the economy. The goals of the unit are to teach students about the Japanese economy and to use the study of the Japanese economy as a medium to teach basic economic concepts.

3. *Ninth Grade Social Studies Oral History Project.* In this program, which is conducted in a ninth grade state history course in the largest high school in the county, students learn about the Depression of the 1930s through interviewing a number of people who were alive during that period.

260

4. *Use of Jeans Factory by Capstone Economics Students.* Since 1985, high school students have used The Jeans Factory, a simulation developed at the University of Kansas Center for Economic Education. In this microcomputer simulation small groups of students manage a blue jeans manufacturing factory and learn such economic concepts as supply, demand, capital investment, and labor productivity.

5. *Other activity.* In addition, Marion County teachers use a variety of economic education materials and strategies, such as a third grade space colony unit, a middle school program using the newspaper to teach economics, a second grade auction simulation, the entire range of Joint Council curriculum materials including the *Master Curriculum Guide* series, and the *Give & Take* and *Trade-Offs* videos.

In all these cases the common experience of teachers who engage in in-depth economics is that after having time to learn of curricular options, they freely choose to use certain materials or pedagogical strategies. Usually, nothing is more guaranteed to fail than presenting a busy teacher with materials or suggested methodology with little consideration for appropriate teacher preparation time or teacher input. When possible, Marion County teachers are also given the opportunity to observe other teachers in the district who have successfully implemented in-depth classroom economics programs.

EVALUATION

Although a systematic program evaluation over and above routine teacher-made tests is one of the most difficult aspects of a comprehensive DEEP project, it is absolutely vital for success. In implementing an evaluation program, we experienced two probably universal problems. Any attempt to evaluate instructional programs usually encounters some level of apprehension on the part of teachers, and it is important that program administrators articulate the goals of the evaluation process before the process begins.

A second and greater problem in the implementation of an evaluation program, which we suspect to be particularly true of rural districts, is that of scarce financial and human resources. Testing is particularly time consuming and costly for rural districts that do not have full-time testing specialists available. However, a strategy that should be avoided at all costs is that of making teachers responsible for the entire evaluation process. We tried this strategy in 1984 with faculty in the lower elementary grades, and morale problems occurred because the task was viewed as unwelcome extra work. It is strongly recommended that a district testing specialist, a building administrator, a consultant, a university center staff member, or someone outside the classroom be responsible for evaluation administration.

In Marion County, evaluation administration has been a major responsibility of the part-time DEEP consultant. This individual, working in conjunction with the UTC center and local schools, prepares copies of tests, schedules testing times, and is responsible for delivering or mailing completed test forms to the UTC center. Still, due to limited resources, all DEEP students are not evaluated each year. We rotate testing among DEEP schools and place particular emphasis on evaluation in new schools.

Formal evaluation of economic education in Marion County is limited to grades 3–12. A variety of instruments are utilized including the Joint Council's *Basic Economics Test* and the Kourilsky Economics Questionnaire for grades 3, 4, and 5; the Joint Council's *Test of Economic Knowledge* in junior high school; and the Joint Council's *Test of Economic Literacy* in high school.

In several cases where evaluation instruments were not available—as for the *Trade-Offs* videos, for example—UTC center personnel constructed evaluation instruments. Scoring as well as data analysis is also a responsibility of UTC center personnel. The following evaluation examples drawn from the 1987–88 school year illustrate the various approaches to, and uses of, evaluation data in the Marion County program.

Formal evaluation is conducted to help determine if economic instruction results in cognitive gains for students. We use pretests and posttests with students in the DEEP program and, when given the opportunity, also match DEEP students with control groups who have no economic education in their social studies classes.

In 1987–88 third grade Mini-Society students at Jasper Elementary School were matched with third graders in a non-DEEP Marion County school. The average pretest (Kourilsky) class means of both groups of third graders were, when converted to percentages, approximately 30 percent correct. When posttest class means were compared, the Jasper Elementary third grade class mean was 60 percent correct, compared to the control group's mean score of 35 percent.

While experimental-control group comparisons often yield these kinds of results for us, occasionally DEEP and non-DEEP class means are approximately the same after instruction. When this situation occurs, attempts are made to influence DEEP teachers to modify their instructional approaches.

A very useful purpose of evaluation has also been to assess whether new combinations of economic education materials and teaching strategies make any difference. During the 1987–88 school year, for the first time fourth grade classes at South Pittsburgh Elementary School received instruction in *Trade-Offs* and then participated in a Mini-Society simulation. Form B of the *Basic Economics Test* was administered at the end of economic instruction. The raw score class mean for the BET was 22 correct answers out of 38 questions.

The data were compared with the national mean in the 1981 *Basic Economics Test: Examiner's Manual* (Chizmar & Halinski, 1981) for fourth, fifth, and sixth grade rural students who had received economics instruction, which was 20 correct answers out of 38 questions. Since Marion County students were younger than the students in the national rural sample with which they were compared, but they achieved higher test scores, we believe that a combination of *Trade-Offs* and Mini-Society is an efficient instructional approach to use in that particular school.

In general, since DEEP's inception, Marion County students' knowledge of economics has averaged from 20 to 30 percent higher at all levels when compared with control groups who are in other Marion County schools that are not, as of yet, DEEP schools. Also, class means of DEEP students in our original schools are rising now, compared to the scores of DEEP students at the same level in those schools that were tested two and three years ago. It is felt this is, at least in part, a result of the fact that current students have been exposed to a systematic economics instructional program in earlier grades.

Our evaluation strategies are not particularly sophisticated and probably never will be because of a shortage of human and economic resources. However, we have gained useful information from the evaluation component that has resulted in the improvement of economic education in the district.

CONCLUSIONS

This description of the Marion County program should be helpful to rural educators considering the implementation of a comprehensive DEEP program. It is recommended that those responsible for DEEP leadership in rural schools consider the following recommendations based on our experiences:

- Before beginning DEEP, develop a cadre of teachers in the district trained in economic education.

- Structure the required economic content for which teachers are responsible in such a way that enthusiastic faculty can go beyond minimal standards, while teachers not particularly enamored with DEEP do not feel overly threatened by the program.

- Given the usual demands on rural faculty and central office staff time, consider using a retired teacher or business person as a part-time DEEP consultant.

- Expand the program gradually so as to better ensure effective teacher in-service.

- In designing a DEEP evaluation program, clearly articulate goals of evaluation to the faculty and avoid burdening classroom teachers with more work.

REFERENCES

Chizmar, J. F., and Halinski, R. S. (1981). *Basic Economics Test: Examiner's manual.* New York: Joint Council on Economic Education.

Goodlad, J. I. (1984). *A place called school: Prospects for the future.* New York: McGraw-Hill.

Kourilsky, M. L. (1983). *Mini-Society: Experiencing real-world economics in the elementary school classroom.* Menlo Park, Calif.: Addison-Wesley.

19. ECONOMIC EDUCATION AND EDUCATIONAL REFORM: PARTNERS FOR AN ECONOMICALLY LITERATE FUTURE

by Marilyn Kourilsky and Lory Quaranta

The nationwide movement to educate K–12 students in economics continues to make excellent progress in the areas of institutional requirements (mandates), identification of curricula, and general political and public support. But how well are we, as a national network of economic educators, meeting the challenges of modeling educational reform for the 1990s? Specifically how and to what extent does the current economic education movement measure up to the four key imperatives of modern educational reform, and what particular suggestions and recommendations can be implemented to activate the priorities of educational reform through economic education?

ECONOMIC LITERACY AND THE ECONOMIC EDUCATION MOVEMENT

The major goal of the economic education movement is to create an economically literate citizenry. Economic literacy encompasses two dimensions that are often enmeshed: the ability to invoke the correct tools in making personal and aggregate decisions (e.g., weighing what I am getting versus what I am giving up when choosing among alternatives) and the ability to understand economic systems (e.g., understanding what determines prices, how money facilitates exchange, how an individual is impacted by inflation, how a country is affected by a budget deficit). The first (and perhaps most important) dimension enhances rational decision making and benefits all individuals from the time they are first cognizant that they are empowered to make choices. The second dimension allows one to understand the economic system in which s/he lives and functions and the particular cause-and-effect relationships associated with his/her economic behavior.

Whereas economic literacy is the goal, economic education is the process—the delivery system through which economic literacy is achieved—and the youngsters in today's K–12 classrooms are the target audience for attaining this goal. Those individuals engaged in the formal delivery of economic education span a large cast of collaborative players including curriculum writers and other developers of materials, teacher trainers, teachers, and expert evaluators. To what extent is our cast of economic educators advancing the imperatives of the current educational reform movement? In order to truly represent a model of reform both internally and to other disciplines, we must critically examine our strengths and weaknesses with respect to the reform imperatives and implement those activities that will reinforce the strengths and remedy the weaknesses.

EDUCATIONAL REFORM IMPERATIVES

A Nation at Risk (National Commission on Excellence in Education), issued in 1983, was followed by a wave of consortia, task forces, and documents, reflecting a growing concern about the quality of education in the United States. As a result, four major themes have emerged as priority imperatives for the United States' educational system. These include the growth and enhancement of (1) collegialism among educators, (2) professionalism in education, (3) research-based classroom practice, and (4) equity-based classrooms.

Collegialism refers to effective and positive networking within a profession whereby ideologies, materials and resources, experiences, and concerns are articulated and shared. Educators are viewed as interdependent and cooperatively connected—part of a collaborative team.

Professionalism refers to the vigorous pursuit of common standards of care and excellence, autonomous decision making, and accountability for those decisions. As educators we must strive for increased professional stature for teachers, thus enhancing their career satisfaction and external credibility to society at large.

Research-based classroom practice refers to the act of translating and implementing into daily practice what we have gleaned from the research on teaching and learning.

Finally, equity-based education is represented as a fundamental goal of a democratic society, whereby students are guaranteed a quality education regardless of gender, ethnicity, socioeconomic level, religion, or other variables.

These four priority areas provide a reform framework for evaluating the current educational process for specific subject areas and disciplines and for generating change recommendations that will strengthen the discipline's participation in the mainstream of educational reform.

Collegialism as a Reform Imperative

A positive enhancing aspect of any profession is what Shanker (1985) calls "a well established formal set of collegial peer relationships" (p. 15). Collegialism has emerged as one of the imperatives of current educational reform. In his landmark study of American schools, Goodlad (1984) identified collegialism as a necessary ingredient for professional growth and achievement. The teachers he observed appeared not to be working together on problems pertaining to their own schools, including the collaborative improvement of pedagogy. Lieberman and Miller (1984) note that the very act of teaching is invisible to one's peers and that teachers behave as if they live and work in a vacuum. "Although they may work in isolation, they are part of a larger context, and it is this connection that is hard to understand from the outside, and often not considered from the inside" (p. 90). Even when large numbers of teachers are being trained in a group setting, they typically "go through the programs individually rather than as members of cohort groups" (Lanier & Little, 1986, p. 549).

The Holmes Group explains in their reform document *Tomorrow's Teachers* (1986) that "good teachers must be knowledgeable but they have few opportunities to use that knowledge to improve the profession, or to help colleagues improve" (p. 15). They emphasize that teachers have a great deal to offer one another if given a model in which to provide insights and make collective decisions.

One of the most compelling arguments for infusing the profession with a greater sense of collegialism is voiced by Griffin (1986), who maintains that collegialism and collaboration are related to ownership. An individual who has played a role in formulating and carrying forward the efforts of a project, rather than being the passive recipient of a set of externally imposed specifications, "will probably feel a strong commitment to bring it to successful fruition" (p. 12).

To what extent does the current pool of economic educators promote collegialism within its network of participants, presenting and sharing ideas, materials, resources, and experiences? It is in this area—*activating and promoting* collegialism—that the Joint Council on Economic Education excels and provides a role model for other disciplines. The

Joint Council, the centers for economic education, and the collective efforts represented by DEEP projects reflect a nationwide, collegially based group of dedicated economic educators. In particular, DEEP represents quality involvement which extends along the entire range of participants: professionals in the field, principals, teachers, and students. All have an articulated role and perceived value both in the process and in the finished products. They have the feeling of ownership and participation advocated by Griffin, Goodlad, Lanier, and others. However, we can go even farther in enhancing collegialism by developing systematic programs of peer interaction/coaching and formal collaborations among DEEP districts. The major recommendations we have for increasing an already strong spirit of collegialism in economic education would be these:

1. Increase the levels of peer interaction at the school site and district levels, where peer feedback can be given in response to the delivery of instructional sequences. This may involve peer coaching, role modeling of different pedagogical techniques by mentor teachers, or geographically based peer tutoring. If teachers have a network of local support, in conjunction with and following in-service training, the success of their implementation efforts will be strengthened. For example, research suggests that following teacher training, peer coaching enhances the transfer of the skills and strategies necessary for successful classroom implementations (Fullan & Pomfret, 1977; Joyce & Showers, 1988).

2. Create a DEEP newsletter in which successful DEEP school districts throughout the nation describe their staff development programs, curriculum implementations, and other school improvement projects related to economic education.

Professionalism as a Reform Imperative

A major imperative of the current educational reform movement involves establishing teaching as a formally recognized profession, both internally among educators themselves and externally as perceived by society at large. By profession we mean a group of individuals committed to a unifying pursuit and to an articulated standard of excellence; they have a sense of autonomy, a deep knowledge base, and an internalized commitment to a common standard of excellence, all of which translate into a high professional self-concept and a strong sense of competence.

268

Other key dimensions of professionalism are the willingness and the ability to make informed and critical decisions. "A professional is a person who is an expert, and by virtue of that expertise is permitted to operate fairly independently, to make decisions, to exercise discretion, to be free of most supervision" (Shanker, 1985, p. 10).

Initially, then, we profile the professional as one who exercises autonomous decision making in the promotion and attainment of professionally defined goals and standards. While most would agree with this profile, a significant component of professionalism is often overlooked—accountability. Not only does a professional uphold standards, promote a core set of goals for the betterment of his/her constituents, and make judicious decisions, often in an autonomous context, but also a professional is willing to be held accountable for his/her actions and decisions (Sedlak, 1987).

The Carnegie Forum, in *A Nation Prepared* (Carnegie Task Force on Teaching as a Profession, 1986, p. 58), promotes the concept and necessity of professionalizing teaching. The forum calls for the creation of a professional environment for teaching in which "professional autonomy is the first requirement." In this environment, "teachers will have to have comparable authority [to doctors, architects, etc.], in making the key decisions about the services they render." The Carnegie Forum continues, "teachers have to be prepared to accept a greater degree of accountability in return for increased discretion."

In his discussion of educational reform, Griffin (1986) addresses the need to replace the current "paraprofessionalization of teaching," wherein the intellectual and substantive components of teaching are largely ignored. At present he believes the tendency is to reduce teachers to the status of specialized technicians within the school bureaucracy, whose function then becomes one of implementing and managing prespecified curricula, rather than developing or critically appropriating curricula to fit specific pedagogical concerns.

At what stage do we find economic education in promoting the professionalization of teaching? It seems helpful to assess its progress in relation to each of the criteria identified above—standard of excellence, autonomous decision making, and accountability.

A key aspect of the professionalism of teaching lies in the standard of excellence adhered to by its members, often referred to as the "Standard of Care" (Bruno, 1988). Economic education has advanced strongly in the establishment of scope and sequence goals and objectives for students.

However, we have not articulated a Standard of Care that would clarify our common goals as economic educators and establish a shared vision of what the professional teacher is trying to achieve in the classroom.

With respect to providing an environment in which teachers can exercise autonomous decision making, we as economic educators have the farthest to go. It is still typical to observe a workshop that consists of an economist presenting the equivalent of his/her college sophomore course in economics, perhaps followed by an elementary or secondary teacher presenting a show-and-tell lesson in which s/he has inserted economic principles. Teachers do not observe (or have role-modeled) a repertoire of pedagogical strategies for conveying the economic content. In fact, the only approach they usually see role-modeled is the lecture method. How then can they decide whether to teach the material in a didactic format, through media, using simulations or role playing, employing computers, initiating inquiry, etc. (Kourilsky & Quaranta, 1988)? Teachers cannot make sound decisions about how to teach economic concepts to their students if their alternatives—in this case, repertoires—are limited. In fact, most teachers without specific training use a very narrow range of practices (Medley, 1977; Sirotnik, 1983) and "expand that repertoire only when substantial and carefully designed training is provided" (Joyce & Showers, 1988, p. 56).

In the area of accountability, economic educators are perhaps the farthest along in promoting the professionalism of teaching within our field. In terms of accountability for student mastery in economics we show leadership among the many disciplines. We have standardized tests in economic literacy for elementary- and secondary-level students. We have recently amassed significant and useful baseline data on student populations. However, we have not pursued accountability of teachers with the same commitment or rigor. Currently, most teachers at best take an economics test designed for high school students. There is no ongoing assessment of their pedagogical strengths and weaknesses, and with respect to their economic knowledge, there are no procedures invoked for distinguishing between lack of information and misinformation. Without such data it is difficult to hold teachers accountable because we are unable to identify why learning is breaking down and how the situation may be remedied.

The following five recommendations are designed to enhance the role of economic education in promoting the further professionalization of teaching:

1. Extend assessment to broader population domains encompassing teachers, mentor teachers, and teacher trainers (including economists). Tests should be designed for each of these groups on economic content and pedagogy, especially learning theory. The Ph.D. economist, for example, may be knowledgeable and even brilliant with regard to economic theory, but illiterate with regard to teaching and learning theory. The professional economic educator must excel in knowledge of both economics and *how to teach* economics.

2. Establish scoring procedures like the Modified Confidence Weighted–Admissible Probability Measurement (MCW–APM) (Bruno, 1988) which help us diagnose the strengths and shortcomings of teachers in terms of whether they possess full information, partial information, or misinformation (or lack information) with respect to each principle tested. Depending on these diagnoses, we may want to employ different training strategies to remedy any weaknesses in their knowledge base (economics or pedagogy) before they pass on their informational weaknesses to new generations of students.

3. Initiate and support ongoing collaborative evaluation teams (including economists, learning theorists, teachers, and students) in which curriculum materials are screened and critically assessed. Criteria should include (a) *content*, in terms of the accuracy and validity of the materials from an economic viewpoint; (b) *coverage*, in terms of the proportion of the materials that is actually devoted to economics; (c) *bias*, in terms of hidden agendas; and (d) *appropriateness and effectiveness*, in terms of subject matter, sequencing, and instructional strategies. Given the existing network which is knowledgeable and dedicated, such a project would be highly feasible, and the result could have a significant impact on the effectiveness of classroom instruction. A "Consumer Report in Economic Education" might be a long-term goal with the additional benefit of encouraging the producers of curriculum materials to have them evaluated before they are placed on the market or, better yet, before they have assumed their final form.

4. Propose a draft Standard of Care for economic education in the classroom—visions of what each teacher might strive to achieve.

Such an articulation might include preliminary guidelines like the following. An effective and creative economic educator

- selects, designs, and evaluates economic curriculum materials and resources based on the needs and interests of all students of economics.
- expects all students to learn, participate, and excel in economic education.
- commands a broad repertoire of instructional strategies which enhance learning of economic concepts and accommodate individual variations in learning.
- encourages the active and inquisitive involvement of all students in the learning of economics.
- displays a high level of commitment to the profession of teaching economics and to professional growth through in-service training and participation in staff development activities.
- exhibits skill, confidence, and ingenuity in designing classroom experiences that interest and challenge all students to understand economic concepts.
- role-models effective and intelligent decision-making skills and provides opportunities for all students to develop similar skills.

While most economic educators would agree with guidelines such as those just listed. a formally stated Standard of Care would nevertheless have a positive unifying effect, focusing the profession's attention on common goals and educating the external community as to what it may expect from a *professional* economic educator/ teacher.

5. Train the trainers. Many economists will be better able to make decisions about how to teach various concepts if they themselves are trained in learning theory and see a variety of techniques in action. Additionally, mentor teachers and field coordinators will be better able to help and monitor classroom teachers if their knowledge of economics is advanced to a higher level of the cognitive domain.

In sum, steps taken to increase accountability, to promote an articulated Standard of Care, and to increase autonomous decision making will serve to strengthen the entire field of economic education. Building on our hard-won achievements to date, we can activate reform in the professionalization of economic educators.

Research in education, including findings on effective teaching and on student achievement, has progressed significantly in the past decade. A reform imperative has emerged, calling for this research to be translated into practice. While researchers in education have stepped up the pace and have improved the quality and applicability of their research efforts, the field as a whole has not been as successful in interpreting, translating, and disseminating the findings within the profession. As Derek Bok (1987), president of Harvard University, states, "any viable approach [to reform] must presumably combine an emphasis on teaching with a vigorous program of research" (p. 80). In other words, we can no longer view research and practice as separate domains; rather we must strive to enmesh the two to increase both classroom learning and teacher effectiveness.

There must be a willingness, says Marsh (1987), for educators to "see themselves as better research consumers, and so to join in networks where they can receive substantial contact and training about research on teaching" (p. 362). An integral part of both pre-service and in-service training, then, should be an action-oriented commitment to disseminate and apply relevant research findings in any given subject area.

Research in education should actively involve teachers and administrators in all phases and should encourage a spirit of inquiry and problem solving in its application. As Brophy and Good (1986) explain, "Rather than trying to translate [research] into overly rigid or generalized prescriptions, teacher educators should present this information to teachers within a decision-making format that enables them to examine concepts critically and adapt them to the particular contexts within which they teach" (p. 370).

To what extent do we, as economic educators, effectively conduct and apply research, and how successfully do we do so within a teacher-centered decision-making context? In assessing our strengths and weaknesses in this area, we need to look closely at two major classes of teacher decisions: what to teach (content-based decisions) and how to teach (decisions about learner and teacher behaviors). In the developing, test piloting, and field testing of economics curricula we have earned high marks. The Joint Council at large (as well as various state councils) has done a highly commendable job in establishing a comprehensive scope and sequence framework for the economics curriculum. We must invest significantly more effort, however, in the application within our scope and sequence designs of relevant modern research about developmental levels and age appropriateness.

Currently, the linking of concepts, skills, and objectives with particular grade levels has been established by polling the opinions of designated experts in the subject field. For example, the concept of inflation may be deemed appropriate for economics students at a certain grade, as determined through the opinion polling of economists and economic educators. Instead, it would be more valuable and appropriate to determine what students are developmentally ready for and capable of, based on the most current psychological research. We could then draw from our own discipline and conduct cost-benefit analyses. We might ask ourselves this: What is the *benefit* to the student of learning this particular concept at this specific grade level versus what is the opportunity cost of the instructional intervention required at this particular grade level for the student to master this particular concept? For example, we may be *able* to teach comparative advantage to first graders, but what are we giving up in order to teach it? It may be that we must give up six weeks of instructional time in order to teach the concept, while in the ninth grade it would take one class period. In general, the time we might allocate to teaching certain economic concepts at a particular grade level could well be more effectively devoted to the teaching of other economic concepts more developmentally appropriate to the grade level.

Another aspect of curriculum development (especially related to scope and sequence delineations) that has received increasing attention through pedagogical research is the distinction between independent and dependent sequences (Hunter, 1989). To increase student mastery and long-term memory processing we must differentiate between those curricular concepts/components that need to be presented sequentially (dependent sequences) and those that need not be presented in any fixed order (independent sequences). For example, we may teach the economy of Brazil before or after we teach the economy of Russia (an independent sequence). However, one would not teach the elasticity of demand before students correctly understand the concept of downward sloping demand (a dependent sequence). While the scope and sequence frameworks of economics may implicitly infer the dependency of certain concept sequences, to date we have not clearly differentiated which sequences are dependent and which are not, and the importance of the teacher's ensuring mastery of all preceding concepts before moving forward to the next concept of a dependent sequence.

In turning from content decisions (what to teach) to decisions about learner and teacher behaviors (how to teach and how to promote learning), we have a growing body of research that can strengthen economic education—research that is applicable from the training arena to the classroom. As Hunter (1982) states,

> If you deliberately use principles of learning which research indicates are accelerants to student achievement, you will have power to increase your students' motivation to learn, the speed and the amount (rate and degree) of their learning, and their retention and appropriate transfer of that learning to new situations requiring creativity, problem solving, and decision making. (p. 23)

Some research results based on learning principles have already found their way into economic in-service and pre-service training. For example, motivation, mentioned above, is generally built into training workshops and is usually promoted in existing curricula. Additionally, economic educators generally model enthusiasm and personal interest in their subject area, which in turn increases student motivation. However, three areas of research on how to teach from which our economic education and teacher education endeavors could derive particular benefit are modeling theory, brain lateralization, and the generative theory of learning.

In modeling we systematically build on the learner's natural in-clinations to use the teacher's actions and behaviors literally as a model—thus increasing mastery. In our workshops we routinely violate this learning principle by *advocating* certain behaviors or approaches (e.g., simulation), while *modeling* another (usually the lecture method). Research has repeatedly shown that usually what students *see* will have a more powerful influence than what they hear. In the workshop setting then, if participants experience the lecture method for presenting economic concepts, it is highly unlikely they will act on any alternative approaches that are verbally recommended. We cannot, for example, expect teachers to employ inquiry-based or experience-based approaches if what is modeled is the didactic method of instruction.

Brain lateralization refers to the specializations of the left and right hemispheres of the human brain. Research indicates that left-brain functioning is linear, sequential, and based primarily on verbal processes. Right-brain functioning involves spatial relationships, holistic analysis, and imagery.

In economic education, in both in-service and classroom settings, we do not adequately address and integrate right- and left-brain processing. For example, it has been found most effective for a teacher to introduce a concept or instructional sequence with a verbal presentation (left-brain emphasis), followed by an integrative graphic presentation (right-brain emphasis) (Kourilsky & Wittrock, 1987). Workshops in economic education can significantly enhance learning and retention both through modeling and by advocating such dual hemispheric processing.

The generative theory is an important aspect of cognitive information processing models and refers to the importance of enhancing learning by progressing from what is familiar and known to the new and unknown. Students generate new meaning consistent with what they already believe and understand. As Wittrock (1986) explains, "Learning and memory are facilitated when the learners construct images and verbal representations that relate old memories to new information, especially in organized and sequential ways" (p. 311).

Brophy and Good (1986) report findings that indicate that "students learn more efficiently when their teacher first structures new information for them and helps them relate it to what they already know" (p. 362). In our workshops in economic education and in the economics classroom we need to make fuller use of findings based on the cognitive model of generative learning.

Clearly there is significant untapped potential for the application of research to economic education. Our specific recommendations are the following:

1. Establish one or more teams—consisting of an economist, learning theorist, developmental psychologist, lower elementary school teacher, upper elementary school teacher, junior high school teacher, and high school teacher—to analyze the scope and sequence of economics in terms of dependent sequences versus independent sequences, appropriate developmental readiness for introducing each concept, and optimal stages in the K–12 curriculum for extending the concept (once it has been introduced) to higher levels of the cognitive domain. The results of these deliberations should be published as addenda to the appropriate scope and sequence documents. All members of the above teams would have to be well versed in the discipline of economics to analyze and interact effectively.

2. Include information (and practice) on the what and how of modeling, brain lateralization, and generic learning in economic

276

education workshops, and provide experience-based examples of the concepts/theories in action. For example, divide workshop participants into duads or triads to illustrate the teaching of specific economic concepts according to the learning precepts described above. The workshop facilitator could then provide feedback to the participants on the quality of their implementations of designated learning principles.

We need to keep abreast of current and relevant research, and we need to apply it at the workshop level, in our design of the curriculum, and to economic instruction methods in the classroom. As we more effectively apply the current research to our what-to-teach and how-to-teach decisions and derive the consequent teacher education and classroom instruction benefits, we will serve as a role model for other disciplines that have been underutilizing their research findings.

Equity in Education as a Reform Imperative

A final and far-reaching reform imperative calls for the provision of equity in education. At one time educational equity was narrowly defined as equal access to opportunities. For example, society provided homogeneous, tax-supported schools for students from kindergarten through high school. Today we would emphasize that our multicultural society with its diverse socioeconomic groups makes such simple-minded policies inequitable. We can no longer pursue an educational policy where we assume "one size fits all." As stated in *A Nation at Risk* (National Commission on Excellence in Education, 1983), one catalyst in the modern education reform movement, the twin goals of equity and high-quality schooling have a profound and practical meaning for our economy and society, and we cannot permit one to yield to the other either in principle or in practice.

Without a strong and unanimous commitment to equity, we will, as Goodlad (1984) notes, fall far short of viewing students as the real clients of schools and of doing what we can do to make schooling fulfill the function of individual development and responsibility.

Promoting equity in education may be accomplished in large part by setting uniformly high expectations for the learning and achievement of *all* students, paying special attention to at-risk populations, and teaching from a multicultural perspective.

277

One of the most consistent findings in research on effective teachers is that students in classrooms in which the teacher *expects* all students to learn achieve at a higher level than do students in classrooms in which the teacher does not hold uniformly high expectations (Stipek, 1988). Regardless of ethnicity, gender, socioeconomic level, or other variables, teachers must expect each student to achieve if we are to move our goal of equity closer to reality. Unfortunately, the classroom practices inspired by these findings are often limited to giving special attention and compensatory assistance to students whom teachers perceive to be disadvantaged. Such perspectives are potentially damaging (Stipek, 1988).

We are continuously reminded that equity has not been achieved when we look at the alarmingly high dropout rate in the United States and the disproportionate number of annual dropouts who are minority students. Approximately 700,000 people leave school each year in the United States; urban public schools have the highest dropout rates—up to 50 percent in some cities (Sharradan, 1986). To reverse this trend, at-risk populations must be specifically addressed by each discipline (Gollnick & Chinn, 1986).

Last, to achieve equity in education, teachers must teach from a multicultural perspective. A multicultural perspective is a state of mind, a way of seeing, and a point of view that receives direction from a set of beliefs about multiculturalism in American history and society. A teacher must see that culture, race, sex, gender, religion, socioeconomic status, and exceptionality are potentially potent variables in the learning processes of individuals and groups (Davidman & Davidman, 1988).

The three aforementioned areas of emphasis for achieving equity, then, provide a foundation or stronghold on which each educator can build. If we teach from a multicultural perspective and eradicate bias and favoritism from our dealings with learners, we improve our ability to hold high expectations for all students, thereby making notable gains with our at-risk populations.

Where do we stand as a discipline in terms of commitment to and delivery of equity in education? Specifically, how effectively do we promote this goal in the classroom, in our in-service training, and in the development of classroom learning materials?

In terms of high expectation levels of students, we need to improve in two important directions. One is in exposing teachers to the research on high expectations of students and in encouraging teachers to look at their own biases and differential expectations of students. The other direction has to do with our own attitudes toward and expectations of economics teachers in the classroom and in in-service workshops. In general, economists tend to perceive teachers of economics as lacking analytic and quantitative ability. Many economists "water down" the economic content of their workshop presentations to teachers; for example, they often do not even attempt to depict demand and supply graphically; present elasticity of demand, supply, or income; or even distinguish between the individual bank and the banking system in terms of credit expansion. In this and other subtle ways, we may communicate to our teachers that we expect less of them than they are capable of understanding and mastering. We must role-model consistently that we have high expectations of the teachers' ability to grasp concepts, present content effectively, and move the teaching of the discipline forward.

With at-risk populations our heart is certainly in the right place, and we have made some progress. Programs that provide early intervention and highly engaging instructional experiences in economics, such as Kindereconomy, Mini-Society (Kourilsky, 1983) and *Choices and Changes* (Joint Council on Economic Education, 1987) have addressed at-risk populations. However, as a network we need to expand in this area and to accumulate more information on the learning styles and proclivities of the specific at-risk populations we are endeavoring to reach. For example, nonminority students respond more favorably to methodologies that emphasize quantitative/analytical explanations and independent student activities, whereas at-risk students respond more favorably to heuristics, explanation by example, and group tasks. Most instruction in classrooms has favored field-independent styles of learning, yet at-risk students are typically more field dependent in their learning styles. As economic educators, and as educators in general, we need to accommodate differences in learning modalities as suggested above (Gollnick & Chinn, 1986).

As for our efforts in advocating multiculturalism, while many of our curriculum resources reflect multicultural sensitivity, more depth is needed in this area. In our presentations and our resources, representation by diverse ethnic groups, females, older people, etc., is limited and often comes off as tokenism. In some cases the representation or examples are too blatant to be real. More balance is needed to make materials congruent with reality, while presenting a broader portfolio of contributions and participations by all cultural segments of our society.

Given where we are in promoting equitable outcomes of student learning, we recommend these steps to activate related reform:

1. Include research findings on teacher expectations in our in-service programs, emphasizing the significant correlation between high teacher expectations and students' achievement levels. Workshop activities may specifically call for teachers to self-evaluate in this area and strategize cooperatively on ways to maintain high expectations for all students. For example, in in-service training we could advocate and role-model both field-dependent (i.e., cooperative learning, peer tutoring, etc.) and field-independent modes of instruction, discerning and distinguishing between them. By such accommodation to learner styles, we move teachers toward reprogramming lower expectations they may possibly hold.

2. Consistently role-model high expectations of teachers in their role of learners in economic education workshops. Economists and educators, as much as possible, should collaborate to ensure that such expectations are integral to their presentations.

3. Compile and disseminate information on successful programs for at-risk students; information should include programs both within and outside the discipline. Consortiums on curriculum development should spotlight such programs and push for their expansion, especially at the elementary level. By studying and dovetailing with effective programs that have been successfully implemented, we can maximize our efforts and strengthen our contributions to at-risk populations nationwide.

4. Conduct curriculum development in economic education, taking into account both minority and nonminority perspectives, values, learning styles, and needs. A multicultural perspective should be promoted both in workshops and in our generated programs and materials. Checklists should be used to monitor our materials on the basis of such criteria as being culturally diverse, nonstereotyping, and nonageist; at the same time we should strive for more authentic and realistic ways to reflect pluralism in our materials.

SUMMARY AND CONCLUSION

Economics as a discipline and economic education as a dynamic and significant movement have the opportunity and potential to activate key education reform imperatives at this pivotal time in the United States.

Professionalism and collegialism will energize and strengthen the profession internally and its perceived status externally. By translating research findings into classroom practice, we will do much to increase our effectiveness in teaching economics. Finally, with equity as a unifying pedagogical and societal goal, we can make a significant contribution to the reform of our schools and what happens inside them. As Jesse Jackson (1988) says, "Believe in our children. Believe in your ability to teach them and their ability to learn."

True reform, as we see it, is more than just commitment or ideology. It is the willingness to alter, enhance, and reform the system from within in the hopes of improving the conditions and outcomes for all involved. We believe that as economic educators we have the vision, the resources, and the energy to conceptualize, plan, and activate educational reform nationwide and, in so doing, increase the economic literacy of our citizens.

REFERENCES

Bok, D. (1987). The challenge of schools of education. *Harvard Magazine* 89(5):47–80.

Brophy, J., and Good, T. (1986). Teacher behavior and student achievement. In *Handbook of research on teaching.* 3d ed., ed. M. C. Wittrock, 328–75. New York: Macmillan.

Bruno, J. (1988). Instructional audit. *Urban Review* 20(2):95–107.

Carnegie Task Force on Teaching as a Profession (1986). *A nation prepared: Teachers for the 21st century.* New York: Carnegie Forum on Education and the Economy.

Davidman, L., and Davidman, P. (1988). Multicultural teacher education in the state of California: The challenge of definition and implementation. *Teacher Education Quarterly* 15(2):50–67.

Fullan, M., and Pomfret, A. (1977). Research on curriculum and instruction implementation. *Review of Educational Research* 47(2):335–97.

Gollnick, D., and Chinn, P. (1986). *Multicultural education in a pluralistic society.* 2d ed. Columbus, Ohio: Charles Merrill.

Goodlad, J. I. (1984). *A place called school: Prospects for the future.* New York: McGraw-Hill.

Griffin, G. (1986). Clinical teacher education. In *Reality and reform in clinical teacher education,* ed. J. V. Hoffman and S. A. Edwards. New York: Random House.

The Holmes Group (1986). *Tomorrow's teachers: A report of the Holmes Group.* East Lansing, Mich.: The Holmes Group, Inc.

Hunter, M. (1989). *Mastering coaching and supervision.* El Segundo, Calif.: TIP Publications.

————— (1982). *Mastery teaching.* El Segundo, Calif.: TIP Publications.

Jackson, J. (1988). In pursuit of equity, ethics, and excellence: The challenge to the gap. In *Kaleidoscope.* Boston: Houghton Mifflin.

Joint Council on Economic Education (1987). *Choices and Changes.* New York: the Joint Council.

Joyce, B., and Showers, B. (1988). *Student achievement through staff development.* New York: Longman.

Kourilsky, M. (1983). *Mini-Society: Experiencing real-world economics in the elementary school classroom.* Menlo Park, Calif.: Addison-Wesley.

Kourilsky, M., and Quaranta, L. (1988). *Effective teaching: Principles and practice.* Glenview, Ill.: Scott, Foresman.

Kourilsky, M., and Wittrock, M. (1987). Verbal and graphical strategies in the teaching of economics. *Teaching and Teacher Education* 3(1):1–12.

Lanier, J., and Little, J. (1986). Research on teacher education. In *Handbook of research on teaching.* 3d ed., ed. M. C. Wittrock, 527–69. New York: Macmillan.

Lieberman, A., and Miller, L. (1984). *Teachers, their world, and their work: Implications for school improvement.* Alexandria, Va.: Association for Supervision and Curriculum Development.

Marsh, D. (1987). Faculty development for preservice teacher education: A research utilization perspective. *Teaching and Teacher Education* 3(4):357–63.

Medley, D. (1977). *Teacher competence and teacher effectiveness.* Washington, D.C.: American Association of Colleges of Teacher Education.

National Commission on Excellence in Education (1983). *A nation at risk: The imperative for educational reform.* Washington, D.C.: U.S. Government Printing Office.

Sedlak, M. (1987). Tomorrow's teachers: The essential arguments of the Holmes Group report. *Teachers College Record* 88(3):314–25.

Shanker, A. (1985). The making of a profession. *American Educator* 9(3):10–17, 46, 48.

Sharradan, M. (1986). School dropouts in perspective. *Education Forum,* 15–31.

Sirotnik, K. (1983). What you see is what you get: Consistency, persistence, and mediocrity in classrooms. *Harvard Educational Review* 53(1):16–31.

Stipek, D. (1988). *Motivation to learn: From theory to practice.* Englewood Cliffs, N.J.: Prentice-Hall.

Wittrock, M. C. (1986). Students' thought processes. In *Handbook of research on teaching.* 3d ed., ed. M. C. Wittrock, 297-314. New York: Macmillan.

20. FUTURE REQUIREMENTS FOR PROGRAMS AND MATERIALS

by June V. Gilliard

In developing curriculum and instructional materials we make certain assumptions about the students for whom the materials are intended, the teachers who will be using the materials to provide instruction, what is being taught in related curriculum areas, the institutional setting in which instruction will occur, and how new curriculum materials are introduced and implemented in schools. We seldom make these assumptions explicit. Indeed, as developers, we may not be totally aware of the assumptions governing our actions at a given point in time.

Changing conditions in the schools compel us to take a long and hard look at what we do and to ask if this is what will be needed in elementary and secondary schools in the year 2000 and beyond. The actions we take in planning future economic education programs and materials will depend on the assumptions from which we begin. My purpose here is to make explicit the basic assumptions that govern our materials development efforts and to examine these in light of current proposals for curriculum reform and conditions that are likely to prevail in schools in the early decades of the twenty-first century.

ASSUMPTIONS UNDERLYING MATERIALS DEVELOPMENT

The goal of DEEP is to effect qualitative and quantitative changes in the economic instruction provided in elementary and secondary schools. Thus, it is not surprising that many of the assumptions that govern the development of the Joint Council on Economic Education's programs and materials are closely tied to the DEEP model for curriculum change. Nor should it be surprising that over the approximately 25-year history of DEEP, changes in the model have generally resulted in changes in assumptions about the kinds of materials needed to effect desired changes in school curricula.

Factors other than the requirements of DEEP influence the development of Joint Council programs. Researchers on educational change have found that characteristics of a curriculum innovation can affect implementation in schools. Thus, to a great extent, the fate of a new program may be determined by decisions in the early design stage.

Influence of the DEEP Model

The introduction of DEEP in the mid-1960s represented a break with traditional views on the role of economic education in the K–12 curriculum. Heretofore, economic instruction in most school districts was limited to a one-semester, elective economics course offered at the twelfth grade level. DEEP encompassed a view that economic instruction should be provided for all students. Further, inasmuch as the acquisition of economic understanding is a developmental process, economic education should begin in the early grades. To assure the availability of economic education to *all* students, the teaching of economics should be integrated into the required social studies program for elementary and secondary schools.

The DEEP "experiment," the forerunner of today's DEEP model, embodied a grass-roots view of curriculum change. It incorporated the most recent research on the process of change in schools. This approach was based on the following premises: (1) curriculum decisions are largely a matter of local autonomy, (2) teacher commitment is essential for the implementation of curriculum change, and (3) commitment to change results from teacher participation or involvement in basically all phases of curriculum development. Subsumed under the latter premise is an assumption that teachers, with assistance from content experts (economists and economics educators), have the knowledge, skill, and time to develop innovative curriculum materials (Giacquinta, 1973; Havelock et al., 1969; Miles, 1964).

Materials published by the Joint Council in the early and mid-1960s supported this view of curriculum change. In general, these materials were of two types: (1) those designed to assist teachers and administrators in the development of new elementary and secondary school curricula and (2) those designed to be used by teachers in planning classroom instruction.

Evaluation of the DEEP experiment revealed that the grass-roots approach did not consistently result in high-quality curriculum products. School systems that had access to "talented writers, curriculum specialists, and economists successfully produced high quality materials"

(Psychological Corporation, 1970, ch. 6, p. 4). When these resources were lacking, however, the materials produced tended to be characterized by "poor economics, poor writing, and narrowly local interests" (Psychological Corporation, 1970, ch. 6, p. 4). Furthermore, the evaluators found that constraints on teachers' time contributed significantly to the observed dysfunctions in the experimental model.

The issue of locally developed curriculum materials was addressed in the first *DEEP Handbook for Curriculum Change* (Symmes, 1969). "The DEEP process," Symmes wrote, "does not necessarily mean locally written pupil and teacher material" (p. 17). Rather, involvement in materials adoption or adaptation was viewed not only as sufficient for generating commitment to change, but also as a more efficient use of teachers' talents and time.

Where were school systems to get the needed economic education materials if they were not to create them themselves? Commercial publishers provided an array of textbooks for use in the senior high school elective economics course. Few economic education materials were available from this source, however, for use in the elementary grades. The variety of materials appropriate for programs utilizing an integrative approach was also far from adequate.

The early 1970s saw a shift in the Joint Council's publications program. Clearly there was still a need for materials to assist school practitioners in the development of economic education curricula and in instructional planning. Yet the implementation of DEEP in many school systems required something more. It required models for integrating economics in the required K–12 social studies program; instructional programs and materials for elementary schools were also needed. The initial response of the Joint Council resulted in the development and publication of the *Master Curriculum Guide for Teaching Economics in the Nation's Schools* and *Trade-Offs*. The former is a multivolume series designed to provide school systems with guidance in structuring content for the K–12 program. It also includes model lessons that teachers can use for integrating economics in a variety of social studies units and courses. *Trade-Offs*, a film/video series intended for use with 9- to 13-year-olds, helped to fill the void in economic education materials for children enrolled in elementary schools.

Trade-Offs represented several "firsts" for the Joint Council. It was the Joint Council's first video/film series, the first comprehensive and sequentially developed instructional program, the first program to

285

present and systematically apply an explicit model for economic decision making, and the first Joint Council consortium effort. This last factor contributed significantly to the early implementation of the program. It is also worth noting that the method used to finance consortium products greatly reduces implementation costs for each school.

The mere existence of new and innovative curricula and instructional materials is not sufficient to effect change in what is taught and learned in schools. New materials can effect change only if they are used by teachers in planning and providing classroom instruction. Thus, developers of new programs must be concerned about factors that affect the rate at and the degree to which such programs are implemented and eventually institutionalized in schools.

Characteristics of Educational Programs

Researchers have found that certain characteristics of curriculum materials affect their rate and degree of implementation. Chief among these is the compatibility of the program with the values, goals, and structures of the target institution (Miles, 1964). Since the mid-1960s, it has been commonly accepted that the greater the congruence between a proposed innovation and the values and goals of the target system, the greater the likelihood the innovation will be adopted. The concept of compatibility encompasses not only the notion of congruence between the innovation and the institutional goals, but also the idea of congruence between the innovation and the target group's decision-making structure, communication system, and structured use of time and space (Crawford, Kratochvil & Wright, 1972; Miles, 1964).

Studies conducted by Crawford, Kratochvil, and Wright (1972) and Giacquinta (1973) indicate that the complexity of a curriculum innovation (i.e., the degree to which the innovation is difficult to use and understand) also affects its implementation. Complexity is assessed in terms of (1) the number of components in the innovation, (2) the number of skills practitioners must learn before the innovation can be implemented, and (3) the number of procedures required to maintain the innovation. The greater the number of new skills and procedures required by an innovation, the less likely the innovation will be installed in the target system. This occurs because complex innovations tend to place an excessive cognitive and emotional burden on professional personnel and require an inordinate amount of time and energy for implementation. Complexity may also affect the cost of new programs. Costs are generally increased when the use of an innovation requires extensive in-service training or other special arrangements. The negative aspects of a complex innovation are reduced when the innovation is accompanied by instructional materials and built-in implementation supports such as teaching guides and in-service training materials.

A third major characteristic affecting the implementation of an innovation is its relative advantage over prevailing practices or other alternatives under consideration. Measures for assessing the relative advantage of a curriculum innovation include the effectiveness of the innovation for achieving specified goals, its monetary cost compared to the cost of alternative programs, and user perceptions of social reward. In the past, potential adopters of curriculum or instructional innovations have found that data on program effectiveness are not always available, and rarely are the developers able to provide data on user perceptions of social reward. Consequently, decision makers have tended to rely heavily on cost as a determining factor.

The extent to which the Joint Council has been attentive to factors associated with compatibility, complexity, and relative advantage is revealed by taking a brief look at past practices for producing and introducing new curriculum products.

Perhaps the greatest hurdle that had to be overcome when DEEP was first introduced in the mid-1960s was to convince administrators and teachers of the need for economic education. Today 28 states mandate the teaching of economics in some form; of these, 16 require at least a semester course in economics for high school graduation (Highsmith, 1989a). In the remaining 22 states that do not mandate economics, statements of educational goals at the state and school district levels often express the need for students to develop an understanding of and appreciation for the American economic system. Recognizing the need for economic education, however, is only a first step in the process of implementation. The commitment of resources is an essential second step if economic education is to become a reality in the system.

Most Joint Council instructional programs and materials are designed to enable teachers to simultaneously achieve objectives for economic understanding and objectives in other priority curriculum areas. For example, newer programs for elementary schools such as *Econ and Me* and the *Exploring the Marketplace* series are designed to foster economic understanding and at the same time facilitate student application of basic

287

communications and mathematical skills. Old and new programs for elementary and secondary schools emphasize the development of decision-making skills. Although the materials generally include suggestions for the use of innovative instructional techniques, it is assumed that in a majority of schools instruction occurs in classrooms with a teacher and 25 to 30 students meeting in regularly scheduled time periods of 45 to 50 minutes each.

The extent to which teachers find Joint Council programs and materials easy to use is in large part dependent on their knowledge of economics. Unfortunately, only a small percentage of teachers have had formal training in the discipline (Highsmith, 1989b). To compensate for teachers' general lack of training in economics, most Joint Council programs and materials have built-in supports such as teacher manuals and in-service training materials. Additional support is provided for school systems enrolled in DEEP through the Joint Council's affiliated network of state councils and centers for economic education.

While data on the classroom effectiveness of older programs such as *Trade-Offs* (Agency for Instructional Television, 1981) and *Give & Take* (Agency for Instructional Technology, 1986) are available to schools, the collection and compilation of comparable data on more recently published programs will take several years. The lack of evaluation data may be partially offset by the inclusion of clearly stated learning objectives and suggestions or materials that teachers can use for determining the extent to which the objectives have been attained.

Current proposals for educational change have the potential to effect far-reaching changes in the nation's schools. To the extent that they effect changes in institutional values, goals, and structures, so, too, will they require changes in the assumptions that govern the development of future curricula and instructional materials.

THE CALL FOR EDUCATIONAL REFORM

National and international assessments of young people's knowledge in the late 1970s and early 1980s underscored shortcomings in the educational outcomes of the nation's schools. The response to what was quickly labeled a "crisis in American education" came in a number of different forms. More than 275 state and national task forces were formed to address problems associated with schools and schooling; prestigious national panels established to study various aspects of the educational system issued 18 book-length reports, each containing recommendations for "fixing" the schools (Orlich, 1989). Between 1983 and 1989 state legislatures enacted more than 700 statutes affecting nearly every aspect of the educational system (Timar & Kirp, 1989; see also Chapters 5 and 19 in this volume).

Questions pertaining to what to teach and how to teach it are perhaps the most fundamental questions in education. In its report on the state of American education, the National Commission on Excellence in Education (1983) was highly critical of elementary and secondary school curricula and offered recommendations for strengthening instruction in the basic academic disciplines—English, mathematics, science, and social studies. In the years since the report was issued, 45 states and the District of Columbia have altered requirements for high school graduation, and almost universally the changes have resulted in increases in required courses (Pipho, 1986). The professional associations and subject area organizations responded to the report and to other critics of the educational system by establishing task forces or national panels to develop curriculum guidelines for kindergarten through twelfth grade.

Current national proposals for reforming the social studies curriculum, if implemented, will effect significant change in what is taught in elementary and secondary schools. Most prominent among these are the reports of the Bradley Commission on History in the Schools (1988) and the National Commission on Social Studies in the Schools (1989). The influence of the former on local and state curricula is already evident, most notably in its influence on the social studies curriculum recently adopted by the state of California (California State Department of Education, 1988). The report of the National Commission on Social Studies in the Schools (1989) was only recently completed; thus, it is too early to predict the impact this will have on school curricula.

An examination of curriculum proposals at both the state and the national levels indicates several new trends in social studies education. The most apparent are an increased emphasis on history and geography, a modification of the expanding horizons approach at the elementary level, and an increase in the number of courses required for high school graduation. With respect to economic instruction, most of the new curriculum proposals recommend the infusion or integration of economics in studies of history and geography and the inclusion of either a required or an elective course in economics in the last year of high school. The idea of integrating or infusing economics in studies of

289

history and geography is not new. What has changed is the specific content drawn from history and geography to serve as the core of the social studies program and also as the context for economic instruction.

Changes in curriculum areas other than social studies have potential for affecting economic education in elementary and secondary schools. A shift in curriculum emphasis, the introduction of new topics, or the development of new instructional procedures can broaden (or reduce) opportunities for economic instruction. For example, the curriculum recommendations proposed in the panel reports for Project 2061 (Appley & Maher, 1989; Johnson, 1989), if implemented, would open new opportunities for integrating economics into the study of science. Implementation of the recommendations for reforming the mathematics curriculum (National Council of Teachers of Mathematics, 1989) could effect change in the presentation of mathematical concepts and processes in economic education materials, particularly those designed for use in the elementary grades.

In addition to concerns about the effects of the reform movement on curricula, the teaching profession, and school structure, planners of future educational programs must also be attentive to demographic trends that are currently effecting change in the student population. Hodgkinson (1988b) contends that a change in the composition of students moving through the educational system is likely to effect change in schools far more rapidly than are the visions and efforts of reformers.

IMPLICATIONS OF DEMOGRAPHIC TRENDS

Today, approximately one-fourth of the young people enrolled in the nation's schools are labeled as "at-risk" or "educationally disadvantaged." Characteristics most frequently associated with being educationally disadvantaged include belonging to a minority racial/ethnic group, living in a poverty household, living in a single-parent family, having a poorly educated mother, and having a non-English language background (Pallas, Natriello & McDill, 1989).

Due to differential birth rates and changes in patterns of immigration, the proportion of minority school-age children is expected to increase considerably over the next several decades. Today, 30 percent of all school-age children are minorities; if current demographic trends continue, it is predicted that by the year 2001, 48 percent of the school population will be members of minority racial or ethnic groups

(Hodgkinson, 1988b). Hodgkinson (1988a) summarizes the situation as follows:

> The extreme heterogeneity of today's school-age youth represents a major challenge to our educational system. Nor is the challenge likely to abate anytime soon. Fully two-thirds of the world's immigrants gravitate to the United States [and] it is likely that immigration will continue at a high level for some years to come. (p.12)

Expansion of the Hispanic population is expected to bring with it a corresponding increase in the number of children whose primary language is not English (Pallas, Natriello & McDill, 1989). In 1982 the proportion of school-age children speaking a primary language other than English was 2.5 percent. Predictions are that this percentage will triple in the early decades of the twenty-first century.

Changes in the structure of the American family are also having an impact on the educational system. Today only 7 percent of households conform to views of the traditional American family—a working father, a housewife mother, and two school-age children (Hodgkinson, 1988a). Increasing numbers of children are raised in single-parent households, many of which are headed by women who lack sufficient job skills for gainful employment. The latter development is a major factor contributing to the increase in the incidence of poverty among children (Hodgkinson, 1988b; Pallas, Natriello & McDill, 1989).

A fourth change in the school-age population noted by demographers is the increase in the number of children diagnosed as physically or emotionally handicapped (Hodgkinson, 1988b). This trend, if continued, will present yet another challenge to the educational system.

The students enrolled in elementary and secondary schools in the early decades of the twenty-first century, Hodgkinson (1988a) contends, "will be drastically different from students today, with a greater variety of backgrounds, languages, values, and abilities than ever before" (p. 11). Assuming that current demographic trends continue, the net effect will be a significant increase in the percentage of students from those groups that schools heretofore have served least well (Goodlad, 1984).

PLANNING FOR THE FUTURE

We began by asking if past assumptions form a valid basis for planning economic education programs and materials for the twenty-first century. The ultimate effect that current demographic trends and recommendations for reform will have on schools is still unclear. Many of the reforms recommended have yet to be tried in schools. Others are in the earliest stages of implementation, and the extent of their "staying power" is unknown. Nevertheless, certain trends do warrant our attention in that they have potential for effecting significant changes in our assumptions about characteristics of curriculum and instructional innovations that make them more or less likely to be implemented in schools.

Of particular concern are the reforms intended to effect change in educational goals, values, and institutional arrangements. Most prevalent among these are proposals for change in what is taught and learned in schools. For example, what effect will implementation of proposed reforms in social studies education have on the teaching of economics in elementary and secondary schools? Will the expansion of history and geography instruction have a significant effect on the quantity and quality of economics taught in kindergarten through twelfth grade? Similarly, to what extent will (or should) modification or abandonment of curriculum practices associated with the expanding horizons approach affect economic instruction in elementary schools?

One can raise similar questions about the impact of changes in curriculum areas other than social studies—e.g., business education, vocational education, and so forth. Will the changes result in an increase in the windows of opportunity for teaching economics, or will they result in the closing of existing ones? Either outcome has implications for what we do in planning future programs and materials.

Changes are also taking place in the teaching of thinking, decision making, and basic communications and mathematical skills. To what extent should planners of future economic education programs be concerned with the development of student abilities in these areas?

Needless to say, we cannot plan future educational programs without consideration of the students who are to use them. What effect will or should changing demographics have on the content and pedagogy of economic education programs? We might also ask, What can we do in designing new programs to help teachers deal with the new diversity that is expected to characterize schools in the twenty-first century?

The questions raised so far relate almost exclusively to the issue of compatibility. Questions addressing the issue of complexity focus largely on proposals for reform in teacher education and certification and the extent to which these result in changes in teachers' knowledge of the content and methods of economic instruction. A change in teachers' knowledge can have a significant effect on needs for in-service training as well as on teachers' perceptions of the difficulty or ease with which they can implement a particular innovation in their classrooms.

Attentiveness to the characteristic of relative advantage raises questions pertaining to the role of evaluation in the development of future economic education programs. What kinds of evidence will prospective users require as proof of program effectiveness?

The foregoing questions are illustrative of the kinds of questions that need to be asked in planning future programs and materials. They help us to become aware of the assumptions we make and to test these against the reality of the nation's schools. They also remind us that program development is not an end, but a means for attaining a far more important goal. Our ultimate goal is to effect quantitative and qualitative changes in economic instruction, kindergarten through twelfth grade. This will occur only if what we produce is implemented in the classroom.

REFERENCES

Agency for Instructional Technology (1986). *Give & Take: What the research is saying.* Research Report 95. Bloomington, Ind.: the Agency.

Agency for Instructional Television (1981). *Trade-Offs: What the research is saying.* Research Report 82. Bloomington, Ind.: the Agency.

Appley, M., and Maher, W. (1989). *Social and behavioral sciences: Report of the Project 2061 phase I social and behavioral sciences panel.* Washington, D.C.: American Association for the Advancement of Science.

Bradley Commission on History in the Schools (1988). *Building a history curriculum: Guidelines for teaching history in the schools.* Washington, D.C.: Educational Excellence Network.

California State Department of Education (1988). *History–social science framework for California public schools, kindergarten through grade twelve.* Sacramento: California State Department of Education.

Carnegie Task Force on Teaching as a Profession (1986). *A nation prepared: Teachers for the 21st century.* New York: Carnegie Forum on Education and the Economy.

Crawford, J.; Kratochvil, D.; and Wright, C. (1972). *Evaluation of the impact of educational products, final report.* Palo Alto, Calif.: American Institute for Research.

Giacquinta, J. (1973). The process of organizational change in schools. In *Review of research in education,* ed. F. N. Kerlinger, 178–208. Itasca, Ill.: F. E. Peacock Publishers.

Goodlad, J. I. (1984). *A place called school: Prospects for the future.* New York: McGraw-Hill.

Havelock, R., et al. (1969). *Planning for innovation.* Washington, D.C.: U.S. Department of Health, Education, and Welfare.

Highsmith, R. (1989a). *A survey of state mandates for economics instruction, 1989.* New York and Washington, D.C.: Joint Council on Economic Education and NFIB Foundation.

———— (1989b). A report of research on the status of economics teaching in the nation's schools conducted by the Joint Council on Economic Education. Typescript.

Hodgkinson, H. (1988a). The context of 21st-century civics and citizenship. Paper presented at the National Conference on Citizenship for the 21st Century in Washington, D.C., 5 October.

———— (1988b). The right schools for the right kids. *Educational Leadership* 45(5):10–15.

Johnson, J. (1989). *Technology: Report of the Project 2061 phase I technology panel.* Washington, D.C.: American Association for the Advancement of Science.

Mathis, C. (1987). Educational reform, the aging society, and the teaching profession. *Journal of Education* 169(1):80–98.

Miles, M. (1964). *Innovation in education.* New York: Teachers College, Columbia University.

National Commission on Excellence in Education (1983). *A nation at risk: The imperative for educational reform.* Washington, D.C.: U.S. Government Printing Office.

National Commission on Social Studies in the Schools, Curriculum Task Force (1989). *Charting a course: Social studies for the 21st century.* Washington, D.C.: the Commission.

National Council of Teachers of Mathematics (1989). *Curriculum and evaluation standards for school mathematics.* Reston, Va.: the Council.

Orlich, D. (1989). Education reforms: Mistakes, misconceptions, miscues. *Phi Delta Kappan* 70:512–17.

Pallas, A.; Natriello, G.; and McDill, E. (1989). The changing nature of the disadvantaged population: Current dimensions and future trends. *Educational Researcher* 18(5):16–22.

Pipho, C. (1986). States move reform closer to reality. *Phi Delta Kappan* 68:K1–K8.

Psychological Corporation (1970). Evaluation report: Developmental Economic Education Program. New York: Joint Council on Economic Education. Typescript.

Symmes, S. S., ed. (1969). *DEEP handbook for curriculum change.* New York: Joint Council on Economic Education.

Timar, T., and Kirp, D. (1989). Education reform in the 1980's: Lessons from the states. *Phi Delta Kappan* 70:504–11.

21. THE NEXT STAGE OF THE DEEP PROCESS

by Francis W. Rushing

DEEP is celebrating the twenty-fifth anniversary of its piloting in 1964. It has been an evolving process of getting economics taught in the classrooms of American schools. The challenge of this chapter is to describe the next stage of the DEEP process. However, one cannot look very far into the future without reflecting on the past. This chapter looks at DEEP in the context of education in the United States over the last two decades. It briefly analyzes DEEP in contrast to other social studies programming and the efforts to increase science education. Finally, it reviews the DEEP case studies published in this volume to determine how the DEEP process functions. These contrasting examples of curriculum change efforts, along with the empirical evidence of economic learning, lay the foundations for responding to the question of where DEEP should go in the 1990s.

THE DEEP MODEL AND AN EVALUATION

Hahn (1977), in writing on the diffusion of social studies innovations, describes DEEP as a problem-solver model of curriculum change and diffusion:

> The process begins inside a system with a felt need. If no need is perceived, then the rest of the change process does not occur. The second stage is problem diagnosis, which may be accomplished with the help of an outside consultant. Next come search and retrieval stages, which frequently, though not always, take the problem solver outside the immediate system. Following this come the selection of a solution, and, finally, its application. If the solution does not meet the problem, the process is started again; if it does, it becomes part of the regular program of the system. (pp. 146–47)

A more formal presentation of each stage of the change process is shown in Table 21.1.

TABLE 21.1
Principles to Consider at Each Stage of the Change Process

AWARENESS	PERSUASION	TRIAL AND ADOPTION	IMPLEMENTATION
Felt need	Compatibility with needs and values; reduced complexity	Training and materials	Continuous training
		Principal's support	Continuous monitoring
	Support of opinion leaders, gatekeepers, and potential advocates		Mutual adaptation
			Advocates

Source: Hahn & Rushing (1981).

The various aspects of the change process can be briefly described:

1. AWARENESS

Create felt need. Obtain data on the need for improved economic literacy among students through local needs assessment; combine this with presentations about economic education's goals; create a climate conducive to change by convincing decision makers of the need to modify the curriculum, instructional activities, or teacher preparation.

2. PERSUASION

Emphasize compatibility with needs and values, and reduced complexity. Use personal forms of communication to persuade people that the proposed new approach is compatible with local needs and values, and show how economics programs will produce gains in areas of local emphasis and how the approach will appeal to students, but also show how new programs can be uncomplicated and easy to use.

Enlist support of opinion leaders, gatekeepers, and potential advocates. Target the approach to match the particular needs, values, and concerns about complexity of groups whose support is needed. Recruit inside advocates within the school system who will continue to promote better economic education (i.e., teachers, parents, school board members, the DEEP coordinator); identify opinion leaders who influence the opinions of others in the system, taking into consideration how the new approach to economic education might appeal to their needs and values; and involve gatekeepers whose official approval is needed for change in the planning as well as the implementation stages.

3. TRIAL AND ADOPTION

Provide training and materials. Base new programs on teacher training which includes developing or adapting materials to meet local needs.

Enlist the principal's support. This can set the positive tone necessary to overcome difficulties and to obtain time, money, and resources.

4. IMPLEMENTATION

Ensure training, monitoring, adaptation, and advocates. High mobility and frequent changes in teacher assignments necessitate the availability of *continuous training* for teachers who are not involved with innovations; *continuous monitoring* after change has been made should be sustained by training, adaptation, and problem solving to achieve success; *mutual adaptation,* so that any changes made to the innovations fit the participants' particular needs, is the key to successful implementation; and, once gained, maintaining the support of *advocates* is necessary to assure continued support for economic education in the community and school system.

The initial and key element in the change process is creating the felt need. The Joint Council on Economic Education's network of councils and centers of economic education has marketed DEEP as a response to the need for economics to be infused into the schools' curricula (i.e., to solve the economic illiteracy problem). DEEP as a process is both easy and difficult to "sell." It is easy because as a process it is general, and to be a DEEP school system requires only that a system acknowledge that economics is desirable as a curriculum component and that DEEP is an appropriate process to accomplish this objective. Selling DEEP is difficult because its generality seems vague. Thus, to many school administrators and teachers, DEEP begins to have meaning only when specific economics programming is demonstrated to be classroom effective.

The earlier phases of DEEP, 1963–1983, placed emphasis on teacher-developed materials for adoption within the classroom. The idea was that when the teachers developed or adapted materials, they assumed ownership and thus became advocates for those materials within the school system. During the later parts of phase two and in the third phase of DEEP, 1984–present, the Joint Council has assumed a much greater role in materials development for various grade levels, and school system personnel have only modified the materials on the margin.

No conclusive research has tested whether teacher-developed or "packaged" materials have greater staying power within DEEP schools (Hahn, 1977, p. 147). Another question focuses on the teacher as innovator or implementor and the high teacher turnover in many school systems: Does the DEEP process innovation endure longer than the product innovations? There is no empirical evidence with which to respond to these questions. However, a survey of teachers of economics shows they still are interested in more and better economics materials for the secondary classrooms (Soper & Walstad, 1988, p. 89).

Lessons from the Social Studies

Marker (1980), in a study on why schools abandoned the "new social studies" materials developed during the 1960s and 1970s, makes some observations relevant to economic education (although economic education is not in the "new social studies" classification). Marker concluded through interviews of administrators and teachers in Indiana school systems that

1. The more unrealistic a user's expectations of the innovation materials, the more likely the innovation is to be abandoned.

2. Innovations are often adopted due to the efforts of a major advocate; when that person no longer promotes the innovation, the innovation is likely to be abandoned.

3. Innovations employed in a manner different from that intended by their developers are more likely to be abandoned than are those that are implemented as their designers intended.

These observations seem to provide some good guidelines for

economic education. Don't oversell the materials. Validate through testing what learning the materials can actually deliver. Second, as the model requires, make sure that there are inside advocates for economic education and that these people will sell the programs. Finally, make sure that teachers are trained in the effective use of materials or programs. Teacher innovation is desirable, but must be monitored because bastardized materials may lose their effectiveness. A classic example is seen in the development of "modified" mini-societies that invalidate Kourilsky's (1983) designed learning experience.

Marker's observations on abandoning of materials are interesting in the DEEP context because of the requirements of the DEEP process to be adaptable. The decision to abandon economics material in K–12 may reflect a variety of possible reasons. First, the materials may have become dated—films, printed materials, teachers, student bodies, administrators, and even communities change over time. What made sense five or ten years ago may require abandonment because of declining enrollments, changing racial or ethnic profiles, declining reading and/or mathematics skills, etc. The materials may require too much teacher training or perhaps too much class time. One of the strengths of DEEP is that it is not a single set of materials, and school systems can adopt the most appropriate programs and materials for their student population.

Lessons from Science Education

A parallel to the DEEP model is the progress of curriculum change in science education. Science education in the United States has come under tremendous scrutiny as the performance of U.S. students has deteriorated vis-à-vis past performance (SAT scores) and as compared to students in other nations.

SRI International (1987a) undertook an assessment of past National Science Foundation (NSF) involvement in developing and disseminating curricula in science. The science evaluation parallels that of our DEEP assessment with regard to key variables affecting the likelihood of widespread adoptions of curricula:

- compatibility of the course with existing curricular frameworks and sequences; where courses in the past had no natural niche in existing curricula, the distribution of such courses was not extensive;

- extent of teacher exposure and training in the concepts, skills, and approach embodied in the course;

- level of difficulty at which the content is set, in terms of both its fit with the nature of the student population being taught and the demands it places on the teachers;
- logistical demands of the course and their compatibility with the support level and overall conditions of the classroom.

The frustration of science educators over the assessment results in the teaching and learning of science is high. This is due in part to the very large resource commitments to science education. The National Science Foundation alone spent over $1 billion on precollege science education between 1956 and 1985. Of this total, over $600 million were expended on teacher training and another $224 million on curricular development (SRI International, 1987b). These totals overwhelm the dollars expended since 1950 on increasing economic literacy (by all sources—state, local, business, and Joint Council on Economic Education).

Shakhashiri of the National Science Foundation at a press conference in 1987 observed, "One of the key missing pieces is a consistent and coherent science curriculum for all students. Not another physics course or chemistry course or biology course, but a consistent and coherent pattern of basic science education throughout elementary and high school." This echoes the dream of economic education as well.

Case Studies on DEEP Systems

The case studies on DEEP systems in this volume are good sources for reflection on the DEEP process. If we utilize Table 21.1 as a guide, we can draw some conclusions from the cases.

DEEP in the Inner City Schools (Cleveland)

The Cleveland Public School System is a large school system that seems to be deficient in several of the principal elements of the change process noted above. Cleveland school district supervisors and coordinators seem to work within a highly structured environment in which change is achieved slowly, if at all. The stimulus for change was external to the system, which would indicate that the "felt need" had not been achieved, at least for key personnel within the school district. The Cleveland system is willing to adopt curriculum changes as long as external funds flow into the system; however, when funding ceases, change retrogresses or, in fact, ceases. The problems in the Cleveland

300

system persist in spite of outstanding planning and support from the Cleveland Center for Economic Education. This case should alert all economic educators to the problems associated with the introduction of new curricula into school programs, particularly when superimposed on the system without any real commitment from within the system itself. The programs that become fads get superficial support and a rash of enthusiasm, but sooner or later they begin to wither for lack of nurturing and commitment from teachers and administrators.

The principles violated here come under the area of persuasion—the need for support from opinion leaders, gatekeepers, and advocates. Thus, the high school course in the Cleveland public schools seems to suffer from a multiplicity of problems: the lack of continuous teacher training and updating and the lack of continuous monitoring through the evaluation of the curriculum and the identification of problems. Finally, the Cleveland Public School System, perhaps more than some suburban or rural school systems, suffers from high attrition rates among its teachers; therefore, it appears it is almost on a treadmill of training to achieve minimum competency in economic education.

The East Cleveland city schools' DEEP experience seems to have obtained much broader support from the system than was the case in the Cleveland public schools and, through energetic and forward-looking DEEP planning, has achieved somewhat better results. The awareness, persuasion, and trial and adoption steps of the process seem to have been accomplished, and the success rate of DEEP is relatively high. However, economic educators must recognize the inherent problems of inner-city education and must sell the DEEP process with sensitivity to the unique needs of inner-city schools as well as to the special set of problems with which school administrators and teachers must deal. "Success" is not an absolute. In many ways it must be measured relative to what level of economic education would have been achieved in the absence of DEEP.

The Urban Experience (San Antonio)

In the case of San Antonio, the felt need was the course that the Texas State Assembly mandated for all secondary schools. As is almost always true when economics courses are mandated, no implementation funds were allocated, nor were changes made in the pre-service requirement for social studies teachers. The school systems, therefore, were receptive to the centers for economic education which could provide a systematic approach to meeting the mandate effectively.

301

In the San Antonio case, the "persuasion" needed was to overcome a somewhat negative environment resulting from integration suits and countersuits. The school systems, because of this environment, were extremely reluctant or—to put it another way—risk averse with regard to new curricula and curriculum changes. The center in this case made a rational judgment to identify a small school district as its first DEEP project and, through its success, expand to other districts. What seemed to be lacking in these districts was a systematic evaluation of the learning outcomes. The success of the program was measured by the notoriety that certain components of the DEEP program received in the education community and the publicity received in the press.

The Large City District (Omaha)

This case clearly demonstrates the importance of key school personnel in advocating and energizing a DEEP school system. In this instance a school official made the case for economics to the business community and cultivated support within the school system to establish a DEEP program. Omaha has outside support through private financial contributions and participation by business and university personnel.

Even the Omaha success cannot be taken for granted. Pressure on the system mounts for reallocations to other curriculum areas such as geography, mathematics, science, history, and global studies. All lend themselves to close linkages to economics, and the system should seek curriculum materials that cover more than one curriculum area.

Economic Education in Suburban Districts (Clovis, California)

The DEEP process began for Clovis not from within the school district, but from without—with university center personnel and a businessman. The "felt need" rippled out from this locus. A financial grant got it started and helped sustain it. There was little economic education within the curriculum, so to sell DEEP was less of a challenge than designing and implementing the program.

DEEP in a Rural School District (Marion County, Tennessee)

This case reflects another variation on the DEEP process. The rural county school system was "sold" on DEEP by a center director who helped finance, train, and develop DEEP within individual schools. The spread of DEEP to the entire school system was slowed by the limited number of personnel both within and outside the system. This constraint exists in urban as well as rural areas when a center's personnel are spread too thinly across the system, particularly during the formative first two years of DEEP.

The five DEEP case studies point to the great diversity among school systems in the United States and to the multiplicity of approaches to creating an effective DEEP system. The DEEP model provides the needed structure to guide the process, while allowing the flexibility to adapt to unique local conditions. DEEP therefore receives good ratings as a model of curriculum change. (Another question that could be asked is whether DEEP delivers economic education to students. Michael Watts provides a review of this research in Chapter 6 of this volume.)

THE NEXT STAGE

In the sections on evaluating the DEEP process, it was concluded that DEEP is a viable curriculum change model. It is a good example of the problem-solving model. DEEP, however, is not a static model, and it has changed over the last 25 years. Yet it has retained its positive characteristics, while continuing to have some drawbacks as well.

Among the positive aspects of DEEP are the following:

- DEEP is implemented by a system within the philosophical framework that exists. No controversial new philosophy is used which must be defended before parents, teachers, or administrators (e.g., it doesn't have the stigma of Man: A Course of Study).

- DEEP is a well-developed model. It has been piloted, analyzed, tested, and restructured throughout its existence.

- Materials developed are basically educationally sound and designed to permit teachers flexibility in their implementation.

- The model's flexibility permits a school system to control the pace and breadth of its economics program to reflect its resource base.

- DEEP leaves the school system in control of the process of curriculum change.
- DEEP provides a broad-based support system, including the local centers and state councils on economic education and the Joint Council on Economic Education.

- DEEP expands the resource base of a system with consultants, free materials, and community and state financial support.

Pitfalls do threaten the success of DEEP. Perhaps the largest is the possibility that a system may only superficially adopt DEEP, glean short-term benefits (e.g., materials, some teacher training), and then be a DEEP system in name only. The system may not generate the internal advocates for economic education, thus rendering the model disjointed or ineffectual because of halfhearted commitment. Finally, teachers, unless they personally buy into DEEP, may feel pressed to raise economics above other social studies subjects and may react with poor-quality or, at best, uninspired instruction (Rushing, 1975).

The DEEP process should prepare a school system to continue effective education after three to five years of being a DEEP system. Yet few systems have generated a self-sustaining energy. For instance, the Atlanta Public School System, an original pilot system in 1964, still requires substantial time, energy, and resources from its sponsoring center for economic education. The Atlanta case seems to be typical, rather than extraordinary.

The 1990s will be a fourth phase for DEEP. But how should it change? The discussion above points toward several changes necessary in DEEP.

A Case for Economic Education

As a problem-solving model, DEEP requires that a "felt need" be identified and embraced. Historically, the felt need has been generated at the school level, usually by a center or council director. By 1989 about 1,800 school systems had declared themselves to be DEEP systems. However, DEEP should be based on a national call for economic education, rather than on a system-by-system piecemeal approach.

The case for economic education has not been made on a national scale. In spite of a 40-year history of good work by the Joint Council on Economic Education and other economic education groups (Junior Achievement, Foundation for Teaching Economics, etc.), there is no national consensus that economic education is an educational imperative. This was most dramatically demonstrated when the national assessment debate in the Congress of the United States erupted, and economic educators were astounded to learn economics wasn't comparable to history, English, mathematics, science, or even government. If economic education is so intuitively obvious as a life skill, why

304

do economic educators have to sell it, resell it, and stand in the store to make sure it isn't taken off the shelf?

The Joint Council on Economic Education took an important step toward making the case for economic education at the Paul Volcker press conference at the American Economic Association meeting in December 1988. The dismal data on the dismal science were hung out before the public, but where is the follow-through? Economic educators under the leadership of the Joint Council should map a strategy for selling the country on economic education. The felt need has to be national in scope and strong in intensity.

One strategy might be to extend the number of states that mandate economics. There are arguments against forcing teachers to teach economics, but with one legislative act the "felt need" for economic instruction is identified. Currently 28 states mandate economic instruction of some sort—18 mandate economics, 10 consumer education, and 7 both free enterprise/economic education and consumer education (Highsmith, 1989).

More Research

DEEP has to expand its research component. This is not a call for substituting the research, development, diffusion, and adoption model for the DEEP model, but rather for building linkages with research into DEEP. The what, how, and when elements of economic education ought to be research based. New programs and materials should reflect what research tells us are the best scope and sequence, teaching methods, and teacher training. No new materials should be disseminated that have not been thoroughly tested. Evaluation should be an integral part of all that is done. Major studies in this direction have occurred in the last five to seven years. However, the evaluation of learning outcomes above shows how shallow our evaluation has been of the overall effectiveness of economic education in DEEP (Walstad & Soper, 1988, 1989). We must broaden and intensify evaluation. The current reform movement has made evaluation a more accepted part of education than it historically has been and thus economic educators will be swimming in the mainstream.

More Training

DEEP should redouble its efforts in training DEEP personnel—center directors, DEEP coordinators, and classroom teachers. In education, people make the difference. DEEP requires that the leadership (usually council and center directors) be trained in the DEEP process and be trained as effective economic educators—not just economists or educators, but *economic educators*. Teachers need more content instruction by their own admission. Better training for key personnel in DEEP helps develop outside and inside advocates for economic education as well as competent personnel to execute the curriculum.

Less—Not More

Some measure the success of DEEP by the number of school systems that have adopted DEEP and the percentage of students within these DEEP systems as compared to the total number of students in grades K–12. A better measure would be the increase in economic understanding within the student population. If the latter measure of success is adopted, DEEP would have to make some adjustments in focus:

1. Focus on getting one economics course somewhere in the secondary curriculum. Evaluation data show this is the best way to get students to learn economics (Walstad & Soper, 1988).

2. Introduce a model set of materials for economics teachers, and train them to use these materials effectively. The Joint Council is already moving in this direction with the capstone economics course and the development of economic and entrepreneurship education materials. It may be easier to "sell" a set of materials if it is well developed, meets a mandated need, and has good teacher training and evaluation components. Fewer good course materials may achieve more economic learning than more and more infusion materials and auxiliary activities (Soper & Walstad, 1988; Walstad & Watts, 1985).

3. Limit the number of DEEP systems serviced by a center for economic education to those that can be properly serviced with the resources available at the center. The statistics on DEEP for 1989 are superficially impressive (1,800 DEEP systems), but one suspects the 300 centers for economic education are overwhelmed. The average of six DEEP systems per center seems to be too many, unless, of course, a significant number are either inactive or marginally active. Many center directors teach in their college, are expected to do some kind of research, and tend to their center responsibilities. Many directors have only 25 to 50 percent released time for center activities, and some have no released time at all. The

306

DEEP model, if it is to be successful, requires greater intensity as the process matures. One suspects that more often than not center directors find themselves short on time, money, and assistance.

DEEP, therefore, must expand the trained personnel to support it. One model would be a "master teacher program" as conducted at Georgia State University. Another more expensive and less self-sustaining approach would be an expanded center network or more professionals on the staff at the centers.

The success of DEEP as measured by learning outcomes will require another order of magnitude of resources than is currently being funded. These resources will be forthcoming only if the case for economic education is made nationally and if the private and public funds devoted to achieving economic literacy are increased.

Part of the National Education Reform

As economic educators, we face the systemic problems of U.S. education. Our counterparts in science and mathematics, and in reading and writing, express many of the same frustrations we do. Ours are greater because most Americans buy into the basic principle that science, mathematics, reading, and writing are educational necessities. As economic educators, we need to form strategic alliances to face the common core of problems. Let us see what others have learned and, in turn, reach out to share what we know. (Indeed, why not share our knowledge of the problem-solving curriculum change model?) Why not do joint research in effective teaching? Learning theory? Evaluation techniques? All educators need to address an even more fundamental question: Is a national curriculum desirable? Finally, we need to explore whether our educational system is the problem, rather than the solution.

If the suggestions above are implemented, DEEP will continue to evolve in the 1990s. The measure of its success will be the increase in economic learning that America's youth achieve. The DEEP delivery system of councils and centers for economic education will be strengthened through more and better training for council and center directors and classroom teachers, better quality control over materials and services delivered, research on all aspects of teaching economics, and more resources to permit the centers and councils to do the jobs they are capable of doing. The evaluation of DEEP will take place in an environment more receptive to its goal because the public will be convinced that Americans need to be economically literate. However, those who profess to be economic educators must be prepared to expend even more energy, must call on their creativity, and must organize the resources and provide the leadership to get the job done. "Success" is not static—it will always be at some higher level of economic understanding than exists today. The challenge will continue into the twenty-first century.

REFERENCES

Hahn, C. L. (1977). Research on the diffusion of social studies innovations. In *Review of research on social studies education 1970–1975* , 137–51. Bulletin no. 49. Washington, D.C.: National Council for the Social Studies.

Hahn, C. L., and Rushing, F. W. (1981). Building an effective economic education program using principles of successful adoption and implementation. In *Economic education: Links to the social studies*, ed. S. S. Symmes, 28–41. Bulletin no. 65. Washington, D.C.: National Council for the Social Studies.

Highsmith, R. J. (1989). *A survey of state mandates for economics instruction, 1989.* New York and Washington, D.C.: Joint Council on Economic Education and NFIB Foundation.

Kourilsky, M. (1983). *Mini-Society: Experiencing real-world economics in the elementary school classroom.* Menlo Park, Calif.: Addison-Wesley.

Marker, G. W. (1980). Why schools abandon "new social studies" materials. *Theory and Research in Social Studies* 7(4):35-57.

Rushing, F. W. (1975). Promoting curriculum change in economics: A model. *Southern Social Studies Quarterly* 1(2):34.

Soper, J. C., and Walstad, W. B. (1988). The reality of high school economics: The teachers' perspective. *Journal of Private Enterprise* 4(1):89–90.

SRI International (1987a). Opportunity 2b—To recast the content of middle and high school science curricula. In *Opportunities for strategic investment in K–12 science education.* Vol. 1, *Problems and opportunities.* 93.

――― (1987b). Program funding history, 1952–1986. In *Opportunities for strategic investment in K–12 science education.* Vol. 2, *Groundwork for strategic investment,* Part Four.

Walstad, W. B., and Soper, J. C. (1989). What is high school economics? Factors contributing to student achievement and attitude. *Journal of Economic Education* 20(1):23–38.

――― (1988). A report card on economic literacy of U.S. high school students. *American Economic Review* 78(2):251–56.

Walstad, W. B., and Watts, M. (1985). Teaching economics in the schools: A review of survey findings. *Journal of Economic Education* 16(2):135–45.

22. VISIONS FOR THE FUTURE

by Stephen Buckles

This volume is a success story. But it is not a story without problems and challenges. The 25-year history of DEEP is one of significant growth in the numbers of school districts enrolled in the DEEP process. It is one of impressive development of curriculum and teaching materials by DEEP schools, local centers for economic education, state councils on economic education, and the national Joint Council on Economic Education. It is a story of accomplishments in terms of teacher training and increased student economic literacy.

Twenty-five years ago, economics was not a significant part of the elementary and secondary curriculum. Now, 40 percent of the nation's students are enrolled in DEEP systems. One-half of the nation's students are enrolled in school systems that require a separate high school economics course for graduation. Two-thirds of the nation's students live in states that require some type of economics to be integrated throughout the curriculum. Many students in other states are enrolled in schools that require or offer separate high school courses and infuse economics throughout the curriculum.

The Joint Council and its network have developed a set of curriculum and teacher materials that allows school systems to integrate economics and to design a separate course. There are 271 college and university centers for economic education to assist schools in the DEEP process. Many of those have staff members whose full-time assignments are to work directly with DEEP schools.

The vast amount of empirical research shows that the essential components of DEEP are effective in creating economic literacy. If a school district requires a separate course for graduation, infuses economics throughout the K–12 curriculum, and has teachers who have participated in substantive economic education programs, its students will graduate understanding basic economic concepts.

There are also problems in economic education. Not all DEEP districts are successful in making sure that students achieve economic understanding. The Joint Council network does not always have sufficient resources to train large numbers of teachers, to assist the districts with curriculum change, and to provide the continuing consultation and training necessary to sustain the initial results. Nor is there widespread recognition of the need for economic education. Some teachers and administrators argue that the school curriculum is full. There are other subjects competing for space in the curriculum, many with considerable public support. Finally, because DEEP is a process, it is difficult to describe to school administrators, teachers, and funders in order to get them to support the program.

The success stories in this volume and the stories about the problems tell us that internal commitment to economic education, sustained follow-up, teacher education, and high-quality, easy-to-use, and adaptable teacher materials are necessary for success. We know that almost 2,000 school districts have at one time indicated an interest in making a commitment to economic education through DEEP. We know that the commitment has not always been sustained. We know that the challenges of having districtwide success in the very large districts are immense. We know that the delivery system has not always been able to continue the follow-up on initial curriculum change or to offer the needed teacher education. But this evidence provides us with guidance as to where we should go from here.

If we envision a nation where the vast majority of the nation's schools are providing economic education, the quality of which is sufficient to permit students to graduate from high school truly economically literate, we must change our methods. I believe that it is clear what must be done to achieve that vision. The Joint Council and its national network must continue to emphasize growth in the number of DEEP systems.

More important, we must increase our efforts to improve the quality of current and new DEEP systems. In this effort the Joint Council should be undertaking three primary tasks:

1. Enhance the national awareness of the need for economic education and the commitment to institutionalizing economic education within school systems.

2. Improve the set of teaching and curriculum materials necessary for effective economic education programs.

3. Improve the quality and ability of the delivery system to work with current and future DEEP schools in achieving the goal of universal economic understanding.

310

NATIONAL AWARENESS AND COMMITMENT

The definition of a national curriculum appears to be an emerging national trend. The National Assessment of Educational Progress, the National Council for the Social Studies, the Bradley Commission, and other groups are leading that drive through recommendations for specific content or testing in subject areas. When economics is not included in those recommendations, the challenge of convincing school districts and teachers of the importance of economics is that much more difficult. Generating resources to change the curriculum, to educate teachers in economics, and to sustain effective teaching of economics requires the commitment of curriculum designers and teachers.

The Joint Council should over the next five years devote considerable resources to increasing national awareness of the need for economic education. Efforts should be made to work closely with all groups in the process of recommending national curriculum models or national testing. We should also encourage national spokespersons to emphasize the importance of economic understanding and the role of economics in the curriculum.

We can show that the DEEP process, when done correctly with sufficient resources, does result in increased economic understanding as measured by scores on standardized tests. However, we have not done enough to demonstrate that this increased understanding does make a difference in how we perform as consumers, workers, and citizens. Additional resources need to be devoted to developing research that examines alternative outcomes of economic education.

State mandates requiring a separate course and infusion and providing resources for training teachers can be effective in generating quality programs. The Joint Council should increase its efforts to establish state mandates where appropriate.

A NATIONAL PROGRAM

The development of economic education curriculum materials has evolved from a local process to one of national leadership by the Joint Council and its network. With the publishing of the scope and sequence document, *Economics: What and When,* there now exists an organizing plan for all curriculum materials.

In addition, there exists a set of curriculum materials, teaching guides, and audiovisual materials that comes close to providing a national program for economic education. Some of the materials, however, are outdated or do not fit the scope and sequence. And there are some "holes" in the range of materials that need to be filled.

The Joint Council is beginning the process of developing the complete set of materials, along with model teacher education programs. Each component of the national program will be designed to fit into the scope and sequence. The materials and the overall program will be easy to use and easy to adapt to local interests and needs.

DEEP is a flexible process of curriculum change. A clear national program, with DEEP at its core, may make widespread acceptance of economic education a realistic goal.

QUALITY OF THE DELIVERY SYSTEM

In the last five years the number of students enrolled in DEEP systems has grown significantly, now with 40 percent of the nation's students enrolled in DEEP systems. Some areas of the country will continue to expand over the next five years. We fully expect that the enrollment of students in DEEP systems will expand at least at a rate of 2 percent per year over the next five years.

Future growth in numbers will be difficult. Most very large systems are already DEEP districts. It is much more expensive per student to add smaller districts. The number of centers for economic education is limited, and many are fully employed in servicing current DEEP systems. If we expect to improve current DEEP systems' effectiveness, more resources will have to be devoted to current DEEP districts.

The Joint Council should increase the resources it allocates to improving the quality of its delivery system. If successful, these efforts should increase the ability not only to expand the number of districts enrolled in DEEP, but also, more important, to better service current DEEP districts and to enhance the effectiveness of current DEEP efforts.

Efforts to improve the delivery system should focus on generating more resources for state councils and university centers and on enhancing their abilities to engage in curriculum consulting and teacher education. More resources will permit centers to engage in more concentrated efforts with individual school systems and to provide more teachers with the proper background in economics. The use of associate or field directors who work closely with school systems must be expanded. We should also develop more model teacher-training programs and offer national curriculum institutes to better prepare individuals actually doing the teacher education.

In no other discipline does there exist a delivery system like the one in economics. It is a model with a national office, state councils to generate state and local resources, and university-based centers for economic education to work closely with school systems to change the curriculum and assist teachers through an organized process, DEEP.

The model is in place. We know what is needed to be successful. The challenge now is to learn from our successes and our failures—and to build on them.

INDEX

314

318

319

322

LIST OF TABLES AND FIGURES

THE CONTRIBUTORS

Willie Mae Beattie, former teacher and DEEP consultant, Marion County Schools, Tennessee.

Terrel H. Bell, former U.S. Secretary of Education and Professor of Educational Administration, University of Utah.

Judith Staley Brenneke, Managing Partner, Rational Education Associates, Cleveland Heights, Ohio, and former Director, Cleveland Center for Economic Education, John Carroll University.

Stephen Buckles, President, Joint Council on Economic Education, New York.

James Dick, Co-director, Center for Economic Education, and Associate Professor of Education, University of Nebraska at Omaha.

Lucien Ellington, Associate Director, Center for Economic Education, and Associate Professor of Education, University of Tennessee at Chattanooga.

June V. Gilliard, Director, Curriculum and Instruction, Joint Council on Economic Education, New York.

Sanford D. Gordon, former President, New York State Council on Economic Education.

Karen Hallows, President, Missouri Council on Economic Education, and Assistant Professor of Economics, University of Missouri–Columbia.

Peter V. Harrington, Director, Indiana Council for Economic Education, and Professor of Economics, Purdue University.

Henry J. Hermanowicz, Professor of Education and former Dean, College of Education, The Pennsylvania State University.

Marilyn Kourilsky, Director, Center for Economic Education, and Dean, Teacher Education, University of California, Los Angeles; and President and Executive Director, California Council on Economic Education.

Don R. Leet, Director, Center for Economic Education, and Professor of Economics, California State University, Fresno.

Michael A. MacDowell, Vice President, Hartwick College, Oneonta, New York, and former President, Joint Council on Economic Education, New York.

Peter G. Mehas, Education Secretary, Office of the Governor of the State of California.

Bonnie T. Meszaros, Associate Director, Center for Economic Education, University of Delaware.

Steven Miller, Director, Central Ohio Center for Economic Education, and Assistant Professor of Education, The Ohio State University.

James B. O'Neill, President, Delaware Council on Economic Education; and Director, Center for Economic Education, and Professor of Economics, University of Delaware.

Lory Quaranta, Field Coordinator, Teacher Education, University of California, Los Angeles.

Francis W. Rushing, Associate Dean for Research and Professor of Economics, College of Business Administration, Georgia State University.

Mark C. Schug, Executive Director, Wisconsin Council on Economic Education, and Professor of Education, University of Wisconsin–Milwaukee.

Warren Solomon, Social Studies Curriculum Consultant, Department of Elementary and Secondary Education, State of Missouri.

John C. Soper, Professor of Economics, John Carroll University, and former Director, Cleveland Center for Economic Education.

S. Stowell Symmes, Executive Director, DEEP Office, Joint Council on Economic Education, New York.

Kenneth Wade, Bureau Chief, Social Studies, New York State Education Department.

William B. Walstad, Director, National Center for Research in Economic Education, and Professor of Economics, University of Nebraska–Lincoln.

Michael Watts, Director, Center for Economic Education, and Associate Professor of Economics, Purdue University.

Edgar S. Woolard, Jr., Chairman, E. I. duPont de Nemours & Company, Wilmington, Delaware.

Howard R. Yeargan, Director, Center for Economic Education, and Associate Professor of Economics, Southwest Texas State University.